Stanislavski in Ireland: Focus at Fifty

To David,

Love & luck with
this work.

Best,
Joe Devlin.

Deirdre O'Connell, Founder of Focus Theatre
(Photograph by Fergus Bourke)

Stanislavski in Ireland: Focus at Fifty

Edited by

Brian McAvera and Steven Dedalus Burch

Carysfort Press

A Carysfort Press Book
Stanislavski in Ireland: Focus at 50
Edited by Brian McAvera and Steven Dedalus Burch
First published in Ireland in 2013 as a paperback original by
Carysfort Press, 58 Woodfield, Scholarstown Road
Dublin 16, Ireland
ISBN 978-1-909325-43-2
© 2013 Copyright remains with the authors
Typeset by Carysfort Press
Cover design by eprint
Printed and bound by eprint limited
Unit 35
Coolmine Industrial Estate
Dublin 15
Ireland

CONTENTS

ACKNOWLEDGEMENTS

We would like to acknowledge the unstinting help given to us by a very wide range of people. The President of Ireland and his wife invited a very large of number of Focus individuals, past and present, to their official home Aras an Uachtaráin on Bloomsday 2012. Almost everyone contributed reminiscences in relation to the Focus, and both the President and his wife, individually, went to considerable lengths to help the theatre. And Sabina Coyne Higgins very graciously welcomed Steve Burch and his wife Deborah Parker and gave us a hefty two hours for her interview for this book. Numerous writers, actors and directors and teachers helped us. In particular, Joe Devlin, who was and is the driving force behind this project, has been unusually generous both in terms of his time and organization. We are grateful to playwright Iris Park and her husband Greg who set a very high bar as hosts for Steve and his wife Deborah during their stay in Dublin.

Of course, we could not possibly have accomplished our mission without the keen eyes and judgement of Lilian Chambers and Dan Farrelly at Carysfort. It would be a poorer book without their input.

Lastly, yet very much not the least, we are indebted to the friendly and very helpful staff at the National Library Archives, without whom we would have struggled, largely unsuccessfully, to find this material. *The Irish Times* on September 27, 2003 reported:

> The inimitable figure of theatre director and actor Deirdre O'Connell flying up and down Dublin's Leeson Street, clipboard under her arm, black shawl around her shoulders, came vividly to life again this week when her papers were presented to the National Library. Given that, in 1997, Michael D. Higgins called O'Connell (1939-2001) the greatest single influence in Irish theatre since the 1960s, this archive, when catalogued, will be a huge resource for anyone interested in Irish theatre in the 20th century.

We can attest to that.

In spite of all the help we received, any errors in fact belong exclusively to us.

Steven Dedalus Burch
Brian McAvera

[**From Joe Devlin**, who facilitated much of the research and many of the interviews:]

I would like to thank the following, without whom none of this would be possible: the O'Connell family, Brian Bourke, Anonymous, the Board of Focus Theatre, Alastar Mac Aongusa, Llew at John Moore's University in Liverpool, Olive Buckley, Phyllis Mooney, Tony Layng, Alex McCullagh, Karl McCaughey, Sebastian Stephenson, the Dublin City Council, Ray Yeates, Sarah Shardellati, The Friends of Focus. Additionally I must acknowledge Terry Connaughton and Ranelagh Arts Centre for supplying Focus Theatre with a free office for a year. And finally my thanks to Nollaig Fahy, to Kevin O'Brien, President of Focus Theatre and Chairperson for twenty-five years, and to all the artists, theatre crews, friends and supporters who gave of themselves without financial reward and without whom the work would never have happened.

Joe Devlin

List of Photographs

Cover Photo: *Mother Teresa is Dead* with Elizabeth Moynihan and Catherine Byrne (Photo by Alex McCullagh)

Frontispiece: Deirdre O'Connell, Founder of Focus Theatre (Photo by Fergus Bourke)

The Focus Theatre & Acting Studio – Fifty Years of Love

'Acting is an act of Love.' Deirdre O'Connell

Fifty years ago Ireland's ground breaking theatre, the Focus Theatre & Acting Studio, was founded by an act of Love. In 1963 a young Irish American actor, Deirdre O'Connell, left her home in New York City and travelled to Dublin City where she met with and fell in love with Dubliner Luke Kelly. They were both immensely passionate about the arts. Deirdre had studied her acting craft under the tutelage of Lee Strasberg at the world famous Lee Strasberg Institute New York City. Luke was the lead singer of the legendary Irish folk band, The Dubliners, and one of the rising stars of the music industry. These young lovers, who were in their early twenties, set out on their mission together to establish a new ground-breaking theatre and acting studio in Dublin that would introduce the Stanislavski acting system to Ireland and Europe.

Deirdre had not only learned her craft from a great master, who had trained some of the most prolific actors including Anne Bancroft, Dustin Hoffman, Montgomery Clift, James Dean, Julie Harris, Paul Newman, Al Pacino, Robert De Niro, Marilyn Monroe, and Arthur Miller (Marilyn & Arthur were Deirdre's classmates), but she was also deeply inspired by her experience of working with the greats in the world of theatre. She harnessed the power of these experiences to challenge her own abilities and creativity, and that power in turn gave her the strength to go beyond the edge of her comfort zone to achieve her mission.

Luke knew that in order to achieve their mission many obstacles and challenges had to be overcome. A suitable site would need to be located, plans drawn up and funds raised. Luke worked tirelessly to overcome the challenges they faced. He even enlisted the support of his fellow band members of The Dubliners who, as it happened, were all professional tradesmen prior to becoming members of the band. Luke and Deirdre had found a suitable building, but it required substantial refurbishment. When The Dubliners returned from a successful tour of Germany they donated enough funds to buy building materials, and together they physically rebuilt and refurbished the building that would house the theatre and studio.

In April 1963 the Focus Theatre's Acting Studio was founded and in 1967 the Focus Theatre opened its doors to the public for the first time and presented its first production *Play with a Tiger* by Doris Lessing. The theatre then went on to mount nearly 400 productions, including record-breaking runs of classics such as Ibsen's *A Doll's House* and of contemporary plays such as Auburn's *Proof*, running for six months at a time. The Focus introduced Irish audiences to plays by Beckett and Shepard for the first time, as well as new writers such as Gianina Carbunariu, Vassily Sigarev, Malachy McKenna and Conall Quinn.

Many of Ireland's leading theatre and film artists started their career at the Focus Theatre, including Gabriel Byrne, Tom Hickey, Johnny Murphy, Sean Campion, Olwen Fouéré, Joan Bergin, Sabina Coyne, Bosco Hogan, Gerard McSorley, and Mary-Elizabeth Burke Kennedy. In the late 1970s Burke-Kennedy pioneered the use of mask and mythology in performance at the Focus Theatre. Tim McDonnell won the Obie Award in the 1980s for his performance in *Diary of a Madman* directed by Deirdre O'Connell.

Following Deirdre's death in 2001 (Luke had died in 1984), Tim McDonnell became artistic director until his retirement. In 2002 Joe Devlin took over as artistic director and has continued the tradition of producing plays from world theatre and developing new writing. Joe also now runs the acting studio. In 2004 and 2005 Focus Theatre won the Spiegeltent Award at the Dublin Fringe Festival. In 2006 the venue was temporarily closed pending refurbishment. In 2007 Focus Theatre worked as full-time Stanislavski advisors on Pantakin's award-winning production of *L'Utima Casa* at the Biennale, Venice. On the 45th anniversary of the Focus in 2008 the Deirdre O'Connell Archive opened at the National Library of Ireland and *Hold the Passion*, a documentary on her life and work, premiered at the Cork Film Festival. That same year the Focus won the Writers' Guild of Great Britain Award for the Encouragement of New Work for its production of Brian McAvera's *Picasso's Women*. Focus Theatre's programme now includes touring (national and international), site-specific productions, co-productions, and outreach nationwide projects.

By the time the Focus Theatre opened its doors to the public in 1967, Deirdre and Luke were husband and wife. They had worked tirelessly and selflessly together to create and deliver their dream. But they were not alone in building their vision and achieving their mission. There were thousands of people who were drawn to the mission of The Focus Theatre & Acting Studio. These kind and generous people gave their time, energy, know-how and money. In the case of The Dubliners, they gave their all, including their blood, sweat and tears.

But, there is something else that unites every person that was, and is, connected to The Focus Theatre & Acting Studio and, that is LOVE. Without the Love shown by our Founders, Supporters, Sponsors, Audiences, Friends, Actors, Directors, Playwrights, Crew, Staff, Chairmen and the Board Members for the arts, acting and theatre it is a fact that the Focus Theatre & Acting Studio would not have come into being.

The inspirational author Kevin Roberts once said, 'Love cannot be demanded or commanded. It can only be given. Like power, you get Love by giving it.' The Love that every single person gave so selflessly during the last fifty years to the Focus Theatre & Acting Studio to help create and shape it is a real and true Act of LOVE. Ireland and its people owe them a debt of gratitude. We must all be grateful indeed for their Love.

Nollaig Fahy
Chairman, Focus Theatre & Acting Studio, March 2013

1 | An Introduction in Search of an Audience

Brian McAvera and Steven Dedalus Burch

In 2002 Christopher Morash published a very well-received book entitled *A History of Irish Theatre* 1601-2000. On page 248 he noted that 'from 1967 onwards the tiny Focus Theatre in Dublin, headed by Deirdre O'Connell, struggled heroically against an almost complete absence of resources to train some of the leading Irish actors of the late twentieth century in the techniques of Stanislavski'. This is the only mention of the Focus theatre in the book, apart from a name check on page 271 in a paragraph which mentions eleven other theatres, whilst also noting that, at the point of writing, there were forty subsidized companies and almost fifty non-subsidized ones.

Histories of theatre, perhaps inevitably, tend to concentrate on particular playwrights, particular productions and big-name theatres, just as histories of acting tend to focus on famous actors and famous performances. As a result the real history of theatre is edited out in favour of the supposed highlights, and, often, a few big subsidized companies get the credit for the work of others.

There is a real need for serious critical spadework to be done in the province of Irish theatre. We need dependable histories of the smaller companies, many of which lasted for only three or four years. In Northern Ireland for example Interplay, Replay, New Writers' Theatre and the Youth Drama Movement (to name only a few of companies during the 1980s) all contributed substantially to the development of New Writing but you will not find any of them even mentioned in Morash's history. We also need histories of itinerant acting companies, of directors, and of training for theatre (or the lack of it) in all its forms.

This book on The Focus Theatre is an attempt to excavate elements of our buried history. There are numerous books on the Abbey Theatre in Dublin, the Lyric Theatre in Belfast and, more recently, much writing on a few big subsidised companies like the Druid or Rough Magic. But as Morash noted there *was* 'an almost complete lack of resources', and spaces such as The Abbey Theatre did not attempt to provide them. It was left, as usual, to the dedication of smaller companies, and in particular to The Focus, to provide proper training for that bedrock of the theatre, the actor. Naturally, this being Ireland, the money went to those who did not provide training, and rarely went to those who did! Equally naturally the credit for training actors did not go to the trainers!

There is little point in becoming annoyed at the unfairness of a historical situation, but there is considerable point in providing detailed information on the spadework done by companies such as the Focus so that future historians have an opportunity to rewrite the cartography of Irish theatre. Even a glance through the List of Productions from 1967 onwards will indicate the diversity of plays produced and the range of well-known actors who passed through The Focus's Stanislavski training school. What it will also indicate is the way in which the emphasis of The Focus changed when Joe Devlin took over in 2002: as well as the classics so beloved by Deirdre, under Devlin there was a distinct shift towards the production of new writers and thus new work.

Numerous people have been interviewed, or have otherwise contributed towards the production of this book. Steven Burch has collated many of these interviews with a view to providing a wide range of reminiscences, interpretations and anecdotes which flesh out the more academically-orientated essays. Our gratitude to all these artists who enthusiastically shared their memories of The Focus then and The Focus now cannot be overstated. Mary Moynihan, who had previously written a thesis on the history of the Focus and who is herself a noted director, has provided a succinct history of the theatre during the Deirdre years as well as an article/interview with one of the leading members of the Focus during that period. Continuing the narrative, Joe Devlin, having first provided what one might call a spiritual biography of his journey in theatre, then focuses sharply on his own tenure in the theatre, in the process providing a social and political context.

This is amplified by the playwright and director Brian McAvera's account of how he came to work at the Focus despite his discontent with acting standards in Ireland, and by Steve Burch's detailed interview with the playwright/director which explores the social and political contexts of working in Ireland and looks at the relationship of the Artistic Adviser and the Artistic Director.

A number of case studies are provided such as that of the playwright Jimmy Murphy in relation to the Focus production of his play *The Hen Night Epiphany,* or the actor and director Cathal Quinn discussing his productions of Beckett as well as his acting role in McAvera's *Francis & Frances.* The playwright and director Elizabeth Moynihan contributes a memoir of the period in which she was trained by Deirdre O'Connell, and in addition, we reproduce a number of the acting exercises developed by O'Connell as well as a number of articles/interviews written about the theatre at various times in its past. Playwright, director, actress, and teacher of the second Stanislavski studio at The Focus, Mary Elizabeth Burke-Kennedy adds a lovely memory of a long-ago very late night tech rehearsal of Strindberg's *The Father* directed by her husband Declan Burke-Kennedy and cast with Deirdre, Jimmy Murphy, Frank McDonald, and Tim McDonnell, entitled *The Tern.* We have also tried to provide a wide range of visual material, be they stills, programmes, posters or other memorabilia, in the belief that images conjure up 'period'.

Forthcoming from all this activity is an anthology of new original plays which Focus premiered over the years to be published separately. And finally we have included in the appendices a rather wonderful reminiscence by former president Mary Robinson on her brief time taking a class at Focus's Stanislavski Studio.

It was a time. And it continues to be.

2 | Loving the art in yourself

Mary Moynihan

After spending five years in New York, training and performing with theatre practitioners such as 'Erwin Piscator, Saul Colin, Lee Strasberg and Allan Miller'[1], American-born Deirdre O'Connell (1939-2001) came to Ireland and founded the Stanislavski Acting Studio of Dublin in May 1963.

The Stanislavski studio was so named as the type of training that Deirdre wanted to bring to Ireland. It was based on the theatrical theory and techniques of the Russian Theatre practitioner, actor and director Konstantin Stanislavski (1863-1938), founder and theatre administrator of the Moscow Art Theatre and creator of the Stanislavski system of actor training, 'the most influential system of acting in the Western World'.[2]

The Stanislavski approach is a system of training, not a specific style of acting, that aims to provide the skills necessary for the actor to develop the inner life; the emotional and sensory life of the character. There is a commitment to ensemble acting and teamwork and work characterized by a truthful and deep 'moment-to-moment aliveness'[3] in performance, generating theatre that is creative as opposed to

---

[1] Focus Theatre Programme, *Buried Child* by Sam Shepard, Focus Theatre, August 1994.

[2] Edited by Martin Banham, *The Cambridge Guide to Theatre* (USA: Cambridge University Press, 1992), p. 923.

[3] Lee Strasberg, *A Dream of Passion, The Development of the Method*, edited by Evangeline Morphos (Great Britain, Methuen Drama, 1989), p. 38.

representational. The work is rooted in the actor's sense of self and the development of the 'sensual and emotional capacity of the actors'.[4]

Under supervision, the actor works on areas such as relaxation, focus and concentration, imagination, physical action and a belief in it, sense memory, emotional memory, the creative flow, and the use of objectives and given circumstances, exploring how these areas help to train the actor's inner creative state in order to create truthful behaviour on stage. The actor develops the skills necessary to recreate, through the senses, the conditions conducive to a creative state before beginning work on a role. Stanislavski's approach to actor training is based on continuous observation of successful acting practice and is not a rigid approach. As he said himself, 'create your own method'.

The Stanislavski Acting Studio was originally set up by Deirdre, an actor, director and teacher, for the purpose of training a permanent company of actors and directors and this resulted in the opening of the Focus Theatre, and the planned development of the Stanislavski Studio four years later in September 1967 in Pembroke Place, off Upper Pembroke Street, Dublin 2.

The Focus Theatre opened its door on September 29, 1967 with a production of *Play with a Tiger* by Doris Lessing which ran for four weeks. The opening of the 72-seat Focus Theatre 'was a dream realized for the late Deirdre O'Connell'[5]. Over the next 45 years, from its opening in 1967 to its closure in 2012, the Focus Theatre and Stanislavski Studio produced over 300 plays by internationally-renowned playwrights such as Henrik Ibsen, August Strindberg, Lillian Hellman, Doris Lessing, Tennessee Williams, Arthur Miller, Jean Genet, Marguerite Duras, Athol Fugard and Samuel Beckett, as well as training and showcasing the work of many well-known Irish actors, directors and writers, 'thus becoming an important part of late 20th-century Irish theatre history'.[6]

Beginnings

Eleanora Deirdre O'Connell was born to Irish immigrant parents on June 16, 1939 in the South Bronx district of New York City. Deirdre was one of five siblings. Her father Michael J. O'Connell was born in Glengala, Co Sligo and her mother, Nellie Taafe, came from Banteer in

---

[4] Interview with Deirdre O'Connell, Artistic Director, Focus Theatre by Mary Moynihan, April 22, 1999.

[5] www.nli.ie/pdfs/mss%20lists/140_FocusTheatre.pdf, p. 5.

[6] www.nli.ie/pdfs/mss%20lists/140_FocusTheatre.pdf, p. 5.

Co Cork. After finishing school, Deirdre won a scholarship to attend night classes and study at Erwin Piscator's New York Dramatic Workshop, 'and her parents encouraged her to pursue her passion for acting. While performing in one of the various productions at the Dramatic Workshop's Repertory Theatre, she was spotted by Lee Strasberg and invited to join the Actor's Studio where she discovered the Stanislavski system, which was to become her lifelong passion and the Focus Theatre's artistic policy'.[7]

By 1963 Deirdre had completed her formal education in theatre and had also become a 'life member' of the Actors Studio in New York which she attended for two years, 'one year while completing my course in the Erwin Piscator Dramatic Workshop and then visiting for a second year before coming to Ireland'.[8]

Deirdre believed that having a desire to find a sense of truth in her performance naturally drew her 'towards Erwin Piscator, Saul Colin and eventually Lee Strasberg, all of whom worked with different points of emphasis'[9] through the Stanislavski system where the aim was the development of the inner life: the emotional and sensory life of the person or character you were going to become eventually.

According to Deirdre she devoted a substantial part of her life to teaching and using the Stanislavski system because:

> I was drawn towards the concept of at least attempting, if not always achieving, to recreate the moment every night and within myself, to make it possible for the actor to relive, to recreate, not just for oneself but as a means of communication for the audience, that it could be done, alive, afresh, anew every night and even at that tender age I did see the difference between representational theatre and what I regard to be creative theatre.[10]

When Deirdre O'Connell arrived in Dublin in 1963 at the age of twenty-three her main aim was to establish a full-time repertory company 'and the only way to start a company was to train one'.[11] As

---

[7] www.nli.ie/pdfs/mss%20lists/140_FocusTheatre.pdf, p. 5.

[8] Interview with Deirdre O'Connell, Artistic Director, Focus Theatre by Mariosa de Faoite, July 1994.

[9] Interview with Deirdre O'Connell, Artistic Director, Focus Theatre by Mary Moynihan, April 22, 1999.

[10] Ibid.

[11] Interview with Deirdre O'Connell, Artistic Director, Focus Theatre, by Mariosa de Faoite July 1994, tape 1.

Deirdre said herself she was aware of her skills as a 'communicator'[12] and so she set up the Stanislavski Studio in order to train actors and directors in the Stanislavski System and more importantly to lay the foundation for a permanent repertory company – an objective that led to the founding of the Focus Theatre four years later.

The first studios were conducted at the Pocket Theatre, Ely Place, in Dublin, at the invitation of its director Ursula White Lennon, and commenced in April 1963 after advertised auditions had been held. Early members of the new company included Declan and Mary Elizabeth Burke-Kennedy, Sabina Coyne, Tom Hickey, Tim McDonnell, Frank McDonald, Johnny Murphy, Meryl Gourley and Joan Bergin. According to original studio member and actor Tim McDonnell 'I saw an article in the *Irish Press* with a photograph of Deirdre O'Connell stating that the 'method' was coming to Dublin and that she was about to begin classes in a small theatre called the Pocket Theatre and I ran down immediately and made an appointment to see her the following Saturday. In those days Deirdre held auditions for the studio. She gave you...tests, a test in relaxation, imagination and...depending on how you did, you were either accepted or not. But I think she accepted everyone (laughs). So I went down and saw her and within a month started classes in the Pocket Theatre in Ely Place...It was 1963, we met every Saturday and Sunday and did classes and exercises by Stanislavski, myself and other founder members of the studio including Tom Hickey and Johnny Murphy'.[13]

The Stanislavski Studio was the first actor-training studio of its kind in Ireland. At that time there was no 'Irish Academy of Dramatic Art...no real training in theatre'.[14] The development of the actor's skills has always been at the heart of the Focus Theatre and Deirdre's introduction to Ireland of the Stanislavski system was seen as a radical style of training, which enabled the actor, while being individually supervised, to be trained in how to work on his or her art and develop a conscious acting technique. The deeper the actor's experience of his or her part, selected, controlled and artistically expressed, the fuller the audience's involvement and participation will be. The philosophy of the studio emphasizes the creative role of the actor while at the same time insisting on group or ensemble teamwork as the essence of good

---

[12] Ibid.

[13] Interview with Tim McDonnell (1991) *Focus Theatre Newsletter*, Issue 2, September/ October 1991, p. 8.

[14] Mary Manning, *The Arts in Ireland*, Vol. 3, No. 1, 1975, p. 63.

theatre. This emphasis on ensemble became the hallmark of many Focus productions over the coming years as observed by *The Irish Times*, 'superb acting, a strong sense of ensemble playing'.[15]

According to Tim:

> ...there is no doubt that in the Dublin theatre of that period there was a very deep reluctance to accept training or discipline of any kind, the idea was that an actor basically needed nothing more than natural talent...that has changed nowadays as most theatre schools have absorbed most if not all of Stanislavski's training but back in 1964 this stuff seemed WILD. You may not believe it but for many months the studio had visiting psychiatrists invited by one of the studio members who witnessed the improvisational work and effective memories. It was just an absolutely new thing.[16]

The studio members trained and rehearsed from April to November and the first production by the studio was *For Madmen Only*, an adaptation of Nobel Prize winner Herman Hesse's *Steppenwolf*, staged at the Pocket Theatre on October 7, 1963. With the closure of the Pocket Theatre the following year for development, the studio members had to move elsewhere. The studio then had a number of different bases including the Royal Irish Academy of Music, the Pike Theatre, and the Dublin Shakespeare Society premises then in Fitzwilliam Square. During this period studio members continued to meet twice weekly to work together on the Stanislavski System and to develop skills in improvisation. Public improvisational performances were held in different venues around the city including the Dublin Shakespeare Society venue, the Embankment in Tallaght, and the Project Art Gallery, and also as open-air performances in public parks. Studio members performed in Meryl Gourley's productions of *Calvary* and *Resurrection* by William Butler Yeats, staged at Players Theatre in Trinity College, Dublin. Having to constantly change venue for productions encouraged Deirdre and the other studio members to look for their own permanent premises to house the Stanislavski Studio.

During this period Deirdre O'Connell worked as a singer and actor in order to raise money for a permanent theatre space. As a 'noted ballad and folk singer'[17] she sang in working men's clubs in England,

---

[15] Review by Derek West of *The Balcony* by Jean Genet, *The Irish Times*, April 27, 1992.

[16] Interview with Tim McDonnell, *Focus Theatre Newsletter*, Issue 2, September / October 1991, p. 8.

[17] www.nli.ie/pdfs/mss%20lists/140_FocusTheatre.pdf, p. 6.

returning to Dublin to run the Stanislavski studios and on one of the
visits home she met the singer Luke Kelly (1940-1984), a member of the
Irish music group the Dubliners. They met in

> O'Donoghue's pub, Merrion Row, Dublin, and they were
> married on June 21, 1965. Deirdre also returned to New York
> several times to work in summer season productions to raise
> more money for her project'.[18]

In 1967, after a long period of searching, perseverance and
determination by the studio members, a permanent premises was
eventually found in a lane off Pembroke Street by Declan Burke-
Kennedy – an empty and abandoned clothing-label factory space at 6
Pembroke Place that was in a considerable state of disrepair.

According to Tim Mc Donnell 'I remember people were literally
walking around town in small battalions trying to find a suitable
premises to house the fledgling Focus Theatre Company. It was Declan
Burke-Kennedy who found the place...in Pembroke Place. We had done
the work together, embraced this new system together and the final
conclusion was putting our own theatre together'.[19] A lease was taken
out on the premises at Pembroke Place, organized by Deirdre O'Connell
and Declan Burke-Kennedy and a fund-raising campaign launched to
raise the £3,000 required to renovate and convert the disused space
into a 72-seat theatre. Money came from donations and subscriptions,
including income provided by Deirdre O'Connell and Luke Kelly, from
Mick McCarthy, owner of the Embankment in Tallaght and from co-
founders/studio members Mary Elizabeth and Declan Burke-Kennedy,
and eventually funding was also received from the Arts Council and
Dublin City Council. With assistance from Burke-Kennedy Architects,
the derelict site was transformed into a working theatre space. As part
of the fundraising campaign, in return for £10 or more, friends and
supporters were offered 'the status of patron and an unlimited promise
of free admission to the theatre'.[20]

The opening of the theatre in 1967 was the culmination of four years
hard work and planning. From 1967 until 2012 when the actual building
closed down, the Focus Theatre operated as a venue-based production

---

[18] www.nli.ie/pdfs/mss%20lists/140_FocusTheatre.pdf, p. 6.

[19] Interview with Tim Mc Donnell, Focus Theatre Newsletter, Issue 2,
September / October 1991. Page 9.

[20] Burke-Kennedy, Declan, Booklet *Dublin Focus Theatre
incorporating the Stanislavski studio*, article on The Focus Theatre
by Declan Burke-Kennedy, p. 6.

company, presenting two to three professional theatre productions a year, covering a full repertoire of Irish and international theatre, including the great classics.

Deirdre O'Connell worked as Artistic Director, manager and fundraiser of the Focus Theatre and Stanislavski Studio from 1967 until her death in 2001 as well as acting in most of the major productions presented. The artistic policy of Focus Theatre was to present plays not commonly known in Ireland, which may not have been seen by the Irish public, and plays were never chosen for their commercial value but on the basis of merit. According to Deirdre O'Connell, plays were chosen that featured 'central, very focused relationships, strong characterization and strong, inner-based themes'[21] and this criterion was reflected in the continuing work of the Stanislavski Studio where the emphasis remained on the development of the 'sensual and emotional capacity of the actors'.[22]

The company encouraged new Irish playwrights by presenting an annual lunchtime season of new Irish plays, and over the years showcased the work of Irish playwrights including Mary Elizabeth Burke-Kennedy, Declan Burke-Kennedy, Tommy O'Neill, Tony Cafferty, Ena May, Carmel Winters, Michael Harding, Elizabeth Moynihan, Malachy McKenna and Frank Shouldice.

Mary Elizabeth Burke-Kennedy was to write and direct several successful shows at Focus Theatre including her own *Daughters,* a feminist retelling of an ancient Irish myth; *The Golden Goose* by the Grimm Brothers, which she dramatized and directed; and *Legends* and *Currigh the Shapeshifter,* the latter adapted from the Red Branch legend. Mary Elizabeth is a successful writer, director and teacher of drama who went on to establish the successful Storytellers Theatre Company in 1986.

Throughout the years Focus Theatre supported and at times organized a range of music nights at the venue and off-site, including an annual Sunday Night Music season during July and August. Musicians and performers who took part included Anthony Cronin, Benedict Kiely, Niall Tóibín, Uinsin Ó Donnabháin, Frank Harte, Paul Brady, Paddy Reilly, Paddy Glackin, Liam Weldon, Brídín Gilroy, Donal Lunny, Séamus Mac Mathúna, Tony McMahon, Pearse Hutchinson,

---

[21] Interview with Deirdre O'Connell, Artistic Director, Focus Theatre, by Mariosa de Faoite July 1994. Tape 2.

[22] Interview with Deirdre O'Connell, Artistic Director, Focus Theatre, by Mary Moynihan, April 22, 1999.

Seán Potts, Mick Fitzgerald, Mark Dignam, Mundy, Hugh Doolan, Tom Roche, Joe Molloy, Glen Hansard, Eoin O'Brien, Miriam Ingram, Rosaleen Lynch, Máirtín Byrnes, Christy Moore, Barry Moore, Johnny Moynihan and Roger Doyle. Jazz music nights at Focus Theatre featured artists such as Louis Stewart, Tommy Halferty, Ronan Guilfoyle, Conor Guilfoyle, Mike Nielsen and John Wadham.

The second play presented by Focus Theatre was *Kelly's Eye* by Henry Livings, which ran for three weeks. This was followed in 1968 by a five-week run of *Evening without Angels,* consisting of one-act American plays; Eugene O'Neill's *In the Zone,* Tennessee Williams' *Portrait of a Madonna* and William Saroyan's *Hello Out There.* In July 1968 Focus Theatre presented a double bill of *Miss Julie* by August Strindberg and *The Wedding* by Anton Chekhov, followed by the company's fifth production, Lillian Hellman's *Toys in the Attic* in October. February 1969 saw the opening of *Antigone* by Jean Anouilh which ran for six weeks followed by a five-week run of *In Camera* by Jean Paul Sartre and then a double bill of new plays consisting of *The Creation* by Lee Gallagher and *Lunch Hour* by John Mortimer.

At that time the *Evening Press* saw Focus as 'one of the most exciting theatrical ventures we have had in Dublin' and *The Irish Times* said 'Dublin Focus Theatre is performing a great service to the city and country by its integrity, dedication and the excellence of its actors'.[23]

Because of the limited number of seats, Focus Theatre often struggled financially. From the beginning the premises housed the Stanislavski Studio, which continued to operate on a weekly basis as a training forum for actors under the direction of Deirdre O'Connell. Studio members paid an average membership fee of £1 per week and this money was often used to pay bills for the Focus Theatre. According to founder member Declan Burke-Kennedy 'it had been agreed from the outset that 50% of the box office takings would have to go towards production and publicity costs and that the remainder would be divided, on a percentage basis, among the actors and stage crew. During the five-week run of *Evening without Angels,* the actors took home an average of about £2 per week for their troubles'.[24] In June 1968 the Arts Council gave Focus £500 as a 'guarantee against losses incurred in the area of production and publicity alone, i.e. excluding the payment of

---

[23] Declan Burke-Kennedy, Booklet *Dublin Focus Theatre incorporating the Stanislavski studio*, article on The Focus Theatre by Declan Burke-Kennedy, p. 8.

[24] Ibid., p. 9.

actors and others'. So while the contribution saved the life of the theatre[25] by helping to pay bills and keep Focus operating, it did not support the actors.

Classics

Despite the financial difficulties during the 1970s and 1980s the Focus Theatre went from strength to strength artistically. The company enjoyed critical acclaim for presenting high quality productions of the powerful classical dramas of the Norwegian playwright, poet and theatre director Henrik Ibsen (1828-1906), Swedish author August Strindberg (1849-1912) and Russian dramatist and short story writer Anton Chekhov (1860-1904). Plays by these authors provided a unique vehicle for the Stanislavski-trained Focus actors to bring to life the fullness of the psychologically-driven relationships through ensemble playing, and a depth of emotion that became hallmarks of Focus productions. Deirdre and the original founder members of Focus created an artistic policy that put the ensemble at the heart of the work:

> From the beginning, the Focus Theatre has attempted to create an all-too-rare example of group art, that is to say a concerted pooling together of individual talents and energy towards a commonly-agreed artistic goal. By its constitution and structure, it is not, and does not desire to be, a platform for individual performers more concerned with their own careers than with the artistic endeavour on hand. It is no surprise, therefore, that the finest Focus productions have been noted for 'teamwork' and 'integrity'; for their clear sense of direction and their 'disciplined performances'.[26]

The works of Ibsen, Strindberg and Chekhov are ensemble plays depicting universal human conditions and emotional crises, exploring the conflict between private and public spheres and the lives of men and women trapped or struggling in various ways to break free and find fulfillment. The psychological depth and complex characterization of the plays were well served by the Stanislavski-trained Focus actors. As Artistic Director, Deirdre chose plays on the basis of having strong human relationships, and the work of Ibsen, Strindberg and Chekhov provided a study of human conflict and an exploration of people's lives and desires and the need to live differently as they pursued goals and dreams that were often in conflict with the society around them.

---

[25] Ibid.

[26] Ibid., p. 3.

Drawn by the sexual tension and intense conflicts that trap the men and women in August Strindberg's plays, Focus Theatre presented three of his works, *Miss Julie* in 1968, *The Father* in 1972, and *Dance of Death* in 1978. All three plays touch on themes of love, class and the power struggles of sexual politics. In the introduction to *Miss Julie* Strindberg wrote that what we need is 'first and last...a small stage and a small house; then a new dramatic art might rise and the theatre might at least become an institution for the entertainment of people with culture'.[27] The intimate nature of the Focus Theatre Space was ideally suited for bringing to life the plays of Strindberg, Ibsen and Chekhov.

In January 1970 Focus Theatre presented *Uncle Vanya* by Anton Chekhov which played to full houses for ten weeks (the company had already performed his play *The Wedding* in 1968). *Uncle Vanya* was followed by Henrik Ibsen's *Hedda Gabler*, which ran for 12 weeks. In this and other Ibsen plays, Focus had great success in portraying the emotional turmoil of Ibsen's characters as they struggled to free themselves from the suffocating conventions of a class-ridden society.

Press coverage for *Hedda Gabler* stated that 'one must once again return thanks to the brave little Focus Theatre for bringing to the Dublin stage the type of quality play which the major theatres steadfastly ignore...This is the only theatre in the country which regularly puts on great plays and I mean the only theatre. It is also unique and exciting in its methods of approaching a play'.[28]

In 1971 the company presented *A Doll's House,* also by Henrik Ibsen, which ran for five months from November 1971 to March 1972. Nora Helmer in *A Doll's House* is a woman searching for freedom and independence. She is trapped in a male-dominated environment and struggles against domestic oppression and the traditional, subservient role of wife and mother. The play reflects a common theme of Ibsen's work, the individual power struggle in opposition to the oppression of a wider social authority, particularly in relation to middle-class society. Themes of sexual identity, desire and the individual struggle for self-determination can also be found in *Hedda Gabler* and other productions by Ibsen presented by Focus Theatre including *John Gabriel Borkman* (1974 and 1991), *Rosmersholm* (1976), *The Lady from the Sea* (1980), *Ghosts* (1985), *Little Eyolf* (1990) and *The Master*

---

[27] Strindberg, August, *Works of August Strindberg: Miss Julie, the Father, Creditors, the Outlaw, the Road to Damascus, the Stronger and Other Plays*. Author's Preface to *Miss Julie*.

[28] Declan Burke-Kennedy, p 12.

Builder (1991). In relation to *Little Eyolf*, Brian Brennan of *The Sunday Independent* (October 1990) wrote that 'it is significant that this traditional staging of a rarely-seen Ibsen turns out to be one of the most satisfying value for money productions to emerge from the Dublin Theatre Festival. The old classic holds its own beside many of its more ambitious rivals and the idea of staging it at all seems almost revolutionary'.

Improvisation

From its inception in 1963 until the early 1970s an important part of the Stanislavski Studio was the development and use of improvisation for public performances. According to Deirdre O'Connell, the studio only did one production from 1963 to 1967 but 'theatrically we kept performing as Ireland's only improvisation theatre'.[29]

In February 1971 the studio members began an innovative programme of Sunday night improvisation theatre:

> ...the studio members inaugurated 'a year long series of improvised performances' which showed 'oodles of resources and ingenuity' according to *The Evening Press* and provide 'an enlightening and stimulating evening for the *Evening Herald*. One of the performers, Mary Elizabeth Burke-Kennedy, described the work as 'nerve-wracking, we would sometimes take a theme and develop it from week to week, like a soap opera. I remember one which concerned an imaginary family in the west of Ireland, near where uranium was supposed to have been discovered, it went on for about 6 weeks'.[30]

The improvisations were unscripted ad-lib enactments on stage, based on a specific pre-chosen theme or issue. After agreeing on the dramatic issue at the core of the work, the actors prepared by setting up and working on character development and relationships beforehand as well as discussing in detail the time and place (where and when) for the improvisation. However

> because it is unscripted an 'improv' has a spontaneous power all its own and often a degree of realism which can be quite

---

[29] Interview with Deirdre O'Connell, Artistic Director, Focus Theatre, by Mariosa de Faoite July 1994, tape 1.

[30] Mary Moynihan, 'The Stanislavski Studio of Dublin. Exploring the use of the Stanislavski System (exercises and programme of actor training) as practised by the Focus Stanislavski Studio', dissertation, 30 April, 1991, p. 12.

unnerving...the actions and words that the audience witness are in no way rehearsed or prearranged.[31]

The improvisations were like plays 'communally and spontaneously created and in that way can take on a richness and an authority which it takes a truly gifted author to possess'.[32] During the live performance of the improvisations the actors used soliloquies to develop the audience's understanding of a particular storyline by moving 'in and out of naturalism at the switch of a particular light, to give a personal view of what was going on, in the sense of some personal story or recollection'.[33]

According to Declan Burke-Kennedy another important element of the improvisation work was:

> ...its immediate relevance to the social context in which it is performed. The issues proposed and embodied by the actors are those which most bear down on them from day to day. Even when the issue is proposed by the audience, the individual interpretation of it is inevitably coloured by the social experience and outlook of each individual actor. It is the fusion (sometimes confusion) of those individual personalities and points of view that constitute the dramatic essence of improvisational theatre.[34]

The public improvisations played a key role in developing the ethos of ensemble playing which the theatre was committed to because in improvisation 'togetherness and co-operation are the basic ingredients and the process, as well as being of dramatic value for the audience, is an experience which continually directs the actor away from the isolationist and virtuoso tendencies that bedevil this most vain of trades'.[35] Public improvisations ceased after the 1970s and were revived briefly during the late 1990s. Improvisational exercises continued to be used extensively as part of the training provided by the Stanislavski studio and in rehearsals for Focus Theatre productions.

In 1986 Deirdre O'Connell received the Harvey's Theatre Award for Outstanding Contribution to Irish Theatre. Another success for Focus Theatre was *Diary of a Madman* translated by Ronald Wilks and

---

[31] Declan Burke-Kennedy, p. 17.

[32] Ibid., p. 17.

[33] Peter Thompson, 'Method in their Madness 21 Years of the Focus Theatre', *Theatre Ireland – Retrospective*, 1987, p. 32.

[34] Declan Burke-Kennedy, p. 17.

[35] Ibid., p. 17.

adapted by Tim McDonnell from the work of Nikolai Gogol, with Tim performing the sole role of Poprishchin, and Deirdre O'Connell directing. Tim was one of the original founder members of Focus Theatre acting in early productions including the first Focus show *Play with a Tiger*.

After being involved with Focus in the early years, Tim moved to the United States to work on building up a successful acting career there. In 1981 in New York Tim was involved in a tragic accident in which he lost the use of his legs and became confined to a wheelchair. After the accident Tim returned to Ireland and in 1987 took to the stage with *Diary of a Madman*, produced by Focus Theatre and first performed at the Project Arts Centre on 28th September to excellent reviews.

Deirdre took the early rehearsals for *Diary of a Madman* in Tim's home with Tim sitting on the bed and they rehearsed for four months, Deirdre visiting twice a week, and eventually rehearsals moved into the Focus Theatre. The play ran at the Project Arts Centre for the Dublin Theatre Festival in 1987 and Tim won the Harvey's Award for Best Actor in the same year. In March 1988 *Diary of a Madman* ran at the Peacock Theatre, Dublin and in 1989 toured to New York and played for 22 performances at the Irish Arts Centre where it again received excellent reviews. Tim won a Best Actor Obie award for his performance in New York in 1989. *Diary of a Madman* was made into a film, produced and directed by Ronan O'Leary, sponsored by RTÉ, and filmed over five-and-a-half days in Ardmore Studios in 1990. In the film Deirdre O'Connell performed the role of Mavra.

Later Years

The 1990s began with a very successful production of *Who's Afraid of Virginia Woolf?* by American playwright Edward Albee directed by Ann Maloney O'Driscoll with Deirdre playing the role of Martha, Sean Treacy as George, and Bairbre Ní Chaoimh and Brent Hearne as Honey and Nick. 'Like its giant forebear, Strindberg's *Dance of Death*, the play begins in hell, and all the revelations and reactions take place within that landscape'.[36] The play first premiered on Broadway in 1962 with Uta Hagan as Martha and Arthur Hill as George, and was made into a film in 1966 with Richard Burton and Elizabeth Taylor, the latter winning an Oscar for her performance as Martha, a 'virago of a wife'.[37]

---

[36] Stanley Kauffmann, *New York Times*, June 24, 1966, Movies.

[37] Ibid.

The emotionally violent production at Focus Theatre received excellent reviews, portraying the depths of a disturbed relationship and the struggle for psychological growth in the face of thwarted ambition, expectation and hope.

> To take on Edward Albee's mammoth work *Who's Afraid of Virginia Woolf?* and attempt to stage it at the tiny Focus Theatre (without Liz Taylor and Richard Burton) could be described as foolhardy indeed...(however) four wonderful actors...have attacked the play and succeeded in wrestling out of it one of the most rewarding night's theatre a Dublin audience can hope to see[38]

and

> Albee's play reaches a shattering climax. The Focus production is one of the best for years...with a portrayal of intense emotional power, marvelously sustained by Deirdre O'Connell.[39]

A particular success during the 1990s was *A View from the Bridge* by Arthur Miller, which opened at Focus Theatre in October 1991 as part of the Dublin Theatre Festival and then subsequently, due to its success, transferred to the larger Andrews Lane Theatre. The 'riveting production has all the elements of classic Greek tragedy'[40] and 'proved a great success...and kept its audience clapping long after the players had left the stage'.[41]

Throughout the 1990s, Focus Theatre continued to produce old and new plays ranging from nineteenth century classics to contemporary world drama – staging work such as Clifford Odets' *Rocket to the Moon* (1990); *The Secret Rapture* by David Hare and *Small Craft Warnings* by Tennessee Williams, (1991); *The Balcony* by Jean Genet, *The Misogynist* by Michael Harding and *Alice Through the Looking Glass* by Lewis Carroll, adapted by Robert Lane (1992); *All My Sons* by Arthur Miller (1993); *Men Without Shadows* by Jean Paul Sartre (1995); *Night, Mother* by Marsha Norman (1997); *Anna Christie* by Eugene

---

[38] Lorcan Roche, 'Fearless Cast Reap Success', *Irish Independent,* 3 January, 1990.

[39] John Finegan, 'Classic Return', *Evening Herald*, 3 January, 1990.

[40] Gerry Colgan, 'A View from the Bridge at the Focus', *The Irish Times,* 11 October, 1991.

[41] Patricia Murray, 'Success for Classic Miller', *The Irish Press* 11 October, 1991.

The 1990s and early 2000s saw a continuation and expansion of the lunchtime season consisting of new Irish writing as well as European and American one-act plays and the production of professional scene study work for public performance. Lunchtime plays often transferred to evening performance and included *Rise and Shine* by Sean McCarthy (1990); *Hello Stranger* by Truman Capote (1991); *Time's Up* by Carmel Winters and Patrick McCabe and *Small Box Psychosis* by Barry McKinley (1992); and two seasons of Tennessee Williams one-act plays in 1995 and 1996 including *Talk to Me Like the Rain and Let Me Listen*, *Auto-da-Fé*, *The Lady of Larkspur Lotion*, *Something Unspoken* and *Suddenly Last Summer*.

Naked Truth: An Evening of Scene Study opened in June 1999 and consisted of scenes from *Little Malcolm and his Struggle Against the Eunuchs* by David Halliwell; *Kiss of the Spiderwoman* by Manuel Puig; *Skylight* by David Hare; *Hedda Gabler* by Henrik Ibsen and *The Lonesome West* by Martin McDonagh.

The last play Deirdre acted in was *The House of Bernarda Alba* by Federico García Lorca, which opened on 11 February 1999 at Focus Theatre. The play was a success for the theatre, running for nine weeks and was directed by Focus-trained actor and director Jayne Snow. The central part of Bernarda Alba was played by Deirdre O'Connell and all except one of the cast of ten actors trained at the Stanislavski Studio under her direction. In the production 'Deirdre O'Connell gives a towering performance as Bernarda – a shuffling monster of bitterness'[42] and 'creates an intelligent and credible performance in the title role'.[43]

A feature film documentary *Hold the Passion* was completed in 2000 by Focus Films, produced by Ann McRory and directed by Ronan O'Leary and premiered at the Cork Film Festival. The documentary was made to commemorate and pay tribute to the life and work of Deirdre O'Connell. It relates Deirdre's journey as artistic director as well as the history of the Focus Theatre and Stanislavski Studio, and contains unique footage of Deirdre's last performance in her role of Bernarda Alba as well as direct interviews with Deirdre and other artists of the Focus Theatre and Stanislavski Studio. Several public screenings have taken place at film festivals and at the IFI cinema in Dublin and the

---

[42] Emer O'Kelly, 'Lorca's Sexual Rage kept in a very clever Focus', *Sunday Independent*, 14 February, 1999.

[43] Gerry Colgan, 'The House of Bernarda Alba', *The Irish Times* 12 February, 1999.

makers of this excellent documentary are still waiting for it to be screened by Ireland's national television station RTÉ.

Deirdre O'Connell died suddenly at her home in Dartmouth Square in Dublin on June 10, 2001 'four years after Focus Theatre celebrated 'Thirty Years of Magic'.[44] Deirdre's funeral service was held in Whitehall Church on the northside of Dublin where, 36 years earlier, Deirdre had married Luke Kelly of the Dubliners. Following a service attended by several hundred people Deirdre was buried in Glasnevin Cemetery. Deirdre was an extraordinary human being and artist and she was mourned and missed by many friends and associates both personally and professionally.

Joe Devlin was appointed artistic director of Focus Theatre in 2002 and artists, including Tim McDonnell, Mary Moynihan, Paul Keely and Ann Maloney O'Driscoll, continued to provide training in the Stanislavski system of actor training.

Between 2001 and 2005 productions included *Tillsonburg* by Irish writer Malachy McKenna (2003) directed by Liam Heffernan, *Jesus Hopped the A-Train* by Stephen Adly (2004) directed by Joe Devlin, *Very Heaven* by Ann Lambert (2004) directed by Bairbre Ní Chaoimh; and *Proof* by David Auburn at Andrews Lane Theatre (2005) directed by Joe Devlin.

In 2004 Deirdre's sister and life-long friend, Geraldine O'Connell Cusack published her book *Children of the Far-Flung*, a 'true account of a remarkable Irish-American family, four generations of emigration and return, from Ireland to New York and back again. It is also the story of the author's sister, the late Deirdre O'Connell, founder and artistic director of the critically-acclaimed Focus Theatre in Dublin, her marriage to popular singer Luke Kelly, her successes and failures, and her remarkable and long-lasting impact on theatre in Ireland'.[45]

In 2006 the Focus theatre venue at Pembroke Place closed down on a temporary basis for refurbishment. For the next four years Focus productions were presented off-site in various venues throughout Dublin. In July 2006 Focus Theatre presented a number of successful productions including *Two Rooms* by American playwright Lee Blessing, directed by Mary Moynihan in Andrews Lane Theatre followed by *Mother Teresa is Dead* by Helen Edmundson, directed by

---

[44] www.nli.ie/pdfs/mss%20lists/140_FocusTheatre.pdf, p.6.

[45] http://www.amazon.com/Children-Far-Flung-Geraldine-OConnell-Cusack/dp/1904148336.

[45] Focus Theatre website September 2012.

Joe Devlin at the Project Arts Centre. The following year Focus Theatre presented at the New Theatre and on tour, *Picasso's Women* by Brian McAvera, consisting of three monologues directed by the author, Mary Moynihan and Joe Devlin. In 2008 the theatre won the Writers Guild of Great Britain Award for the Encouragement of New Work for its production of *Picasso's Women*.

After four years off-site, the Focus Company returned to the Focus Theatre space on June 16, 2010, which was the date of Deirdre O'Connell's birthday. The theatre re-opened with a production of *The Tower* by +Joe Joyce, performed by founder member Tom Hickey and actor Bosco Hogan. New plays that year included the Irish premiere of *Tic* by Irish writer Elizabeth Moynihan (2010) and an Irish premiere of *Orphans* by Dennis Kelly (2010), produced by Smashing Times Theatre Company and Playleft Productions in association with Focus Theatre, and directed by Mary Moynihan. During the 2000s the Focus Theatre identified its artistic policy as having

> a strong commitment to exploring contemporary international theatre practice. The Company's artistic policy is to present the best of contemporary world drama, to develop new plays, to produce world classics and to bring the theatre's work to as wide an audience as possible.[46]

It was during this period that Focus Theatre began to present a range of productions in association with other theatre companies including *Baglady* by Frank McGuinness, produced by Eska Riada in association with Focus Theatre (2010); *Stones in His Pockets* by Marie Jones, produced by Aisling Ghéar Theatre in association with Focus Theatre (2010); and *Hollywood Valhalla* by Aidan Harney (2012) produced by Purple Heart Theatre in association with Focus Theatre at Bewleys Café Theatre.

Legacy

The Focus Theatre venue closed down in April 2012 due to cuts in arts funding. The company was no longer able to pay the rent due on the premises at Pembroke Place and the lights came down for the final time on Sunday April 29, 2012 after 45 years of making theatre. The final evening at Focus was marked by a reception at 7.30pm attended by the President of Ireland Michael D. Higgins and his wife Sabina Higgins and by invited past and present artists and friends of the Focus Theatre

---

[46] Focus Theatre website September 2012.

along with members of the O'Connell and Kelly families representing the late Deirdre O'Connell and the late Luke Kelly. Sabina (nee Coyne) Higgins was one of the original founder members of Focus Theatre and both Sabina and Michael were long-time friends of Deirdre. Sabina was bridesmaid at Deirdre's wedding to the singer Luke Kelly. As supporters of the Focus Theatre, Sabina and Michael paid tribute to all those who had worked at Focus Theatre over the years. Following the reception a performance of *Hollywood Valhalla* by Aidan Harney was held.

Speaking at the reception on the last night, the President said we all owed Ms O'Connell a debt of gratitude because she brought 'the acting techniques developed by the foremost theorist of theatre in the 20th century, Konstantin Stanislavski, to Ireland...The introduction of these techniques was the primary purpose of her coming to Ireland...the result was a unique and invaluable contribution to the creative arts in Ireland'. He said that without the Focus Theatre, Irish people 'would have been deprived of access to some of the finest works that are important for an understanding of our humanity and the purpose of our human existence'.[47]

The Focus Theatre has played an invaluable role in Irish Theatre over the years, presenting over 300 plays, and the Stanislavski Studio has made a significant contribution by providing a unique training in the Stanislavski System to a large number of actors and directors. Many of Ireland's leading theatre and film artists started their careers at Focus Theatre. Gabriel Byrne made his debut in Focus in 1976 in a version of Turgenev's *A Month in the Country*.

Other leading actors and directors to have worked at Focus include Olwen Fouéré, Margaret Twomey, Joan Bergin, Mary Elizabeth Burke-Kennedy, Bairbre Ní Chaoimh, Ena May, Jayne Snow, Tom Hickey, Johnny Murphy, Gerard McSorley, Tim McDonnell, Donal O'Kelly, Ger Carey, Eamon Hunt, Paul Raynor, Liam Halligan, Ken Harmon, Luke Hayden, Brent Hearne, Paul Keeley, Robbie McDowell, Michelle Manahan, Elizabeth Moynihan, Ann O'Driscoll, Paul Roe, Ann Russell-Weakly, and Mary Jude Ryan. President of Ireland Michael D. Higgins once said that Deirdre O'Connell was 'the single greatest influence in Irish Theatre since the 60s'.[48] The Focus Theatre has had a huge effect

---

[47] Fiona Gartland, 'Final Curtain for Focus Theatre', *The Irish Times* 30 April, 2012.

[48] Kathy Donovan, 'Memories in the Focus', *The Irish Times* Weekend Arts, 25 July, 1992.

on Irish theatre, an influence as Irish actor and founder member of Focus Theatre Tom Hickey says is 'quite substantially hidden in strands of Dublin theatre'.[49] Speaking at the closing of the Focus Theatre Tom said, 'I don't know what is going to happen to Deirdre's ghost, because every time I come in here I imagine I'm going to see her walking out of the coffee room. Presumably she'll stay here'.[50]

It is not possible to talk or write about Focus Theatre without referring to Deirdre O'Connell who was the founder and driving force of the place. Deirdre always dressed in black, wearing several layers of black shawls providing an intriguing contrast with her flaming red hair. She carried a wooden clipboard with various scripts attached along with an assortment of black bags slung over her shoulder, containing more scripts, notes and papers and the occasional orange or gift she would spontaneously present to you when meeting. Most days she walked the short journey from her home in Dartmouth Square, gliding along the canal and down Leeson Street, turning onto Upper Pembroke Street and entering under the archway of Pembroke Place laneway to arrive at the nearby Focus Theatre where she spent the majority of her time.

I first heard about Focus Theatre from a friend in 1988. At that time there was a huge demand for places in the studio and no clearly-defined pathway or criteria for joining. Deirdre was a busy woman and sometimes did not follow traditional rules of doing business, such as answering phones or making appointments, unless it suited her. As a stranger approaching Focus, finding a way to contact Deirdre was often difficult and required persistence (perhaps Deirdre's way of seeing how passionate and determined you were!).

Another friend of mine encouraged me to approach Focus. He waited at the end of the laneway as I walked down it slowly towards the large black wooden door of the whitewashed Focus Theatre. As I was about to knock on the door my courage failed. I made to leave when suddenly a gust of wind blew the door open and a voice from the darkness cried out (entering Focus was like entering into Aladdin's Cave) 'Who's there? Come in'. It was a member of Focus, Jarlath Fahy; a group of actors were inside building the set for *A Question of Geography* by John Berger and Nella Bielski. I offered to help out

---

[49] Peter Thompson, 'Method in their Madness, 21 Years of the Focus Theatre', *Theatre Ireland Retrospective* No 15, p. 34.

[50] Helen Donohue, 'Closure of the Focus Theatre', Interview with Tom Hickey, RTÉ News Report, April 26, 2012.

building the set and was then asked to help backstage, which I did. Each evening as Deirdre arrived into the theatre before the show started she would pass me by, a mysterious presence all in black, acknowledging my presence with a kind nod or gesture yet rarely speaking. When the lights came down on a performance at the end of each evening it was tradition to head to Houricans Pub on Lower Leeson Street, sometimes known as the 'Focus Office' (out of necessity as Focus Theatre was too small to house its own office space). One evening in Houricans during the last week of the run I was beckoned over to speak directly with Deirdre about my joining the studio and that was it. It was like being called into the inner sanctum and I was initiated.

Deirdre called core artists who worked full-time at Focus her 'family' and those who visited on a more infrequent basis 'cousins'. I moved swiftly into the heart of the family, acting and directing at Focus Theatre and making many friends that I still have today. It was like a creative commune. After ten years working at Focus Theatre I moved on, as many artists did, but you never really leave Focus and it never leaves you. Working with Deirdre was special.

Deirdre said she was always in mourning for her late husband, the singer Luke Kelly, who died in 1984, a few years after Deirdre and Luke had separated. Deirdre often spoke of Luke and for many years a picture of him hung in the Focus Theatre Green Room where Deirdre would sit perched on top of a high wooden stool surveying her tiny kingdom. Deirdre always remained close to, and received great support from, Luke's family, keeping in touch with Luke's brother Jimmy Kelly and the other family members.

With her extraordinary talent as an actor, director and teacher, Deirdre could easily have chosen to work elsewhere, however, despite the ongoing financial difficulties experienced by the venue, she chose to remain and dedicate her life to the Focus Theatre. Deirdre lived Stanislavski's maxim of 'loving the art in yourself, not yourself in the art' and was truly dedicated to seeking and portraying truth in performance. She had excellent insights into human behaviour and was a great communicator.

Deirdre was a genuinely rare human being, and offstage a very private person, sometimes to the point of reclusiveness. Whether performing in a show or not, most evenings Deirdre would arrive early into the Focus Theatre to check everything was in order. Everyone in Focus helped out, actors putting up posters or answering the phone during the day, studio members cleaning the space or serving teas and coffees in the evening. On occasion Deirdre was not slow in letting you know her mind if something irked her particularly in relation to the preparedness of the theatre space before the audience arrived.

One evening I happened to be on the receiving end of one of Deirdre's rebukes not because of anything I had done but simply because I was the first person she saw when she arrived into the theatre. For some reason she was particularly fired up this evening, so I told her where to go in no uncertain terms, picked up my coat and bag and left. She immediately followed me out to the laneway to apologize and after that we got on like a house on fire. She was never having a go at the individual but simply fussing over the preparedness of her beloved theatre. Sometimes I wondered was she testing us to see what we were made of?

To those of us who knew Deirdre as a friend she was a warm and unique comrade and mentor, always willing to offer a helping hand. She was incredibly generous in sharing her insights and skills as an artist and teacher of the Stanislavski System and an interesting and unique individual to know. I worked on many productions with her and attended countless studios, and in rehearsal or performance she was always professional, courteous and courageous while offstage she maintained her creative eccentricity.

Deirdre consistently encouraged actors to develop their sensory apparatus and she herself was a very sensory woman. Physically she was thin and delicate, yet on and off stage, she had a powerful inner power and presence while also being incredibly vulnerable. Like all of us she was human and suffered her demons yet she followed her dream and has made a rare and unique contribution as an artist to countless individuals and to the world she lived in. I will always remember her with love and appreciation. Thank you Deirdre O'Connell.

Deirdre O'Connell
1939–2001
Founder of the Focus Theatre

3 | The Journey to Stanislavski and Beyond

Joe Devlin

Home life was not easy but if I took anything good from living there it was to try and better myself by reading. Educate yourself. At home there were books everywhere. All kinds of books: history, politics, art, novels, biography, plays and books on acting. Books on acting?!

We lived on a housing estate in West Belfast. Before I learnt to read I would make up stories for my brother Peter. It was the 1970's and the Troubles were in full swing – they were very dark years for everyone. I used to escape into books of fairytales, adventure stories and science fiction – Doctor Who mostly, and books about planets and space travel.

When there were no power cuts we liked to watch TV. Dad's books were subliminally placed behind the television set. Those book spines are emblazoned on my mind. *Napoleon*, *An Introduction to Modern Painting*, *Irish Language Dictionary*, *Complete Works of Shakespeare*, *Complete Works of Oscar Wilde*, *A Dictionary of Political Quotations*, *Trinity* by Leon Uris, a paperback on the U.V.F, (Ulster Volunteer Force), a biography of James Connolly, a *History of the Trade Union Movement*, a book on The Molly Maguires...

As I watched and experienced the thrill of the Doctor and Sarah Jane fighting Sontarans in medieval Britain the message was going in at tea time on a Saturday. Mum loved Hollywood musicals – we watched them as a fatherless family (common for many Irish Catholic families in West Belfast in those days). My brother and I loved 1930's horror movies, the Marx Brothers and Flash Gordon. Outside, bullets whizzed through the windows, cars were hi-jacked, tear gas and bombs exploded. Shootings and assassinations happened and gun battles took place. Road blocks were a common occurrence. People's houses were raided. Innocent men were interned. Buildings were set on fire and sometimes people too. To escape I could fly away in the Tardis, or completely submerge myself in the comic-book world of Superman.

In retrospect a comic-book hero was an early archetype for a terrified child to find some safety in the realm of the imagination. As a child I was emotionally shut down. Post-traumatic stress would be diagnosed later. The experience of the north made me old in some ways – there are things that children should not bear witness to. Survival was not only through books, but by drawing pictures and listening to pop music – they made me feel alive. I particularly loved melody. I had three older sisters who all had records. Anne loved The Beatles, Moya loved Abba and Trish loved The Bay City Rollers. The vinyl on those records was worn to the groove. Paul McCartney and David Bowie on the 1970's transistor radio elated me. My own record-buying days would happen later with Punk music, New Wave, and the New Romantics. I loved to dance to the Top 40 in the kitchen. Oh the joy, the exhilaration of it all.

I liked Dad's art books. He used to go to the second-hand bookshops in Smithfield and bring books home. I would inherit this trait from him in my teens. One book in particular had a black and white reproduction of Millais' *Ophelia* floating in a river. It scared the living daylights out of me but I would pick it up and stare at it for ages. When I was 10 years old I discovered Speech and Drama on a Saturday morning. We performed poetry and acted in Christmas pantomimes. I could now completely escape into my imagination. At secondary school with the help of an inspirational teacher called Kieran Dynan I discovered Shakespeare for myself, as well as Heaney, Keats and Wordsworth. 'The world is too much with us' indeed. It is still one of my favourite sonnets.

Mum and Dad both loved theatre. When I was 12 or 13 they would take me to see contemporary Irish plays such as Graham Reid's *Hidden Curriculum* at the Lyric and Irish classics such as O'Casey's *Juno and The Paycock* at the Arts Theatre in Belfast. I was a teenager in the early 1980's when I first discovered Stanislavski in a book called Building a Character on a shelf in my Dad's study. I couldn't really understand it. But it did prick my interest.

I moved to the Midlands in England in the mid 1980's to live with my sister Anne in Birmingham. My A Level exam results had been poor in Belfast but my social life had been terrific. I also had this brilliant part-time job working in a record shop. I spent all my earnings on books, records and going to rock concerts. There were too many distractions. My sister Anne and her husband, Chris Parr, a TV Drama producer, helped me to get focused to revise for my exams, and create a good work ethic. I revised for English Literature, Art and Art History and had a life-changing year living with them. Dinner conversations were about art, politics, art-house films, serious plays and classical music. Chris even let me into the B.B.C. TV studio to watch TV drama being made at Pebble Mill. Constant visitors to the house included the playwrights David Edgar and John Godber, the latter's Hull Truck Theatre Company, and the director Danny Boyle, to name but a few.

My sister Anne was a playwright. Sometimes she would invite me to go to the Royal Court Theatre to see her work. I was able to meet and talk to actors and directors including a very young Simon Curtis. It was so exciting and I was only 19 years old. It was such a privilege to experience and meet with some of the best professional creative talents working in theatre, film and TV. I would travel to Stratford to see Shakespeare and classical productions at the R.S.C. I saw most of the 1986 and 1987 Seasons in Stratford – about 18 productions over a 12 month period. Tickets were only £4 standing: I was in heaven. After my exams I moved to Stratford and got a bar job, just to see plays including *Macbeth* with Jonathan Pryce and Sinead Cusack; *Romeo and Juliet* with Sean Bean and Niamh Cusack; *Twelfth Night* and *The Merchant of Venice* with Antony Sher; *The Art of Success* with Simon Russell Beale and Michael Kitchen; *The Rover* with Jeremy Irons and Imogen Stubbs; *Hyde Park* with Fiona Shaw; *The Fair Maid of the West* with Imelda Staunton and Pete Postlethwaite. I would travel to London and Paris by means of cheap coach tickets, to visit art galleries. I would also go to see classic plays in London's West End, and touring productions by Michael Pennington's English Shakespeare Company. So, before I started my degree in Theatre Studies and Art and Design, I had a very good grounding in classical theatre, new writing for stage, and a good understanding of the visual arts.

In relation to theatre that I experienced in the U.K I had not seen anything like the standard of acting or production anywhere in Ireland up to that point, except with visiting international productions to the Belfast Festival or the Grand Opera House once a year. From talking to the actors in the Dirty Duck pub beside the R.S.C in Stratford I understood that there was a very serious classical, actor-training tradition that supported the British Theatre industry going back hundreds of years. (However, at that time one of the key issues that was starting to emerge was the invasion of theatre by university academics with wonderful ideas that would compromise the work of the actors and the plays themselves – a trend that would later take over mainstream Irish Theatre.) All of that experience, both on stage and off stage, would later influence my attitudes and the future choices I would make about my own work.

It was only when I was studying for my degree aged 20 at the then Liverpool Polytechnic that I began to try and get an understanding of actor-training, or more specifically the Stanislavski approach. I was emotionally under-developed and not very equipped for life. That would soon change with living independently, and with love, heartbreak, alcohol and more part-time jobs. A retired Stanislavski-based actor from Switzerland called Kim Lauterberg taught us the history of World Theatre and Stanislavski performance for three hours a week. He had a quiet depth and a firm but gentle rhythm. As you might expect from that kind of experience it was really just a taster but he was able to impart some understanding of basic principles of objectives, super objectives and through-lines.

The Stanislavski approach facilitates an actor, allowing him to develop his relationship with himself at an imaginative and bodily level. Once that is established, the actor then builds a relationship with the other actor. This interplay is where the dramatic tension lies. At the time I was too locked into ideas. They were emotionally safe for me to inhabit. Art really should never be safe. I learnt over the years that ideas work better at an implicit level allowing the imaginative and emotional centre to emerge in a production through the dramatic action of a scene or play. It was the 1980's and education at that time was very politically correct – we all lived in our heads not our bodies. The irrational was to be treated with suspicion.

Another of our course tutors was a man very immersed in the 1960s counter-culture even in the 1980s. He was called David Llewellyn or Llew as he was known and who once loaned me his battered copy of 'The Tibetan Book of the Dead'. He kept the flame alive for left-field creative approaches for the actor in the white heat of ideology (such as Marxism and Feminism) that dominated the drama department in the mid 1980s. He was an actor and playwright with an enormous passion for the avant-garde, particularly the work of Jarry, Artaud and Grotowski. John Godber had told me that Llew had been a huge influence on him. While I was on a weekend visit from college to my sister's house in Birmingham, Godber asked me if Llew was having the same impact on my creative journey. I am ashamed to say that I could not answer the question at the time. I just was not ready for what Llew was teaching. I needed certainties in my life. The irrational was just too scary for me to contemplate. I now understand as a middle-aged man that life and creativity are to be lived and understood in its uncertainties and not to a pat ideological formula.

Before I graduated I knew I had got stuck in an ideological cul-de-sac. I needed to change. I spent the next five years working as a professional theatre director in Ireland and re-educating myself with all kinds of actor-training approaches as well as circus theatre and contact dance including trying to get to grips with Artaud's *Theatre and Its Double*, but that would take a while. I also trained with visiting international practitioners such as Philippe Gaulier, Angela De Castro and Andrew Wade. Later, I went back to Liverpool and apologized to Llew. With that, I also learnt that humility is a really important trait in an artist's character. Llew is now Head of Drama in that department in Liverpool (now John Moore's University). Society and education have moved on since the 1980s. The human capacity for the imaginative is greater than ideology. There are some universal creative truths that are eternal whether we like it or not. I learnt that I could hold certain private views offstage but that when it came to directing or performing, those views had to be jettisoned. To impose ideological views onto the creative mind of a performer, or characters and dramatic situations, shuts down the potential exploration of genuine dramatic conflict and the luminosity of the human condition on stage. Censoring a character because of what he says or how he behaves also stops the audience from experiencing areas within their own psyche that they are in conflict with themselves. Somewhere within that tension and discomfort an insight into oneself might happen or a healing could take place. I would learn that empirically.

My own attempts to grapple with Stanislavski as a student were ambitious but gauche and juvenile. I cringe now when I remember how laughably and arrogantly I played Francis Hardy in *Faith Healer* by Brian Friel in a student production directed by Conall Morrison. That experience was terrifying but it did teach me for the first time what it was like to be immersed in a part, and imaginatively how to be in a moment. It was not easy and I used to throw up just before I went on stage. It was my first attempt at Stanislavski and looking back it would have been a very ponderous experience for the audience, to say the least. After that I concentrated more on directing and designing student productions. But I would never stop attending different actor-training courses so as to understand the actors' process.

While living in the U.K. I also started to buy *Theatre Ireland* magazine to keep myself informed of what was happening back home in Irish Theatre. There were new plays by Brian Friel, Tom Kilroy, Tom

Murphy, Tom MacIntyre, Frank McGuinness and others. I started to order the plays in Waterstones in Liverpool to read them. I then read many other plays by those writers so that I could get an overview of what was happening back home. One name kept cropping up – Patrick Mason. He had directed many of the plays that I was reading. I made a mental note.

I applied for the Thames TV Theatre Directors Bursary (for theatre) two years in a row and got down to the last eight, for the four places, both years running. Director Pip Broughton (then Artistic Director of Paines Plough Theatre Company) was very encouraging. Max Stafford-Clarke (Artistic Director of the Royal Court) told me that you do not need bursaries to be a director and that I was just to do it. He also said not to worry as he did not get the bursary when he was starting out. It was a useful experience. Retrospectively, I was not ready as a young man for mainstream British Theatre. I needed to do a lot more work on myself if I was going to be part of that world. However, it did let me know the level that I needed to get to if I was to be a serious director. I had lived in the U.K for five years and felt that if I was going to have a chance of a career it would have to be back in Ireland. As an Irishman living in the U.K in the 1980s I sometimes found the British class system difficult to negotiate, particularly in theatre, and I really did not want to become an ethnic curiosity from a warzone, just to fit in.

A year after I had graduated and with a number of directing credits under my belt including Shaun Duggan's *A Brusque Affair* in the Edinburgh Fringe Festival, Tom Kilroy's *Talbot's Box* in The Belfast Festival at Queen's and a stint as Assistant Director to Roland Jaquarello at the Lyric Theatre, Belfast, I read an advertisement in Theatre Ireland magazine for a Stanislavski residency in Thomastown, Kilkenny, with Mishe Mokeev from Moscow Art Theatre. Mishe had been a scientist and had split the atom. He had moved into theatre because he wanted new challenges. He would apply his scientific rigour to the human condition. He would talk about exploding the moments within the play. Here was my chance to get more in-depth practical experience. We were locked in a mill for two weeks, completely immersed in character. We were working with Chekhov's *The Three Sisters*.

I was there to learn as a director. Mishe told me the best directors train as actors. They understand the process of the actor. Mishe understood me – a verbose, sometimes insecure and eager twenty-something needing to prove himself. He obviously felt those qualities could be used in performance so he cast me as (a young) Vershinin. We improvised on and off text while working on scene studies. He also taught me questions to ask myself as an actor: What were the given circumstances of the play and of each individual character? What initial event starts the events of the play? What are the inner-life conflicts within each character? What are the objectives and super objectives? What are the 'tactics' for the character to get what he wants? Once I had absorbed the questions as an actor he then allowed me to direct scene studies. By the end of the residency he said I had cracked the work and there was nothing more for him to teach me as a director and that I should just get on with putting the Stanislavski work into practice.

What I learnt with Mishe would be the basis for most of my naturalistic work that followed, including my production of *Potestad* by Eduardo Pavlovsky with Mark Mulholland and Kate McClay for the Lyric Theatre which transferred to Andrew's Lane in the Dublin Theatre Festival in 1991. It was performed as a lunch-time show on the set of a production of *A View from the Bridge* produced by Focus Theatre. As we were commuting every day from Belfast to Dublin I was unable to see the Focus production.

Around this time Una McCarthy was running the Old Museum Arts Centre and was very supportive of my work, as were people like Marie Jones, Brenda Winter, Paddy Scully and Ian McIlhenny. In the mid-1990s I wanted to develop and grow more as a director and to try other theatre forms. I was also becoming frustrated by the mono-subject of the conflict in the North. It was hard to escape it. I became Artistic Director of Point Fields Theatre Company in Belfast. It was an unpaid position but it allowed me to get the necessary experience of running a theatre company. I did it for three years. To get more experience of developing scripts for the stage I trained with Andy Hinds.

With Point Fields we were engaging with the themes of the era by commissioning new plays by established writers such as Graham Reid's *Lengthening Shadows* which we eventually did as a co-production with The Lyric Theatre. We were also trying to push the subject matter beyond the obvious Northern Irish conflict, or at least attempting to look at it through a different prism. *The Starving* by Andy Hinds was a poetic male love story set during the Siege of Derry and an allegory for the relationship between Ireland and England; *Pictures of Tomorrow* by Martin Lynch dealt with the disillusionment of old warriors who had fought during the Spanish Civil War. It was a very personal play about Martin's own disillusionment with leftist politics. *Men at their Work* renamed *Shoot the Crow* by Owen McCafferty dealt with power, trust and betrayal on a building site. It reflected Owen's desire to create a new drama that went beyond the political conflict. It was commissioned by Point Fields and developed with us while Owen was writer-in-residence. Pre-production had started on the play. We also had director John Tiffany on board. He was associate director with The Traverse in Edinburgh at the time. However, with funding cuts we could not proceed with the production so I sent the script to Garry Hynes at Druid who produced it the following year.

We were very ambitious for new writing with Point Fields even though we had little or no funding. There was no equivalent of the Royal Court or The Traverse in Northern Ireland. We created a seeding project to encourage more new writing. It was called 'Angels with Split Voices' inspired by a painting by the artist Gerard Dillon. It was my way of dealing with the conflict. When the violence was really bad it became too dangerous to meet artist friends in a city-centre pub like Lavery's, for fear that you might be attacked. It was the innocent people going about their daily lives who were being murdered. I would sit in my flat in South Parade and read Greek classics, listen to classical music, operas and Brit Pop CDs evening after evening, as well as make collages from the newspaper headlines and stories in the papers.

One of the collages became the poster for the first season of the 'Angels' project. We would commission three or four new writers a year to write on a given theme. The first year was on the theme of 'Identity and Place' and dealt with the private and unheard voices of people who were suffering as a result of the conflict. It was also inspired by the private pain of the characters in Wim Wender's film *Wings of Desire* and Ingmar Bergman's *Cries and Whispers* which I used to watch a lot on video during that period. The season featured new work by Owen Mc Cafferty, Gary Mitchell, Glenn Patterson and Ruth Hooley. The short plays touched a nerve with audiences in Northern Ireland as well as with Scottish audiences in Glasgow's Mayfest. The second year was on the theme of 'Sex & Sexuality' with new work by Andy Hinds, Rosemary Magill and Nell McCafferty. In a live radio interview a journalist asked me 'So, sex and sexuality – what has this got to do with living in Northern Ireland?'. I asked her if she had a libido.

I was constantly looking for ways to feed myself creatively. I went to see a production of Benjamin Britten's *Turn of the Screw* produced by Opera Northern Ireland. It had always been one of my favourite ghost stories so I wanted to see the opera version. I liked it very much and wondered how I could learn more about music theatre. Una McCarthy put me in contact with Ion Caramitru who was coming to Ireland to direct Tchaikovsky's *Eugene Onegin* for Opera Northern Ireland.

Caramitru was Romania's leading actor and one of his county's principal directors. He had led the revolution in his country to depose Ceausescu's regime and was later made Vice President. He had started out as an athlete before becoming an actor. He told me that his athletic skills helped him become a good actor with a serious attitude to discipline, bodily strength, fitness and control. Ion took me into his rehearsal room and allowed me to see his process. He would also talk about the need of the performer, whether it be a singer or an actor, to have the facility to create an inner life.

I had also learnt this from the Czechoslovakian choreographer Helen Lewis. She would stress the importance for a dancer to have an inner life. She had survived Auschwitz but her husband had not. One of her imaginative exercises with performers was to get them to find a partner, make a connection, and then lose the partner in the crowd. It created a visceral energy when working with a large group. Another influence was the opera director Javier Lopez Pinon, whom I assisted in Belfast on Donizetti's *The Elizir of Love*, who introduced me to the concept of historical genre performance which he taught in Amsterdam.

This was early 1994 and the conflict in the north had escalated. Sometimes it was frightening to walk around parts of Belfast during this period because of the tit-for-tat murders. You just did not know where assassins would strike next. In the rehearsal room I felt safe and nourished by the power of Tchaikovsky's melody and the singing in the rehearsal room. I can still hear the chorus of voices and remember how the vibration of the sound impacted on my solar plexus and I remember the peace and warmth that the music created and I felt completely connected and saved by the beauty of it. For a moment I thought if only the politicians and the warring factions could experience this too, it might change them – even for a moment.

I wanted to learn more about how to make classical theatre. There were no structures to develop a career, or training opportunities available in Northern Ireland. Ion Caramitru invited me to Romania to see training and theatre production work. I was an observer in the Bucharest Academy where actors train for seven years in all genres of theatre. The production work I was exposed to in Eastern Europe was extraordinary: productions by Liviu Ciulei, Alexandru Darie, Gabor Tompa, Andrei Serban and Silviu Purcarete and many other fine directors. It was the work of Darie that I most connected with. There was real heart in it and a human scale to the productions that perhaps was missing from some of the other larger and more visually ornate work by other Romanian directors. Their work impressed but did not touch me. Darie was trained by Liviu Ciulei the great master teacher whom everyone that I met in Bucharest revered. Ciulei had moved to the U.S.A to run the Tyrone Guthrie Centre but one of his productions was still on at the Bulandra. It was a seven-year old production of Wedekind's *Spring Awakening* and it was still one of the best productions that I saw in Eastern Europe. I knew I was in the right place to learn. I worked for Ion Caramitru in a number of areas including helping him to write speeches in English so he could fund-raise abroad for Romanian Theatre, and ran a project to select Irish plays for translation and production in Romania. Plays included Brian Friel's *Dancing at Lughnasa* and Sebastian Barry's *Boss Grady's Boys*. It was during this time that I became assistant director at The Bulandra to Alexandru Darie or Ducu as he was known. Darie's work was a character/actor-driven theatre with a soulful and eternal quality. He also had developed an ensemble of actors. I got the chance to observe his work in rehearsals on productions of *The Three Sisters* and *Julius Caesar*. He facilitated the talent of the actor and encouraged the work in a particular direction. He constantly talked about the energy and spiritual nature of the space that is to be created through the actor's imagination in order for the world of the play to exist – 'otherwise the work is just dead'. (How often had I experienced dead theatre in the west?!)

If he entered a space he could sense if the energy was dead or alive. I was experiencing how to create the sacred space with the actor, in classical plays. It was an emotional and imaginative equivalent of the classical music I had experienced in Caramitru's Tchaikovsky production – visceral vibration created within the actor's body (instead of singing or using a musical instrument) through the imaginative relationship with himself and with each other actor in a rehearsal room. The energy would stay in the space long after the work had finished.

This experience in Eastern Europe set the bar for me. After I returned to Ireland everything about my own work was focused on creating a sacred space. In the year 2000 it all came together in my first professional production of a classical play – Shakespeare's *Julius Caesar*. When I returned home I had spent a number of years preparing myself to take it on, having seen too many bad Shakespeare productions in Ireland, and I did not want to add to the growing list. I did training courses with voice and language experts Kristin Linklater and Andrew Wade as well as devouring Cicely Berry's *The Actor and The Text*. I road tested my Shakespeare production skills on a student production of one of my favourite plays, *Twelfth Night*, before I would expose myself in a professional arena.

I had had a difficult relationship with my Dad who had died in 1999. The shock of his passing woke up my nervous system. The grief and trauma I experienced with his death was a major key to moving out of my head and into my body. I had attended his cremation but not his burial. I needed to mark his passing in some way. I privately dedicated my production of *Julius Caesar* to him. 'I come to bury Caesar, not to praise him'. My work got better as a director and I received my first Dublin Arts Council grant for Rattlebag, my then company, and Aiden Condron got an Irish Times Award Nomination for Best Actor in the role of Mark Antony. Not a bad achievement with no proper funding. With hindsight I now understand that an artist must have a 'needful' intention (or at least I needed to) to give depth to the work. It is that energy that drives an artist's work. That fuels the company and is received by the audience. Having found my own way into Shakespeare I then started to experiment with other genres and forms. I would collaborate with practitioners such as Jack Walsh in physical theatre, and Sonia Haccius in experimental design, as in *Mansfield Park* from the novel by Jane Austen in a version by Myles Dungan. With the support of the Civic Theatre it became Rattlebag's biggest success in terms of reaching a wider audience. We got an Arts Council increase and had a sell-out national tour the following year. Although *Mansfield Park* was a hit show the production for me lacked any real emotional punch and tended to entertain at a frothy surface level. In my desire for learning and trying out new ways of doing things I had thrown too many styles of acting into the production. It looked great. It sounded great, but emotionally it was thin. I had got stuck in the physical pictures and in the narrative.

The work during that period was not fuelled by an emotional or spiritual 'needfulness' but by a desire to explore how theatre productions and styles work. 'How do I do this?' Or 'What happens if I do that?' It was period of enquiry into the 'plastic' nature of theatre that was necessary for my own development. Those periods are necessary for every artist and need to be supported even if they do not work. It is part of the creative journey. The Arts Council were also now supporting me to develop further. I was given a bursary to explore new theatre techniques, including an introductory course in Dublin on View-pointing with Will Bond from S.I.T.I Company, New York, as well as training with Caroline McSweeney for several months. She helped me facilitate a work-shopped performance piece based on Robert Bly's book *Iron John*. It was never performed in public but it did help with my own development at a physical, imaginative and mythical level.

In 2002 I applied for the position of Artistic Director of Focus Theatre. After a second interview I was offered the post. The general note I was given was not to do anything too radical but to get the organization and the programming into some kind of shape. The first thing I did was to establish contact with Tim McDonnell who was running a Stanislavski acting studio in The New Theatre in Temple Bar, Dublin. By the time I met him I had already had a good twelve years working in professional theatre. I had developed a good understanding of stagecraft across a multitude of genres, and also had experience of different scales of production with the Lyric Theatre, Grand Opera House, and also with Patrick Mason at The Abbey Theatre who allowed me access to his rehearsals of new plays, so allowing me to get a better understanding of language and rhythm and of how the physical aspects of design and space all work together for larger auditoriums. I also had experience with a number of independent productions that toured in the UK and Ireland. However, nothing really was to prepare me for what I was about to experience with Tim McDonnell.

After observing one of his classes I was hooked. Tim is a Master Stanislavski teacher with enormous humility and patience. His understanding of the human condition is far reaching and profound. His understanding of dramatic art is anchored in this. He is completely passionate about creating the experiential in live theatre. For him if this is not happening then there is no theatre at all. He is an inspiring teacher. We would talk for hours and hours about art and the creative process. He agreed to become Head of Studio at the Focus while I ran the theatre.

First of all I need to say that I did not know that serious Stanislavski training was available in Ireland. It was under the radar. (In terms of its presence in Dublin you could be forgiven for thinking that theatre only consisted of the Abbey and The Gate. They had budgets to promote themselves.) I thought I had to go abroad to find Stanislavski training or to do a residency with an international visiting practitioner. I knew nothing about the Focus Theatre when I was living in Belfast. It was only when I moved back from Eastern Europe to live in Dublin in the mid 1990s to work as assistant director at the Abbey Theatre that I took notice of the Focus.

I picked up a flyer that was promoting one-act plays dealing with the IRA and Loyalist cease-fire in the North called *Cease-fire*. I was intrigued. As I was still, at the time, artistic director of Point Fields

Theatre Company, which specialized in new writing in Northern Ireland, I thought I would have a look. *Jack's Too Open* by Paula Clamp was the first production I ever saw in the Focus. It was a lunch-time show by a first-time writer. Although I could tell that the production values were very basic what stood out was the work of some of the actors. Set in the back garden of a house in summer time I could feel the energy and the heat from the stage. It was very sensual. It had all been created through the actors' imagination. I had only ever experienced this level of imaginative work in Eastern European productions. My perception of the Focus at that time was that it appeared to be a closed shop. Nor did it appear to have a relationship with the wider Irish theatre community. So, my visits were infrequent. I only saw about three other shows there before I got the job of Artistic Director. I concentrated on my own work with Rattlebag Theatre Company directing plays at The Crypt, The Civic, The Project and The Playhouse in Derry, the latter theatre being where I directed *Energy* by Gary Mitchell. Shows were toured when possible, and I also taught performance in various schools including the University of Ulster and Trinity College, Dublin as well as directing a new opera *The Fire King* by Kevin O'Connell in Derry and Los Angeles.

Programming The Focus Theatre in the 2000s

When I accepted the job of Artistic Director of Focus theatre I met with the Arts Council in Dublin to inform them that I was going to work there. They were already funding my own company Rattlebag. I asked for an increase in funding for the Focus as we were going to need it during its new phase of development. They allowed me to take the grant from Rattlebag to add to that of the Focus. They also told me that the funding for the theatre had nearly been axed in the previous year. It was the success of a new play *Tillsonburg* by Malachy McKenna at the venue that saved the grant. Elizabeth Moynihan had brought it to Deirdre O'Connell's attention and Elizabeth had also produced the debut run at the venue. I decided to put *Tillsonburg* on national tour in January 2003. John O Brien co-ordinated the tour. It was a big success and sold out in many of its dates North and South of the border. There was a moment when promised funding from a source fell through and threatened the future of the show. The late Mike Diskin in Galway Town Hall stepped in and increased our fee to keep the show on the road.

I was getting on with developing my own programme for the Focus. The general feeling in Dublin at the time was that the venue had become a museum and was raiding the successes from its own past. It was understandable that the organization had done that to keep the identity alive after Deirdre's death. I set about developing a new policy – mainly Irish premieres for what I would call our 'World Theatre Programme'. We would run our new writing programme in tandem with it. It was a deliberate marketing tag to reinvent the venue in the public realm. It worked. We continued to keep our loyal audience but were able to develop a newer and younger one by working with the Dublin Fringe Festival. The 'World Theatre' banner caught on as other better-funded organizations started using it to promote their own programmes. As well as creating more opportunities to bring more Stanislavski trained directors to the fore, such as Mary Moynihan, time was also spent integrating the Focus into the wider theatre community. We presented more visiting companies, which included such successes as Bill Hughes's production of *The Songs of Mama Cass*; Jack Gillhooley's *Shooters* that was developed at the Focus and produced by Purpleheart Theatre; and Cian O Brien's first step into producing at the Focus with Making Strange Theatre's production of *Hedwig and the Angry Inch*. We also had international companies from the United States, South America and Eastern Europe including Green Hours from Romania – they would win Best Production during the Fringe Festival in 2005. Our 'Creative Partnership Scheme' was set up to formalize our working relationships with the other organizations as well as to support emerging directors like Louise Lowe who was working in Ballymun. We provided a free training placement for her actors at the Focus studio.

For the most part mainstream Irish Theatre tended to be literary. Younger directors would also be influenced by the increasingly academic direction of what was going on in London. I would make frequent visits to see a diversity of shows, from musicals to classics and serious new drama. Sometimes I would see more than one show a day over a three day period or go for a 10 day trip. I did this perhaps two or three times a year over a seven to eight year period. Ryan Air was cheap. It was sometimes just 1 euro to fly. I was lucky enough to get really good accommodation deals or crash on a friend's sofa bed. Generally I went to The National, The Globe, The Royal Court, The Donmar Warehouse, and The West End and sometimes to fringe venues or to Shakespeare in The Park. Apart from a handful of stand-alone productions such as *The Master Builder* with Patrick Stewart, *The Three Sisters* and *Journey's End* at the Playhouse, *War Horse* and *The Philistines* at The National, *Brand* with Ralph Fiennes, *Edward 11* at the Globe and Mark Rylance in *Jerusalem* I found I did not connect with a lot of the work. It seemed dead to me. However, The Royal Court bookshop was a great and inexpensive resource for new international plays. Apart from visiting major exhibitions at The Tate, Tate Modern and National Gallery, looking for new international plays to produce at the Focus became my main reason for travelling to London throughout the 2000s.

The Focus venue was working well during my first year. Shows were selling out in the April to October season. I wanted to keep the venue open in the winter months and during quiet periods. We had no money to do so. At least we had a venue. I thought that perhaps some kind of cabaret might work. I started going out to see stand-up comedy to get ideas. One evening I bumped into a very intriguing woman by the name of Anne Lillis. Her stage persona was that of a sweet and polite women with a tongue like a sewer. It was hilarious. Her work was steeped in the shadow side of the performer's imagination. It was very dark and very funny. I would learn later that she had trained in the Stanislavski process at the Focus under Deirdre O'Connell. I invited Anne to come into the venue and put together an alternative programme in which artists could try out new and risqué material that would not be seen in mainstream venues. All of the work would be newly written and rehearsed that week at the Focus and performed at the weekend late at night. There would be little or no advertising, bar a cheap photocopy flyer. It became The Fallen Angels.

It would feature new work by artists such as Simon Toal (his show 'The Friends of Jack Kairo' would be developed from his time in the cabaret and would become an international festival hit in Europe. Simon had also trained with Deirdre O'Connell before going to Denmark to work with Eugenio Barba). With the help of Breifni O'Connell Cusack we would also have unannounced mystery guests including Jack L, Camille O' Sullivan, music legend Ronnie Drew as well as members of The Waterboys. The draw for the big names was as a mark of respect for Deirdre O'Connell's legacy at the venue and to try out new work in front of a live audience. They would get a split of the door. The success of the alternative cabaret took everyone by surprise. Within a month we were selling out through word of mouth. Within nine months The Fallen Angels were winning awards at the Spiegeltent at the Dublin Fringe Festival, and touring the country. It kick-started a whole new scene for alternative cabaret in Dublin.

We were also lucky in hitting the zeitgeist on more than one occasion. In 2004 we produced 'Plays of Changing Europe' a series of play readings from writers from the Eastern block which included *Ladybird* by Vassily Sigarev from Russia; *Stop the Tempo!* by Gianina

Cărbunariu [translated by Paul Meade] from Romania and *The Colonel and the Birds* by Hristo Boytchev from Bulgaria. Our Eastern European Season the following year featured full productions of *Ladybird* and *Stop the Tempo!*. Both writers were banned from having their work produced in their own respective countries. *The Village* called us 'the company to watch this year' in 2005. Mary Moynihan's full length directorial debut production *Two Rooms* by Lee Blessing opened just as another war flared up in the Lebanon; and a revival of *The Kiss* by Michael Harding, featuring Tom Hickey as a priest who gets sexually aroused after kissing a child, opened just as the Ryan Report on sexual abuse was released by the Irish Government. Our 2010 season featured Polish Theatre Ireland's debut production *Scent of Chocolate* by Radoslaw Paczocha which ran alongside The Dublin Theatre Festival's Polish Theatre Season. The Focus based run attracted huge numbers of the Polish community living in Ireland. The show completely sold out. We had given the Polish community in Ireland its first professional theatre platform. We also provided free actor training to one of their actors. It was so exciting to see the birth of a new cultural strand in Irish theatre.

We also explored how to utilize Stanislavski techniques for presenting new work in different ways. One such project was an idea by Sinead Hackett, *The Seven Deadly Sins*. Sinead devised the show with writers Simon Toal and Orla McGovern. It was a site-specific play about a love triangle set in a restaurant, a bedroom, a pub and on the street. The devil took the audience on a journey around Ranelagh village in Dublin and exposed them with humour to our worst human traits. It was a very successful experiment during the Ranelagh Arts Festival and demonstrated that traditional Stanislavski training can be applied to contemporary theatre making practices. It then transferred to the Westport Festival in 2010 and was just as successful with audiences in the west of Ireland. Developing a relationship with Mouth on Fire Theatre Company run by Cathal Quinn and Melissa Nolan we were able to reintroduce the shorter plays of Beckett back into the Focus repertoire including the World Premiere of the Irish language version of Beckett's *Come and Go* translated by Gabriel Rosenstock.

Focus Studio in the 2000s

Tim and I agreed, when I took on the Focus job, that in order to move the acting company forward we would have to restructure the acting studio. It meant having to re-audition many people who had been there for many years. If they could not reach the level we both felt was necessary for them to have a serious career, both within and without of The Focus, they would have to leave. 'Career actors only need apply'. It was a very traumatic transitional time for everyone involved. I hated it but it had to be done. We then set about creating a new pool of actors and worked with a number of the career actors that had already been trained by Deirdre O' Connell.

In the spirit of Deirdre O'Connell's all encompassing generosity we continued to keep an open door policy for anyone who wished to get access to creative training. However, we now differentiated between professional actors and people who just had an interest. The policy became more manifest in the late 2000s with the development of our nationwide out-reach programme which included creative development for people over fifty. The over fifties' group work was then toured into nursing homes in and around Dublin. We also periodically contributed free support-training for actors with Down's Syndrome which was facilitated by the Equinox Theatre in Callan, County Kilkenny. We developed a drug awareness through drama pilot project for inner city schools for twelve year olds which was run by Sinead Hackett, utilizing Stanislavski and Boal techniques. More employment for theatre practitioners was created with those developments. However, with the recent cut-backs the Focus Out-Reach Programme came to an end but in 2012 we introduced 'creativity for beginners' classes alongside our professional actor training studio in the Ranelagh Arts Centre.

I stayed in Tim's studio for six years, observing for the first three, and for the next three I trained as an actor so that I would be able to teach the work. I noted how he helped the artists test and stretch their instruments in the safety of the acting studio with very practical exercises that were to be repeated to create body memory. I watched how novices blossomed into fully-fledged talents and how experienced actors came to refresh and refine their technique and develop more depth of feeling in their bodies. The centre of the studio training was the improvisational work. In a safe environment an actor would explore human experience in its extremes including, for example, bereavement, relationship break-down, betrayal, guilt, and loneliness. The imaginative experiences created in the studio opened up the actors' facility and honed the talent. The loss of my Dad a few years earlier had got me to that point already. Life experience is what informs the artist's imaginative and emotional palette. It also needs to be said that no amount of training is going to make someone more talented. If they have it the Stanislavski studio will draw it out.

I learnt from Tim that with a system, an actor can hit the same dramatic points again and again, night after night. Great actors who have a natural ability but no training sometimes struggle to reach the emotional points consistently. The most important thing he taught me was how to take a contemporary and modern play out of a purely narrative or surface place – actors can hide in the narrative and get away with a surface reading, not revealing anything of themselves or their inner life. For example, questions to ask yourself as an actor working on a part would be: What makes today the same but different from yesterday? In other words what lifts the performance on *this* day out of the ordinary? Perhaps today is the anniversary of the death of a loved one and you wish to mark it. It creates a 'needfulness'. That becomes an unspoken choice or impulse in an actor's performance. It creates an invisible tension that is picked up on subliminally by the audience which creates an understanding that something special is happening even if they do not know what it is. It moves the play into a metaphysical or mythological ritual of shared experience. However, the choices an actor makes must be supported by what is going on in the play. 'Needfulness' can also inform the director's choice for doing the work in the first place, as I discovered with my production of *Julius Caesar*.

The Stanislavski training taught by the Focus allows the actor to illuminate the character in the play through his or her own body and imagination. It reveals something of the human condition in the playing. I already understood this concept from directing Shake- spearean plays. In classical performance an actor needs depth in his or her facility to allow the language to drop deep into the body. The classical actor also needs to develop a mythological imagination. In Shakespearean performance this is all done through the language. The Focus acting studio allows the actor to get there through specific intentions and repetitions of particular exercises. The exercises help the body to thaw over a three-year period, thus allowing for the creation of depth of feeling and emotional resonance. It unblocks 'the blocked actor' (to use a phrase from Declan Donnellan in 'The Actor and the Target'). The voice and imagination is used to get there in the training. However, once this facility has been established within the actor, he or she is able to create, through their imaginative choices, very clear experiences with or without words. To coin a phrase they get there through 'specificity'. In addition, I have seen actors audition for Shakespearean plays one year, who can handle the language but have been unable to reach the imaginative and emotional depth required for delivering the text; then having spent time in the Stanislavski studio, have returned to audition for Shakespeare and nailed the part. The thawing in the body has helped them physicalize the Shakespearean language. Another aspect of the Focus studio which makes it unique in Ireland is that it is also a facility for established artists to keep their creative muscles active between jobs, and it is a space where he or she can work on a role for a show they are doing or are about to start work on and receive positive feedback in a safe and protective environment.

I was able to test what I had learnt with Tim as a director on my production of *Proof*. In *Proof* the actor cast as the fatherless Hal was playing the narrative and skimming over the play. I suggested that the reason why Hal is researching the dead Professor's work was because he has been looking for a way to remember the only father figure who had helped him in his life. The actor took the note and then played the scene. He emotionally burst, his eyes popped and tears came. He had a break-through. What I understood was, for better or for worse, that it was the mythology of our families that gives our work its depth. The Greeks knew this. The creation of 'needfulness' in the actors' imagination creates that mythology in the playing. Thanks to Tim I had found my holy grail for working on contemporary plays.

Proof transferred from the Focus into the larger Andrew's Lane Theatre and ran for six months in Dublin. Both Tom Hickey and Tim McDonnell said that I had taken production work at the Focus to a new level. It was Tim's generosity to share his wisdom that took my work as a director to a new deeper level with contemporary plays. Ion Caramitru was in rehearsals for a show at The Gate. He came to see *Proof* on the first preview, saying that the production was a complicated piece of work and that I had done an excellent job. He then invited me out to direct a show in Romania but for some reason or other the invitation was later withdrawn. It did not matter. His intention was enough. I felt as if I had won an Oscar. The production cost only €10,000 to produce. Its success with Irish audiences was that it delivered an experience. It was a traditional Stanislavski production.

In relation to the design of *Proof*, Sonia Haccius's instinct was to move away from naturalism. I felt that on my first proper production at the Focus I needed to take it slowly with the experimentation. However, the colouring of the set and the costumes were put together in a way that was not naturalistic. The colouring harmonized, and had a painterly quality. Many people commented on it in a very positive way. It was the beginning of moving the design of the shows I directed at the Focus away from obvious naturalism. This would later be criticized by naturalistic purists as productions visually changed and became more abstracted. I refused to be tied down in my own work to what I would refer to as the tyranny of the tea cup. Some of the productions worked; some did not. As an artist I will be firm in my belief that I have a commitment not to stand still in the work I do with my art-form.

I understand why some people were upset by the changes. The resistance to change was rooted in a fear that the training in the studio was not being reflected in the style of the productions. That was never going to be the case for every show. To this day we have not abandoned naturalism. My own belief is that the Stanislavski training gives an artist his or her primary colours. You learn how to create naturalism and then you jump off into more abstract work. To use a painting analogy, you start with Gustave Courbet's realism and arrive at Jackson Pollock's abstract expressionism and move beyond that again. It is the emotional and imaginative palette that you keep going back to. It becomes your base-line and it becomes your anchor. As long as the performer is rooted in what he is doing, whatever way the work is manifested, the spirit of life will be palpable in the work. The human condition will be illuminated whether you perform Greek or Roman classics, Shakespeare, Restoration, Ibsen, Beckett, Sara Kane, or movement-based and visual theatre.

Problems in Theatre

1. Artifice versus truth – do we need both?

In a recent production I directed, one of the actors with an enormous emotional range was playing only anger in every scene as the character was angry having just been dumped by her boyfriend. In real life this is how a person in that predicament might behave. However, in the artificial situation of a play it became difficult to work with, so I suggested that she might only play the anger in one or two moments in the play. It worked. It allowed her to find more colour and range in her playing and helped the other actors as well as the play itself to breathe. So, the actor needs to be able to reach the depth of feeling required but also needs to know how to use it at the right moment.

2. Audience Engagement and Response

We toured *The Hen Night Epiphany* by Jimmy Murphy into districts and communities in and around Dublin. We were very strategic about the title. Jimmy had written a drama with a comedic edge. Five women go into the Irish countryside on a hen night. Over the course of the evening it emerges that the bride-to-be is being physically beaten by her future husband. It takes the community of the women to help the young bride to face the reality of her future life. We wanted mainstream audiences watching TV soaps to leave their living rooms and come out for an evening to see a play. We got our target audience. We were filling three and four-hundred seat auditoriums over a five-week period as well as taking the play into school halls. The mythological or the emotional heart of the play was being experienced by a wide range of people which included men and women aged between sixteen and ninety years old. After the startup run at the Focus Theatre we opened the tour in association with The Ranelagh Arts Centre at the Multi-Denominational School Hall. A woman of eighty-four years of age was sitting beside me. I asked her after the show what she thought. She said 'the tears were tripping me'. I had not noticed but she had been crying silently. She went on to say that she had not been able to cry since her husband died twelve years earlier. He had been violent to her in the early years of her marriage when he was a heavy drinker. He stopped drinking and his violence ceased. But she kept it all a secret from her family and her community. The play helped her at a profound level to start her healing.

In another venue a woman got so caught up in the drama that she started to argue with the actors about violence in the home. Later in the tour a divorced man came to see the show. He said that he had never realized the impact that his behaviour was having on his wife. It helped him to understand himself. He was full of remorse. After the success of *The Hen Night Epiphany* we had hoped to tour the production the following year but our application for funding was turned down. We played one final week in Galway Town Hall's main auditorium in February 2012.

Over the years at the Focus my own work has evolved. My visit to the Moscow Art Theatre in 2004 was a major inspiration when I saw classics by Marivaux produced as physical theatre along with an installation design. The work since 2005 has attempted to go into more experimental areas. I sought out designers such as Sonia Haccius and Ann-Marie Woods who have a unique visual strength. *Mother Teresa is Dead, Picasso's Women* and most recently *The Hen Night Epiphany* all had experimental designs, hopefully adding another mythological layer to the productions. All of those productions had a metaphysical aspect to the design that underpinned the emotional and metaphysical quality that I hoped was being conveyed through the performances of the actors. Instead of the traditional Irish stone-walled cottage, *Hen Night Epiphany's* installation design had a transparent cottage shape floating in the ether. Nothing is solid or certain. Everything is in the moment. The physical reality of the world is breaking down. The house is a classic archetypal image that represents the self in dream analysis. In the play the house is in the countryside in a place called the King's Hill. It is an extension of the central character's chaotic emotional state. It is a visual representation in metaphysical terms. It may also be read as the state of the country during difficult times.

I do from time to time embrace the classic naturalistic work that The Focus is famous for. My most recent work in this genre included new plays *Tic*, a play about a woman with Tourette's syndrome by Elizabeth Moynihan based on the fairytale of *Rapunzel* and *Hollywood Valhalla* by Aidan Harney a play about redemption which contains the *Centaur stealing Ganymede* myth. I will not abandon naturalism but I will continue to pursue more experimentation with genre, style and the metaphysical imagination as well as other methodologies from time to time. I feel that this is necessary so that we do not become museum theatre. I also do not believe in patronizing an audience by spoon-feeding everything to them. For example if an experimental design on a production is challenging then that is a good thing. It has been placed there for a reason. Let people work it out for themselves. That is part of the creative game.

3. Factual background versus the Imagination.

While I was studying for my degree in the 1980s I understood the value of researching and using information to inform creative work. Of course it is important to be informed about background information when working on a play. However, factual information should only be used as a jumping-off point for the imagination and not be used in an impositional manner on a play.

During my rehearsal period for *Jesus Hopped the 'A' Train* by Stephen Adly Guirgis, a death-row therapist from the United States was advising us at a very serious level. We took on board the informational aspects of what he told us of life in that kind of prison. When we played it for the intellectual and social information that was in the play the production was completely dead. We went back to the imaginative reality of the play, the personal needs of each character and the interpersonal relationships between them. The heart and pulse of the production re-emerged.

4. The Problems with Emphasizing Language Over the Experiential

Sometimes an issue that emerges in western theatre, particularly in contemporary drama, is the over-emphasis of the literary at the expense of the dramatic and the imaginative work of the actor. Stanislavski, Artaud and Grotowski challenged this problem. A writer may hear how his script sounds in his head and may want the actors to replicate what he imagines the play will sound like, as if it is a musical score. That is an impossible task. For a start the actor does not know what the writer hears. It also stops the interpretive nature of the actor from coming to the fore. The authentic talent may get buried. So the potential imaginative and emotional connection the actor may make can get shut down. Sonic tone becomes the main experience rather than the emotional power of the drama. The actor cannot do his job and the audience loses out. Both the actor and the audience are short-changed when this happens. The play when read on the page may have musical resonances and perhaps is even shaped like a symphony. There is a real pleasure to be gained when reading a play in this manner at home. However, when it transfers from the page into the actors' bodies it needs to become a dramatic experience in a production. An actor needs to be allowed to take moments in order to make dramatic shifts. The pinning down of these shifts and turning points in this way creates the theatrical through-line of the play. The play is a blue-print. The trained actor fleshes it out imaginatively with the help of the director to realize it at an emotional level. In this way the experiential is created for the audience.

5. Creative Crossroads

After *Jesus Hopped the 'A' Train* opened in Dublin I flew to Crete to spend a week on holiday with Tim in Stavros. I was at a crossroads in my work, having taken naturalism, with Stanislavski, as far as I could, and not wanting to repeat myself I considered giving up theatre and going into healing as a Reiki practitioner. Having bought myself a book on the Greek gods in the local town I would read it on the beach and in bed. Time was spent talking with Tim about performance and art on that trip. I still felt lost.

One evening I decided to go for a walk to the beach. It was a balmy evening and I could smell the sea from the pathway. Reaching the beach I stood looking up. It was a clear evening and the night sky seemed to be very low – almost as if I could touch it with my fingers. The stars seemed unusually very large and luminous. I remember focusing on the stars and thought about the Greek gods from the myths. As I focused on Dionysus I could feel an energy filling me up and completely taking over my body. I felt a heightened sense of sensuality. I had accidentally discovered archetypes for myself.

Archetypes had been brought into the mainstream by Carl Jung as a tool for healing in psychology in the early 20th century. . They lie deep within our subconscious. The four main ones are 'King', 'Warrior', 'Lover' and 'Magician'. The healthy individual will act them out subconsciously. When we act from our 'King' we are mindful of our own sense of power (not in an egotistical way) and self-worth; with the 'Warrior' we defend ourselves and our loved ones when under attack; with the 'Lover' we fall in love; with the 'Magician' we have the power to transform ourselves and the world around us – the archetype of the artist. After that there can be any number of archetypes that may manifest themselves within the imagination.

6. But what do I do with it?

A month later I found myself in Russia observing theatre productions in Moscow and actor-training practices in a school run by Mishe Mokeev. I was travelling with my then Chairman of the Focus, Kevin O' Brien. We both wanted to pay a visit to Stanislavski's house which was not far from Red Square. While visiting the theatre space within the house, the guide had told us that Stanislavski had directed the very first production of Tchaikovsky's *Eugene Onegin*. I thought that was a good omen. We crossed the stage and went into the green room, noticing that the Greek gods were painted on the ceiling. This immediately recalled my experience on the beach in Crete. Photographs were taken. A few weeks later, back in Dublin I was in a workshop with Stewart Pearce. Stewart started the class by saying 'we are all artists and we are all healers'. That was when I realized that I could continue to work in theatre. Stewart introduced me to the practical application of archetypes in relation to performing classical work, specifically in the plays of Shakespeare. It can create a visceral power and a clearly defined stature within the actor's body. It has its limitations when used with Stanislavski technique. But if you do use it, work on your relationship with self and relationship with others first. Then if you need a particular quality in your playing use it sparingly. However, the appropriation of the Dionysus archetype can work as a substitute for sense memory. We used it to create the bawdiness and ribaldry of the three younger drunken women in *The Hen Night Epiphany*.

7. Integrating New Approaches

The most important thing Stewart taught me was how to utilize the elements imaginatively for Shakespearean performance. It was a technique developed by the Mayans to detox illness from the body.

Vocal vibration is used as well as an imaginary appropriation of the four elements of 'Fire,' 'Air', 'Water' and' Earth' within the body of the actor. Imagine the body is split into four chambers. Each chamber houses an element. If you visualize each element and work with the 'aum' sound through each chamber, visceral vibration is created. The actor is able to create energetic flow through the body. It helps to release deeper levels of energy and feeling. It allows for intention and meaning to become luminous in every part of the body. The vibration also impacts on the observer creating a connection and an experience.

Shortly afterwards the Abbey hosted a two-week workshop on a new play called *A Cry from Heaven* by Vincent Woods based on the *Deirdre of the Sorrows* myth. Written in verse it suggested possibilities for a revival of a new Irish classical style in dramatic writing in Ireland. It never happened. The workshop was run by Olivier Py, a French Director who worked with what he called 'the mystic space'. Imaginatively he identified the four points of the compass North, South, East and West in the space. Imaginative use of space in this way is also used in traditional Celtic shamanistic healing rituals.

During the workshop Olivier allowed me to explore the part of an Ulster Warrior in the mythical world of the *Deirdre* play. I was able to put into practice what I had discovered from working with the archetypes and the elements. I was able to draw on what I knew of a notorious loyalist paramilitary figure in Belfast who had been prominently featured in the press. My experience of growing up on a housing estate in Northern Ireland was also extremely useful. As an actor I was able to grapple with how to knit together disparate performance techniques. As well as working on relationships with the other actors playing members of the tribe I immersed myself in the cosmological world of the ancient Celtic warrior. I imagined that the universe was full of mystery and that it was multi-dimensional. With that I found the imaginative reality of the part and the verse language became activated in my body. I had found a breakthrough for myself and was able to take it beyond the literary level of performance. Olivier wanted to cast me in the part which was a terrific affirmation of what I had discovered for myself. It gave me the confidence to continue my research back at the Focus the following year.

8. How do I bring it all together

I returned from Australia in early 2005. I had been visiting family and had an opportunity to do some research into aboriginal art and mythology. I discovered dream-time – an aboriginal belief that we all dream our own lives on another plane and that this existence is the dream. It would later inform my production choices in *Mother Teresa is Dead* in 2006. The period away in Australia had given me time to think about where to go next at a creative level. That spring I started an experimental laboratory, to run in tandem with Tim's work at the Focus Studio. The Focus Laboratory periodically ran for three years. It was set up to explore how an actor could bring together traditional Stanislavski work, classical voice with the elements, archetypes, Shamanic journeying and other performance techniques including the choreographic approach of 'Viewpointing' developed by Anne Bogart.

Stop the Tempo! By Gianina Cărbinariu for the Dublin Fringe Festival was the first play we did after starting the lab. We spent three months on it. We had fused together our traditional Stanislavski work with the elements and choreography. I had also seen Katie Mitchell's Beckett Season for the R.S.C some years before. It influenced the design of the show utilizing darkness and light and torches held by the actors to create the experience of isolation. When the actors and the audience were not in complete darkness the torch light reflected on the actors' bodies became the set design for the show. I was also drawing on chiaroscuro to create the visual architecture in the mise-en-scène. As an experiment it was well worth doing. As a production it did not completely work but we had to start somewhere. Brian McAvera's *Francis & Frances* in 2011 was a more satisfying theatre experience with Focus actor Tara Breathnach and guest artist Cathal Quinn.

In 2009 I took over as studio facilitator at the Focus and continue to teach the Stanislavski actor training programme that I had learnt from Tim. I have also integrated what I had found useful from the laboratory period. The most useful additions to the acting studio training were the integration of 'viewpointing' and the appropriation of the 'elements' for the actors' voices and bodies. It has allowed for more flexibility and diversity in our choice of production, genre of play, performance style and scale of production with the Focus. Most importantly it helps the actors develop a better range in their playing.

Having widened the brief of the training palette to embrace a multitude of genres we have also been able to support new developments with other companies in specific areas when required. Working with Siamsa Tíre (The National Folk Theatre of Ireland) on their new experimental dance theatre project called 'Tearmann' the workshop utilized view-pointing, the archetypes and the elements as well as Stanislavksi improvisation for the creation of the famine-fields sequences. However, the first time we improvised people dying of starvation it was so painful to watch we had to stop. It needed a filter. I remembered Philippe Gaulier, the French clowning teacher, telling me that you must find the pleasure in the playing on stage, otherwise the creative suffering becomes *only* suffering and is therefore unwatchable. I gave the dancers the note to find the pleasure in the 'game' of dying. The note worked and the energy in the workshop lifted the improvisation to a beautiful and compelling performance. It did not compromise the intention. It illuminated the suffering so the viewer could stay with the experience.

In Cork, Asylum Theatre Company was developing a new style of performance called human puppetry. They had asked me to facilitate a workshop to help them work with sound in their bodies while they had their backs to the audience. They utilized the body-chamber work with the four elements to create the sound, using only grunts and vowel sounds placed very specifically in parts of the body and with a very specific intention in their thoughts. The project became *Red Lola,* a re-imagining of the fairytale Red Riding Hood and the Russian novel Lolita by Nabokov. They wore facemasks on the backs of their heads and dressed back to front. The style created a comedic cushion around the production. It was a very powerful piece of work about an underage girl trying to seduce a grown man. The style allowed for a taboo subject, an aspect of the human condition, to be explored in a safe way. When the production was staged it was a very challenging piece of theatre for our politically correct times. It asked the audience to acknowledge the dark areas of their own psyche. The moral of creating this kind of theatre is that it brings into light the dark areas within us all and asks us to take responsibility for it.

Working on 'L'Ultima Casa' at the Biennale in Venice with Pantakin Theatre in 2007 was a different experience again. I became their Stanislavski Adviser on that show. They were a traditional commedia dell'arte mask company and were trying out a new experimental soft body mask in a new production. Traditional masks are made of hard moulded leather. With a specific physical intention and the imaginative appropriation of an animal archetype the performer is able to activate the mask. The natural tension in the leather merges with the human energy field around the body. However, the new soft-material body masks were not working. The actors' energy was not animating them. The body masks looked like soft baggy human skin. So we tried working with human archetypes, the imaginative appropriation of the elements within the body chamber and Stanislavski questions on the relationship with the self, and then the relationship to each other. The actors' bodies became animated. It took the play beyond the Italian language, (which I do not speak). The whole rehearsal room came alive with visceral energy generating from within the actors. At the first preview in front of an audience Manuela Massimi came onto the stage in her elderly Italian Mama body suit. The audience erupted into howls of laughter. She waddled over to the front row and spoke some improvised lines to them. She had her back to me. However, the clarity of her intention was so clear; I was able to understand what she was saying through the luminosity and vibration that was created through her body. The use of the 'elements' came into their own on this production. We ended up winning a production award in the 2007 Biennale in Venice.

Oddly, our Arts Council funding was withdrawn later that year, and then a few months later reinstated by only 50 per cent of the previous amount. We then went on to win The Writers Guild of Great Britain Award for the Encouragement of New Work for producing Brian McAvera's *Picasso's Women* and for commissioning *Francis and Frances.*

I had got to know Pantakin while I was in Venice researching traditional European masks. (I learnt much later that Mary Elizabeth Burke Kennedy had been doing mask theatre at the Focus in the late 1970s and early 1980s but it had not been documented anywhere). I saw their production of *Il Corvo* during Carnivale and was completely transfixed by extraordinary performances and lucidity of the performers in mask. The visual and physical style was beautiful and exotic. It was directed by Michele Modesto Casarin and featured himself and an ensemble of actors that he had trained. Michele was the Artistic Director of Pantakin. The company, structurally, was similar to the Focus in that they had their own theatre space and taught a traditional training programme – commedia mask performance – in their school for professional actors. They also had their own company of actors who were also trained in other genres. They produced traditional classic commedia dell'arte shows like *Don Giovanni* that played in village squares and town halls throughout Northern Italy, as well as their more contemporary production work such as *Il Corvo* and their experimental work such as *L'Ultima Casa*. They also produced circus theatre. They allowed me to tour with them so I could get a better understanding of how the mask work impacted on audiences in productions and how they functioned as an outfit. The actors also worked as their own stage-managers. They were so generous with their time while I was with them. Their touring structure would become the template that I would use for the Focus touring in Ireland, particularly in relation to having shows in rep for a number of years as well as scaling productions up or down according to time of day and venue size. Michele told me that mask theatre as a folk tradition in Europe was best suited to actors using regional dialects. As an experiment the Focus brought him to Ireland to run a free workshop for Irish artists as part of the Thom McGinty Award hosted by Dublin City Council at the Lab. We then planned to do a co-production with Irish and Italian actors but the recession came and the project was put on hold.

9. A conflict of Acting Styles in the Same Production

Different styles of acting can permeate a mainstream production in Ireland. The actors in themselves can be very good and trained in a particular way or they may have raw natural ability. However, the lack of a coherent acting style can have a negative impact on a production. A shared acting vocabulary can give a company coherence and allow the actors to go further at a technical, imaginative and emotional level. Tim would constantly refer to the work of a company or team of actors who have all trained in a similar style as being rather like a jazz band improvising on and off a theme but with everyone working together. There is the pleasure of experiencing 'unity' in artifice. It is primal. When the 'unity' is not there an audience can become aware that something is not right. So, poetics need to apply, not only to a script and production design, but also to the acting style. Eastern European practitioners understand this. That is why they have academies that train directors, theatre critics and the actors under the same roof.

From the 17th Century onwards the education system in the West has been informed by Descartes. He famously said 'I think therefore I am'. Our entire culture has been framed by that statement. It affects everything including our playwriting. The Shakespearean consciousness is completely different: I sense, I feel, I intuit – the non-rational experience of the world. In the 20th Century Stanislavski saw that his own work and Russian theatre in general was lacking imaginative and emotional depth. He developed his theories on acting so as to achieve, in the 20th Century theatre, levels of performance that were achievable in Shakespeare's time. The development of the artist's senses – I touch, I see, I smell, I taste, I hear – informs the artist's humanity and understanding of the universe. It connects the actor at a deeper level in himself so as to create experience to change the audience at a molecular or spiritual level.

10. Yeats's Theories on Theatre

I had researched Yeats's theories on theatre in 2004 after I had been asked to apply for the post of Artistic Director of the Abbey Theatre. His actor training ideas seemed more aspirational than practical. Some might even say that he is responsible for the problems we still need to overcome in theatre making in Ireland today. However, what I did find useful were his ideas on Unity of Being – a philosophy of physical, intellectual and emotional/spiritual development for the artist; and Unity of Image as the artist's use of images to create meaning in his work. His Unity of Culture was a bit more problematic as it would have taken a utopian or totalitarian state to realize it. He did not pre-empt the collapse of the aristocracy and the education of the peasantry moving Ireland towards a more equal society. He could not have foreseen the Celtic Tiger nor the cultural changes brought about during that period with the influx of new Irish peoples from around the world. His 'Unity of Culture' has no place in a modern Ireland. If he called it 'Unity of Experience' or 'Unity through Experience' then it would be inclusive of a diversity of cultures and people of different social standing. What binds a community of disparate peoples together in a healthy society is the shared experiences of all human life at an imaginative and emotional level. The forum for that is live theatre. That is what makes theatre so important and so unique. We can all laugh and we can all suffer pain individually and collectively in a theatre. We can work out our deepest spiritual problems in theatre so that we can heal and move forward in life. That is why theatre is not a luxury: it is a necessity in any society. In an essay entitled 'A People's Theatre', published in 1919 Yeats alludes to a theatre that '...can appease all within us...the Popular Theatre should grow always more objective...and more a discovery of the simple emotions that make all men kin.' This statement for me is his most important comment on theatre. It tends to be overlooked. It echoes Joseph Campbell's writings on the nature of mythology and its use in bringing together the community and healing people at an individual and collective level. That is the purpose of art. It brings a level of awareness to individual people and helps its society to evolve.

Setting aside the mystical language used by Yeats for a moment and focusing on his theories of the Four Faculties of 'Will', 'Mask', 'Creative Mind' and 'Body of Fate': although they are not of practical use to the actor they do have some correlation with Stanislavski's acting ideas. Yeats's ideas are formed from his interior metaphysical experience of his own life. They can only be understood at a conceptual level, making them difficult for an actor to put into practice. Stanislavski is a much more practical teacher and offers very specific tools to help the actor develop the imagination, the senses, creative awareness, depth of feeling, time and place and to be in the moment. He shows us how to apply 'objectives' and 'super objectives'. Yeats's 'Will' is the Stanislavski actor's 'needfulness'; 'Mask' corresponds with 'objective' and 'super objective'; 'Creative Mind' is the actor's imaginative memory and 'Body of Fate' corresponds with the depth of the actor's imagination and the experience created. What can bridge both Yeats and Stanislavski is the imaginative application of the elements within the actor's body and in certain specific cases the archetype to the actor's creative consciousness.

There is a misconception amongst people who have never studied Stanislavski at a practical level that it is only about naturalism and producing the well-made play. The key to Stanislavski, in my view, lies in a quote from *An Actor Prepare s*: 'The fundamental aim of our art is in the creation of the inner life of a human spirit, and in its expression in an artistic form.' The system he developed assisted the performer to get to a Zen-like state – to be in a moment and to develop the facility to create a feeling of imaginative and emotional depth. Certainly that is what the repetition of the exercises that we teach in our studio can achieve. The application of objectives makes active the state of imaginative and emotional depth. The inner state achieved within the performer's body before appropriating the objectives, is the state of openness that can be applied to any genre, style or presentation. When the imaginary appropriation of the elements is integrated into the actor's body, the audience can be given a more lucid and deeply felt experience.

> The central point of the world is the point where stillness and movement are together. Movement is time, but stillness is

eternity. Realizing how this moment of your life is actually a moment of eternity, and experiencing the eternal aspect of what you're doing in the temporal experience – this is the mythological experience.[51]

Conclusion

The Focus after 50 years has an enormous legacy to draw on with its reputation for its commitment to the art of the actor as well as modern classics and new writing. In 2014 the next phase will build on that legacy. The key to the success and existence for half a century of the Focus is the training it offers actors and directors in the studio. It is the actors with that level of illumination in their facility and the ability to create an experience that give the work of the Focus its uniqueness in Ireland. It is also why Irish audiences return again and again to see our work. With a new venue and a new ensemble of artists versed in our classic Stanislavski training we will return to producing one modern classic in our traditional naturalistic style as well as pursuing other kinds of production and genre, exploring new hybrids and experimental works informed by a broader European sensibility of traditions and techniques. The Focus spirit will continue to thrive and will transform itself for future generations of actors and audiences. 2063 is just around the corner.

---

[51] Joseph Campbell with Bill Moyers, *The Power of Myth* (Doubleday, 1988, p.89).

4 | Lineage: Acting and Theatre

Steven Dedalus Burch

In 1972 when I first came to Dublin and studied Irish theatre, it was said that most Irish actors felt they did not have to train, that they were natural performers. There did exist training of a kind, but it was largely like the training one received from the majority of schools and personal teachers: voice training, how to walk, etc.

W.G. Fay and Frank Fay, two brothers who were professional actors at the turn of the twentieth century, were brought to the new theatre Yeats and Lady Gregory founded in order to direct the plays and to train the new company at the Abbey. Such acclaimed actors as the Allgood sisters, Sarah and Molly (Maire O'Neill), the Shields brothers, Arthur and William Joseph (Barry Fitzgerald), F.J. McCormick, and J.M. Kerrigan, all began in the plays of Synge and later with O'Casey. Sara Allgood played the Widow Quinn in the original *Playboy of the Western World* and later originated the role of Juno Boyle in *Juno and the Paycock*. Arthur Shields also played in the *Playboy*, as well as in *The Plough and the Stars*.

To see each of these actors on film is to be given a window on the early Irish theatre. While Sarah Allgood did recreate her performance in the Hitchcock film of *Juno* she does not come off as well as the legend suggests. It may be that she was unaccustomed to playing for the camera in the 1930s. By 1941 in John Ford's *How Green was My Valley*, as the family matriarch, Sarah Allgood gives an extraordinary performance, both grandly and intimately comical and profoundly moving. At the end of the film, when her husband dies, her performance registers as transcendent, it is one of the screen's great acting moments.

In 1947, Carol Reed directed W.G. Fay and F.J. McCormick, the originators of Synge and O'Casey's greatest characters (e.g., Christy

Mahon, Joxer Daly), in a scene in *Odd Man Out*, in which the first fifty years of Irish theatre history comes alive in an astonishing way. Watching this scene one sees the very best of early classical Irish acting (and an extra attraction is the presence in the film, though not in this scene, of the next generation's greatest actor, the young Cyril Cusack.) Shortly after this a new generation of Irish actors in the fifties, including Cusack, Siobhan McKenna, Richard Harris, Peter OToole, and Ray McAnally, also provided great performances on stage in films.

So, the theatre community of Dublin wondered where did this need for the Stanislavski technique come from? Well, great acting has always come from an ability, whether accidental or intentional, to reveal raw emotional truth. But, less than great acting has always relied on the standards of the day of the teaching and training available.

In the early 1970s, when I was in Dublin, my teachers pointed out the lovable and highly popular Abbey Theatre stalwart, Harry Brogan, as an example of a style of acting that was as hammy as it was pleasurable and audiences warmly embraced his performances. But it was a style that fit the plays of Boucicault, as I saw in the 1972 Abbey production of *Arrah na Pogue*, but not the realism demanded by Anton Chekov or Eugene O'Neill.

To understand the importance and the achievements of Dublin's Focus Theatre, I want to explore two separate yet parallel strands of theatre history which came together in a disused garage at 6 Pembroke Place and to see how they played out and contributed to its founding and to its lasting impact in Dublin and beyond.

The System of Stanislavski

In 1963 Deirdre O'Connell founded the Stanislavski Studio, a school in which she could teach and promote the 'System' which was devised by Konstantin Stanislavski from the 1890s to the 1930s. She herself had been a student at the Actors Studio since 1958 and had studied with Lee Strasberg, a legendary teacher of Stanislavski's system which he termed 'the Method.' Over half a century as an actor, director, and acting teacher, Stanislavski devoted his career to assessing acting as a craft and to how it could be taught as such. And the key word here is *craft*.

For much of theatre's history, actors were looked on as being possessed of magic, talent, even genius. Touched by the gods, actors would find something indefinable, something tinged with a deep sense of Truth in their performances. One could not train to be an actor. One was born an actor. One was born with Talent and the only training any actor needed was in projecting and modulating their voice and in their movement. There were tricks of the trade to be learned: cheating out (playing so that one's face was turned out toward the audience even in dialogue with other actors on the stage); crying or laughing on cue; physical bits of business (called *lazzi* in the commedia dell'arte and *schtick* in the Yiddish theatre and in American vaudeville) with which to establish character; dancing and fencing. But acting could not be taught. You either were or were not an actor.

Perhaps no anecdote better puts this case forward than this apocryphal story from the life of Laurence Olivier, once regarded by critics and audiences from the 1940s-1970s as the greatest English-speaking actor in the world. In the 1960s he performed the role of Othello at the National Theatre, utilizing every part of his legendary technical storehouse with which to present the Moor. One night, after a stunning performance, a close friend went backstage to see Olivier. He found the star trashing his dressing room, throwing chairs and screaming in a rage. Attempting to calm down the actor, his friend said, 'Larry, what's wrong! What's come over you? Don't you know that tonight you gave maybe the greatest performance of your career?' Shaking and in tears, Olivier replied, 'I know. And I don't know how I did it!'

Great acting, even good acting, was controlled by an actor's sense of inspiration in the moment. To be divinely touched. So many actors over centuries trusted this axiom, one which made every actor's performance erratic, at least those to whom doing their best work at every performance was their goal. This was what propelled Stanislavski to undertake a study of acting, to treat it as a craft that can be taught, and that can be repeated night after night. Which is not to deny the importance of inspiration, which does occur – but as a craft the actor is freed from relying on it solely.

Stanislavski broke down the 'rules' and founded a system with which to bring each actor to emotional life in performance; to present the actor with a program of analysis of the role and to work on making each actor find and recall an inner truth for their character that can be repeatedly represented. In such areas as Given Circumstances, Sense Memory (or Affective Memory), Through-line (or Spine), Super-Objectives, Magic 'If', and Circle of Attention, the actor can break down the role into these various components and bring a sense of truthful behaviour to the performance. This is what Deirdre O'Connell was taught and what she was convinced that the Dublin theatre needed. Indeed, the task was daunting. Everywhere she turned she was told that the Irish were naturally talented and required no training. The level of acting at the Abbey, at the Gate, and at the Gaiety was fine, except that audiences were getting tired of the 'star' turns their favourite actors would take, earning applause on their entrances: all vocalizing and no inner life.

And yet, acting, great acting, even merely good acting, needs emotional truth, at least by common western standards. Stanislavski defined acting as 'living truthfully in imaginary circumstances' and since the early Greeks such 'truth-telling' has been a part of great acting, no matter the style of playing, the genre of the writing, or the physical and cultural requirements of the role. The Greek actor Polus, cast as Elektra, made his entrance (all the roles in ancient Greece were played by men) carrying the urn of his father, Agamemnon. Elektra's first speech was an emotional speech necessitating all of the actor's resources. As it happened, Polus' oldest son had died recently, so the actor entered carrying the ashes of his son, connecting fully, truthfully with the emotions of Elektra, not representing her sorrow but 'filling the stage with genuine grief.'[52] Stanislavski would have approved and even cheered. Some things cannot be adequately faked.

Stanislavski did not develop his ideas in a vacuum. After he and Nemirovich-Danchenko had opened the Moscow Art Theatre (MAT), they sought out Anton Chekhov, whose second full-length play *The Seagull* had been a disastrous failure in its premier production. Chekhov's plays were something new to the theatre. Less plot-oriented, more character studies, they demanded genuine human behaviour to drive the plays instead of the melodramatic actions of much of the nineteenth-century theatre. Cathartic moments, if and when found, turned on the nuance of speech and of body language. It was about the play's subtext, what remained hidden under the dialogue and in the silences. It was essential for each of his plays that they be performed without attention to the individual ego, that we the audience be immersed in an acting and design ensemble where the world of the play would wash over us with our own recognition. This had been growing in the western theatre since the middle of the century, slowly at first, with actors like Mikhail Shchepkin, Russia's greatest actor, showing the way.

The reputation of MAT grew, along with that of its principal director, Stanislavski. After the Bolshevik Revolution, several of its primary actors, including Michael Chekhov, Maria Ouspenskaya, Richard Boleslawski and others settled in Western Europe and later in

---

[52] *Actors on Acting*, ed. Toby Cole and Helen Krich Chinoy (Crown Publishers, New York, 1970), pp. 14-15.

the U.S., bringing the acting techniques developed by Stanislavski with them.

By the nineteen-twenties certain American actors and directors began to study the System, including Harold Clurman, and Stella Adler (who stepped aside from the students and went to Stanislavski himself). By 1930 they had formed their own theatre company, The Group Theatre, based on the principals of the System and its ensemble playing. Ten years later the Group disbanded and after the Second World War some of its directors and actors re-grouped and started the Actors Studio in New York City in 1947. By the early nineteen-fifties Lee Strasberg had become the leading acting teacher of the Stanislavski system, now called the Method. Actors of the calibre of Marilyn Monroe, Geraldine Page, James Dean, Paul Newman, Al Pacino, Ellen Burstyn, Karl Malden, Eli Wallach, and Ben Gazzara studied these techniques (while others such as Marlon Brando and Montgomery Clift studied with Stella Adler and received their Stanislavski training elsewhere). In 1958 eighteen year old Deirdre O'Connell auditioned for the Studio and was accepted in its program where she trained and eventually co-taught for the next five years.

At this same time a struggle broke out in America over whose training was closest to what the master, Stanislavski, wanted. It was argued that early Stanislavski encouraged actors to go so far into themselves that they lost sight of the fact of performance, whereas later Stanislavski was felt by some as more encouraging actors to invent, create emotional circumstances and bring it out in performance, to work from physical activity first and find the emotional truth from it rather than from starting with emotional truth. A classic example offered is the question: when walking in a forest and one comes upon a tiger, does one become frightened, then scream and then run? Or does one run first and become afraid on the running, when the physical activity may only increase the emotional and adrenal response of abject terror? Strasberg was accused of concentrating solely on Stanislavski's early writings which Stanislavski himself acknowledged later as unsatisfactory. Sanford Meisner, another Group Theatre alumnus, broke with Strasberg and offered training based on the later psychophysical theories of Stanislavski, while Stella Adler affirmed that only she had actually spoken with Stanislavski and she knew his intentions best. O'Connell herself actually broke with the cult of Strasberg by the time she left New York for Ireland in 1963, concentrating more on the full range of Stanislavski's writings.

Because the technique was suited so well to film acting, where projecting character only looked fake, while the camera picked up on the greatest of subtle nuances, the Stanislavski System thrived as film and television became the main forms of dramatic entertainment and small theatres, such as the Focus Theatre, were obviously eminently better situated for this kind of 'realistic' acting.

This was western theatre's second revolution, occurring almost simultaneously with its first revolution to the extent that the two appeared to be such mirror images as to be confused as the same.

The Rise of Realism and the Free Theatre Movement

The first revolution had occurred a generation earlier. The rise of realism throughout the nineteenth century changed the way plays were being written, acted and designed, and even brought in the 'new' art form of the director. This coincided with a growing dissatisfaction on the parts of some practitioners and audiences with the commercial theatre's dominance through melodrama and various spectacles and with local censorship laws. 1887 was the year of the great schism, when the Free Theatre (*Theatre Libre*) Movement began in Paris and spread throughout Europe and North America during the next forty years.

The rise in realism paralleled a rise in technology that made the real world available to masses of people for first time (telephones brought real people, through their voices, to great distances; photography and the phonograph brought their bodies and places of habitation, and again, their voices and sounds through vast distances, even resulting in the invention of a new form of theatre, the travelogue. All of this coincided with a rise in cultural disruption. Immigration from the rural to the urban and from the colonized countries to the colonizers filled cities with teeming masses of humanity. With it came enormous squalor, disease and poverty, along with demands for government intervention on behalf of the sick, the disabled, the unemployed, the underemployed and the underpaid, as well as the enslaved. Prostitution, robbery and assault, and drug and alcohol dependency, along with spousal and child abuse soared in numbers. Liberation movements – for women, for slaves, for the colonized, for workers – popped up from country to country.

Theatre does not lead. It follows. Theatre, however, can be a means of drawing attention to problems. Emile Zola, following the lead taken by Balzac earlier in the century, argued that theatre can be a means of presenting a social ill and examining it as a pathologist would a disease. Auguste Comte presented a philosophy called Positivism which stated that everything in the universe is knowable, and that the duty of science and art was to bring this knowledge to bear on solving these social problems. Fine sentiments, but theatre had become a significant commercial enterprise by the nineteenth century. Theatres grew in size, in audience attendance, and the subject matter for plays was kept strictly at the superficial level. Melodramas were the most popular theatre form at this time (to be replaced in the twentieth century with musicals), and audiences packed these theatres, e.g., the Boulevard theatres in Paris, the West End in London, Broadway in New York.

An amateur French actor, André Antoine, read the essays of Zola and heard about the plays of Ibsen, banned in most cities for obscenity (particularly *Ghosts*). Antoine was a visionary who realized that by staying small (under a hundred seats), he could have a theatre which was not dependent on huge revenues where new writers could experiment in theme and form. In 1887 he opened the *Theatre Libre* (free theatre) in Paris to a subscription audience (no tickets were sold and no advertising in the press kept the censors from wielding their power). He produced plays by Zola, Ibsen, and Strindberg. He was the first to produce evenings of one-act plays (called fifteen-minute plays, or *quart d'heures*) independently from full-length plays. He directed his actors to ignore the fourth wall (he wouldn't even tell his actors where the audience would be sitting until the dress rehearsal). He forced his actors to drop the declamatory style of acting and to concentrate on nuanced behaviour. He dressed his sets with all the details necessary to create a real world on the stage. Word of mouth made his theatre a sensation. The Free Theatre Movement had begun.

Two years later, in 1889, Otto Brahm opened his free theatre (*Freie Bühne*) in Berlin with Ibsen's *Ghosts*. Strindberg and Wedekind and Schnitzler were produced there also. Two years after that, J.T. Grein opened his free theatre in London, the Independent Theatre Society, in 1891, also with Ibsen's *Ghosts*, and he produced the first play by George Bernard Shaw, *Widowers Houses*. Within a decade this theatre became the Royal Court Theatre. Other theatres opened in its wake, sometimes following Antoine's lead, sometimes taking only a few of his ideas, the Moscow Art Theatre and the Abbey Theatre among them. A tour by the Abbey Players to the United States in 1911 inspired an American version of the free theatre movement, called the Little Theatre Movement, beginning the following year with the Toy Theatre in Boston and the Chicago Little Theatre (both in 1912) with the Neighbourhood Playhouse and the Washington Square Players in New York in 1915 (which subsequently evolved in 1919 into the Theatre Guild), and the

Provincetown Playhouse in 1916 (which produced the first plays of
Eugene O'Neill, himself influenced by the Abbey's plays, especially
those of J.M. Synge). Within another two years there were more than
fifty such theatres in the United States.

Other changes occurred in the American theatre at this time. In 1903
George Pierce Baker began teaching playwriting at Radcliffe College
and later enlarged it at Harvard University, titled English 47, which
included a workshop (Workshop 47) to produce the plays. Among his
students were Eugene O'Neill, Sidney Howard, and Edward Sheldon. In
1925 Baker resigned from Harvard and became the head of Yale
University's first Department of Drama. In 1915 Robert Edmond Jones
veered away from the familiar realistic set designs of the time when he
created an 'expressionistic' set for a production of Anatole France's *The
Man Who Married a Dumb Wife* which historians credit as
inaugurating the New Stagecraft Movement.

Since this time, there have been other small theatre movements
dedicated to new plays, to promoting new artistic and social and
political ideas in America, and to creating a new aesthetic which
included other styles beyond realism, among them the Lafayette Players
in Harlem (1915-32), the Civic Repertory Theatre (1926-33), the Group
Theatre (1931-41), and the extraordinary Federal Theatre Project (1935-
39) initiated by Hallie Flanagan to provide work for unemployed
theatre artists and to bring their eclectic art to all Americans during the
Depression.

It was from this tradition, especially from that of the Group Theatre,
that New York-born Deirdre O'Connell came. A visionary like Antoine,
she understood the need to keep her theatre free from the commercial
pressures that afflicted the main stages of Ireland, including the Abbey,
the Gate, and the Gaiety. Dublin had its small independent theatres,
most notably the Pike in the 1950s which premiered the work of
Brendan Behan and gave Samuel Beckett's *Waiting for Godot* its Irish
premiere. Through the Stanislavski Studio, Deirdre O'Connell began a
programme of training in 1963 that produced first-rate actors like Tom
Hickey, Tim McDonnell, Sabina Coyne, Ena May, Gabriel Byrne, and
Mary Elizabeth Burke-Kennedy (also a first-rate director), augmented
by strong ensemble casts in classics by Ibsen (Focus's production of *A
Doll's House* was a phenomenal success, running for five months to
great acclaim), Strindberg, Chekhov, Lorca, and Turgenev as well as
contemporary works by Samuel Beckett, Harold Pinter, Doris Lessing,
and Tennessee Williams.

In a recent email my collaborator Brian McAvera noted that Deirdre O'Connell

> cleared away (or cleansed) Irish acting of its nineteenth century melodramatic roots to give naturalistic acting room to breathe; and then Joe [Devlin] came along and introduced non-naturalistic work, broadening the baseline.

This is true. But the Focus continues to assert itself with its Stanislavski training simply because Stanislavski's training is not limited to the realistic/naturalistic theatre. Stanislavski provided the actor working in any kind of style, from realism to Brechtian epic to Japanese Noh or even the Indian kathakali, with a means of enriching the performance through intentions, or inner actions and of breaking down the script/story by analyzing the circumstances of the moment and articulating that moment through the study of the character/performer's intentions,[53] regardless of the style. And the results of this training? The Focus Theatre, seating only 67, yet continually crammed to the rafters (if it were large enough to have rafters) in production after production, beset with financial woes due largely to the theatre's limited number of seats, has nevertheless continued to remain true to its founder's vision since her death in 2001 and, under her successor Joe Devlin, it continues to do so now on the eve of its fiftieth anniversary, even in new and temporary quarters.

This is the lineage behind the founding and working of the Focus Theatre and provides us with a sense of a great tradition from one visionary to another, all the way to Deirdre O'Connell and the present day on the fiftieth anniversary of the founding of the Stanislavski Studio in Dublin.

---

[53] Bill Bruehl's *The Technique of Inner Actions: The Soul of a Performer's Work*, Heinemann, 1996, offers many excellent examples, especially his work with a Bharatanatyam dancer trained in traditional Indian norms, 10-13.

5 | Interview with actor Margaret Twomey

Mary Moynihan

Mary: Tell me how you became involved in Focus Theatre?

Margaret: I wanted to put on a play for Concern and I was looking for a small theatre in town. I was a Friend of Focus at that time. As a Friend, you could come to a rehearsal or a workshop so I thought I'd come down the lane and ask Deirdre if she would be prepared to rent the theatre to us, not knowing anything about Focus in that regard. Of course she said yes. But she also said 'you can have it for nothing'. I thought that was an amazing gesture because we were expecting to pay maybe Ir700-800 rent. In a way hers was probably the biggest contribution as we made about two thousand pounds.

We filled the theatre and had people queuing up Friday, Saturday, and Sunday. Deirdre came along on Thursday but the space was booked out. The company wanted to try and make a place for her but she wouldn't hear of it. She insisted on making her own booking for Saturday and paying her own way in to her own theatre and I just thought that it said a lot about Deirdre. And not only that, but the studio people helped us to put up and paint the set. Everybody in the theatre was at our disposal. You got this sense when you came in that it was more than just a theatre; it was kind of a family as well. She came to see the play and then in the pub one night she asked me if I would like to come to her studio. That would have been about 1989 and I was there until Deirdre died in 2001. I wasn't there every single Saturday. Sometimes I might be in a show or there might be family things going on. I might be gone for maybe a couple of weeks or months and then I'd be back again. I suppose I was there twelve years.

Mary: The Stanislavski Studio was conducted by Deirdre at the Focus Theatre usually on Saturdays and Sundays and occasionally mid-week, ranging in time from three hours to a full day. There was a format normally beginning with the deep muscle relaxation process, followed by abstract sound and movement and sensory exercises, followed by improvisations and prepared work. Many of the exercises were based on themes given by Deirdre such as a place, an active verb or an emotion. Can you describe your experience of the studio?

Margaret: I had to watch like everybody else, not for terribly long but for a couple of weeks. I sat in the audience and watched the exercises people were doing on stage, like *Justification of an Action*, *Personalization of an Object*, or character studies and the mirror exercises and I was just fascinated. On one particular Saturday she said to me that I could go up for an improvisation exercise called *Loggerheads* that started off with repeating a phrase, and then introduced abstract psychological sound. You talked but you didn't use identifiable sounds or real words. They were all abstract sounds that expressed where you were at, emotionally, in the moment. I thought abstract work was great because it brought you out of the head and you'd arrive at a place that you didn't plan or know was there, a place you'd never get to just by talking. I remember her asking me at the end of the exercise what I learnt in that exercise and I said I learnt that you had to listen more intently. Because you didn't have the words, you had to listen in a different way. She seemed pleased with that so she let me go up the next Saturday to take part in the studio.

There we would normally do the deep muscle relaxation process to start with and then Deirdre would give us a theme, maybe for abstract sound, and then we would explore the same theme through abstract movement and once the movement was established we would reintroduce the sound, so it seemed like you were building up an emotional vocabulary for the day. I remember exploring themes of places like Paris, Hawaii, and Beirut. Sometimes she gave us places I had never heard of but I worked with whatever the word evoked for me. She would sometimes give us verbs such as 'to fear'; it could be something you felt or something that was happening around you. She was very specific; you might do 'afraid' but then weeks later you might do 'to be afraid' which had a subtle difference.

She might give a phrase to use in *Loggerheads,* which she would say without any particular intonation such as 'why would you do that?' We would repeat that phrase back and forth to our partner until it developed into an improvisation on that theme. Somehow what went on in the earlier exercises was there as a residue when I went to do the improvisations, even though I now had a new theme to deal with. I didn't find the improvisation too hard because I was already warmed up through the earlier abstract work, which had awoken the imagination and the emotional vocabulary. For some of the exercises such as the *Justification of an Action* or *Character Study* you could be up on the stage for forty minutes or an hour on your own with no words.

What I found really worked over time was the sensory work. We used to hold an imaginary object and work on it through the senses. It might be the dominant object from our abstract sound exercise, such as a ring or a bag or a shoe. You would explore the (imaginary) object, absorbing and understanding it through the five senses and then behaving with it. An orange couldn't be interesting because it was a round yellow object; you had to get down to its essence, which would be soft, juicy. You began to develop a language of the senses. I taught in Africa and I remember reading that nothing passes through the mind without having first passed through the senses. So I remember thinking at the time, this is a process, you know. If you don't go back to the senses do you fully experience the object? You had to move away from being intellectual once you started dealing with the senses, as it becomes an emotional experience.

There are two things that I always remember about studio. I was up on the stage a few weeks when Deirdre said to me 'I notice about you that when you're in an improvisation you don't actually put out your objective, you wait till the other person does, and then you seek to get your objective in and around their objective'. Now she was speaking solely in terms of drama. You can never have full drama if you don't have conflict and if you're not going to put out your objective you're not going to get that sense of conflict, and will never move to the next stage. Drama is all in the conflict and in the negotiation that happens when both people want to achieve their own objective.

I remember thinking at the time how profound this was because, even though she was talking about the principles of drama, I realized that was how I negotiate life. It never occurred to me that I wasn't directly asking in life for what I wanted, and I remember thinking this has to stop. That was the first glimpse I got into realizing I was not acknowledging myself, so how could I acknowledge a character?

Mary: What do you mean by acknowledging yourself?

Margaret: Sometimes it's not till someone reflects back something about you that you actually think about it. What I really learnt was that in life I tended to try and go around conflict rather then hit it head on: that was my way of negotiating life. I realized that when Deirdre said it. I learnt that, in drama and in life, if you're only going to go around conflict you're never going to move to the next stage and develop the drama. If things are messy you've got to acknowledge that and then you have to negotiate a change or development. In dramatic terms we also learnt that there were many different ways of negotiating a conflict, including convincing or attacking, which weren't always aggressive.

Mary: It could be seductive.

Margaret: It could be anything. It taught you how to listen and hear and you were always encouraged to allow yourself to be affected by the other person's objective. It didn't mean that if I wanted to go to Cork and you wanted to go to Belfast I would keep saying 'No, I'm going to Cork'. I'd listen and ask 'Why do you want to go to Belfast?'. Is there anything in that for me. Is there any good reason why I should be swayed by your argument? So you learned all those skills. I know Deirdre always said this is not a therapy session and we must never use it as such, but you did learn a lot about yourself, and that helped you when you went to study characters.

Deirdre herself was extraordinarily perceptive. I don't think I ever met anyone who was as perceptive as her. So when somebody asked me why I liked Focus, why I kept going back I said, I thought it was because it actually set me free because I learnt about myself. I think most people one way or another found this about Focus. If you weren't truthful about yourself you weren't truthful on the stage and so in getting to some sense of truth about yourself you became free. You have to start by being honest with yourself.

I thought the other great part of her talent was her ability to feedback to you in a profound but simple way the very essence of your problem – the adjustment you needed to make to bring your performance to life. So I think when she said to me about not putting out my objective that was an amazingly useful thing because I possibly would have diluted the conflict in the drama because I wouldn't have realized what I was doing. She could get to the nub and the essence of your particular problem and it was different for everybody. She could see what was holding you, specifically, back. She was so profound in doing that.

I remember after my father died I went to Cork to visit a friend of my father's, who was in hospital. He said 'how do you feel?' and I said 'I think I feel like I am on a bomb site, like I am on a piece of land in Beirut or something'. He said nothing and then I went and spent a few weeks in West Cork and on the way back I went in to see him again and he said 'how's the bomb site?' I hadn't given it much thought and then I said 'oh, I think there's a dresser on it' (a piece of furniture so now it was no longer barren as there were things coming back into the picture) and he said 'well, that's a start'.

Shortly after that I went into Focus and I don't remember exactly what the theme for the day was but Deirdre maybe said Beirut and the whole bomb site image came back. There were about ten of us onstage and in a flash I thought 'no, I'm not going there, I'm not exploring this here'. Then I heard from the depths of the theatre 'Don't disregard your first image Margaret, it might be useful'. I remember thinking 'How does Deirdre know, she's watching ten people, and the thought flashed through my mind in a fraction of a second'?

I am sure she knew everything about each one of us up on that stage, our weaknesses and strengths, but she never referred to them in a personal way. It was always about the creative process. That's what I liked – that great pursuit of the truth and the integrity behind it. It was always about the acting and the art of creation and to get us to go as deeply into it as we could. It was a unique experience, Focus, wasn't it?

Mary: She was very perceptive, it's like she could read your soul, and she could look inside and see what's going on. You never felt you were being exploited; you were vulnerable but you never felt in danger.

Margaret: Never, never, never. And you know that's why I was reading that poem to you, 'somewhere I have never travelled, gladly beyond' by e.e. cummings.

> your slightest look easily will unclose me
> though I have closed myself as fingers,
> you open always myself
> petal by petal as Spring opens
> (touching skilfully, mysteriously) her first rose

That poem says something about someone opening you skilfully and mysteriously and I thought that's what Deirdre did, that verse was so like what she did for people in studio. And then the closing verse, I thought that was 'Deirdre-speak': *I do not know what it is about you that closes and opens; only something in me understands.*

Mary: You mentioned abstract sound as part of the actor training. Abstract sound is expressive rather than realistic, it is non-literal. An abstract sound exercise at Focus was called 'Sounding into' where you are given a place or a word that you have to explore solely through abstract sound, to express your images and emotions only using abstract sound. For example, rather than expressing the conventional sound for weeping you are looking for a more primal, non-verbal sound to express what is going on. During the exercise you explore many different non-verbal sounds and after a period of exploration you become aware of the pattern of sound, refining your sound down to two or three basic sounds that for you most describe the word you are exploring. Can you describe your journey in an 'abstract sound' exercise?

Margaret: I loved 'abstract sound', it was always something that brought me to a deeper place. If she gave you the theme you took it on, you tried to absorb it and then go with the first abstract sound that came into your head, but bearing the theme in mind. You often started tentatively but as you went on and allowed the sound to bring you somewhere else you suddenly realized it was becoming more intense, and that intensity brought you to a deeper place. The psychological sound is great because you can just keep going, it always builds and releases and builds, and you can keep going until you find what you need. In that sense it is easier for me to use psychological sound rather than psychological gesture. 'Abstract sound' wasn't bound by any rules of sound, that's how I understood it. It was something that you felt and you did your best to find a sound or sound pattern that would express how you felt. So if the theme was 'Paris' an image might come into your head of Cancan dancing and you find an abstract sound, it couldn't be music or dance, but you would try to find a sound that would give the rhythm or essence of what you were feeling and then that would bring you to somewhere else. The word and the sound created images. I used to get a series of pictures, maybe an image of the bridges of Paris, and then the people under the bridge, that might bring you to the poor of Paris, so while you might have started out with dance you might end up with something totally different. For me it worked when you got a rhythm that was repetitive and it said in some way 'Paris' to me through abstract sound. It kept me away from the head; it helped me to work through images through abstraction. It stopped me planning and reasoning.

Mary: Were the images you refer to personal or imaginary?

Margaret: Imaginative mostly. Some days it wouldn't be personal at all.

Mary: The exploration of the bombsite could be personal.

Margaret: Yes and I suppose that was an intense personal experience that I wasn't sure I wanted to explore there in studio. Because I had created a Beirut for myself before she gave it to me it was hard to bring my imagination entirely away from it. But what I found was, that even if the image was purely imaginative, somewhere it was embedded in your own emotions, your own emotional space, so I think exploring an image is a kind of a mixture of the personal and imaginative.

Mary: After the sound exercises Deirdre might ask you to express the same place or word through abstract movement, as in a 'mirror exercise'.

Margaret: With Deirdre the mirror exercises mostly worked on a theme, you were trying to find the expression of the theme through your body moving abstractly in space, shaping the theme or emotion in space through body movement.

Mary: And of course the moving body is always creating images.

Margaret: Yes. It's pretty hard to keep images out of the work, it seemed to me.

Mary: Deirdre trained with Lee Strasberg who placed a strong emphasis on personal emotional memory work. What is your experience of the work at Focus?

Margaret: People say that Stanislavski is about recreating an emotion but I remember it as a much more active experience than dwelling on personal past emotion. Past emotions came up of course and sometimes that was a useful place to go if you were having a difficulty but you didn't always use it.

My memory of Deirdre was that, in relation to finding out about character, she liked you to do it through action rather than sitting round a table talking. If something was not working you would discuss it for a while but she preferred and encouraged you to solve it on your feet through action. If something was not clear to you then you would tease it out through improvisation or exercises rather than through a discussion. I think she thought action was where you found truth.

People sometimes think that the truth is telling it exactly as it is but Deirdre's truth was bigger than that, it was about knowing what was real for you, and acknowledging that...arriving at a truth in your performance. And knowing it was different for everybody...your truthful performance of a part may be different from mine. Acting was almost a spiritual thing for Deirdre, a sacred thing. I also think that her generosity with the gifts she had was amazing; she shared any knowledge she had with you. Whether we picked it all up or not is another question. I always thought it was awesome that, if you went to studio on a Saturday at two o'clock and you had work that you wanted her to look at, she'd stay till midnight if necessary to watch it and help you progress it. That was no problem to her as she was very generous with her talents and her time. And what did we pay – a small donation which we threw into a basket, a pound or two, and if we had nothing that was ok too. Nobody knew.

She always came down the lane with all this black flying, and she looked like the most theatrical figure you could imagine and she'd talk to you in a theatrical manner and yet when she sat down to look at the work all that fell away and she became the most practical person you could imagine. Suddenly she would be focused, giving sensible, practical, down-to-earth understandable and deeply insightful direction.

Mary: Was it very difficult to get into the Focus Theatre?

Margaret: After Deirdre gave me the theatre for nothing (for the Concern show) I said to her at some stage that it was an amazing gesture because 'you knew nothing about me, about what I do'. And she said, 'I'm not infallible Margaret, but I'm seldom wrong about people'. And I wonder was that the key, you had to be there for what, in her book, was the right reason.

Mary: And that being?

Margaret: To develop your talent if you had it, to explore the work truthfully, to learn to communicate. There was no point going to Focus if you wanted a quick route to performance. People didn't join the Studio and find themselves on stage the next month no matter how talented they might appear to be. You had to learn the craft, have the perseverance to stay for what she expected of you. A lot of people will tell you that they sat for years watching studio before being asked to join. So you had to be there because you wanted to learn and you felt ready to learn.

Mary: How did you become involved in theatre yourself?

Margaret: When I was in school I went to drama classes with Eileen Hayes in the Fr Matthew Hall and I did pantomimes and the Feis Maitiu. I was from Dublin and went to national school in Glasnevin and then on to Scoil Caitriona where we did every subject through Irish. My mother was an Irish speaker originally from Donegal. She loved Irish culture and music and was always madly interested in drama. When we were kids she used to tell us stories and they turned out to be Shakespeare's stories. She didn't say much about Shakespeare but if she was telling us about *The Merchant of Venice* she would stop and say 'the quality of mercy is not strained'. She would say the speech for her own pleasure, because she loved it. When I went to secondary school I discovered that I actually knew Shakespeare and many of his stories. When we were kids we had one of those fold-up screens and my mother would have us putting on concerts for her. She would announce each item saying, '...and the next item on the programme is a poem from...' or 'the next item is a song from...' She obviously loved drama herself and from a very early age she would bring me to the Abbey and the Gate, and we would listen to Radio plays on a Sunday night.

I continued doing classes and performed regularly but then I got married and went to Africa to work and when I came back I went to drama classes including three or four years with Betty Ann Norton and I acted locally until I went to Focus. I did a lot of work for an ex-Abbey actress, Lammy Baker, she invited me to take a part in a production with St. Thomas' Dramatic Society and I worked with them for many years while my children were small. I went from there to Focus. With St Thomas's we did two big plays a year and went to Drama festivals. We also organized drama workshops which I always attended.

In the early nineties I attended studio in Focus and was lucky enough to get a part sometimes. I also worked outside Focus with other theatre companies. In 1991 I became involved in the founding of Smashing Times Theatre Company with other artists I met through Focus Theatre including you, Mary. I was on the board of Smashing Times Theatre Company and also acted in professional productions presented by the Company including *End of Term* by Maeve Binchy, directed by Focus director Tim McDonnell, which went on a nationwide tour playing in all the major venues throughout Ireland and Northern Ireland. I continued working with Smashing Times Theatre Company and also with Focus Theatre and I still do today.

Mary: You have performed in film and television playing the part of Eileen Bishop in RTÉ's *Fair City* recently. You acted professionally at Focus Theatre during Deirdre's time. Can you talk about Marsha Norman's 1983 Pulitzer Prize-winning play *Night, Mother* presented by Focus Theatre in 1997 and directed by Deirdre? This was a two-hander and you played the mother, Thelma, and Elizabeth Moynihan played your daughter Jessie, a woman in her forties.

Margaret: *Night, Mother* opens with a mother at home settling down for the evening having her cup of tea when her daughter, Jessie, arrives in and tells her that she is going to take her own life that night. The mother tries to persuade Jessie not to do it. They talk about the past and their hurts. They talk about what life means to both of them and the mother says she doesn't care how mundane life is, she still wants to live and that Jessie should want to live also.

As a director Deirdre was very methodical. We did a lot of improvisation exercises before we actually went on to the text. We explored in our own words situations that would arise in the play as well as exploring scenes based on the other characters mentioned in the text but who did not appear on stage. We also did the 'Character Study' exercise and I remember Deirdre saying that the character study exercises and improvisations were great because they would sustain us through the run.

Mary: The 'Character Study' or 'Character Private Moment' exercise used at Focus Theatre explores a significant event in the character's past life (that takes place prior to the play), the repercussions of which are felt in the actual script or text. You choose an event from your past life that is exceptional or formative, it impacts directly on the character in the actual play, and you explore this event by living through it. The actor is alone on stage and the exercise usually lasts thirty to forty minutes. The exercise has a structure with an action as the central heightened or climatic moment of the scene, and you develop a storyline based on your character's biographical details, which revolves around the carrying out of the central action. You justify how you work up to the central moment of the scene, building organically using the pyramid structure – the *before stage*, building up to the central action, the *during stage*, living through the central moment, the *after stage*, coming out the other side affected by what has happened. The climax of the piece should be a moment of revelation in relation to the key event or relationship for your character that you are exploring. You are alone onstage living through and within the fictional circumstances of the storyline. While the storyline is fictional, the component parts must be invested with special significance for the actor, for example the objects used can be personal and the events must be important to you. You set up the character's private space on the stage, a bedroom or sitting room where you are on your own, placing the personal objects and other required items in appropriate places, you position yourself within this private space, do a mini relaxation and then move into the exercise, going through the sequence of events that you have decided in terms of objects and activities and seeing where they bring you to.

Margaret: Mama in *Night, Mother* had a difficult relationship with her husband who is referred to in the play but does not appear, so I created a character study exercise based on the first few days of my marriage as a newlywed. My husband had gone away for the day and was due back shortly. I set the exercise in the sitting room/kitchen area of our home and I had bought myself a new outfit, a nice dress, lovely shoes and a nightdress. The items arrived from the shop all wrapped up and I opened them and tried them on and got myself ready, preparing dinner, setting the table, and I waited and watched for him to arrive home. But he never came and at the heightened moment I undressed and hid the items away and I remember experiencing this huge sense of disappointment. When I started the character study exercise I had no idea where it was going but I could always remember that huge sense of disappointment I felt when I realized my husband was not coming home to me that evening; that he was not interested in me.

And in the play I had a monologue where I said I always felt I was a disappointment to my husband because I was too mundane, that he married a plain country woman and I was never more than that. When I did the monologue every night on stage I could still remember the disappointment I felt in the character study, it was always there, it was just there. Deirdre was right, it did inform the performance, and you didn't have to worry about being fresh because you actually had experienced in the rehearsal room the emotion that was called for in the play so it was always accessible to you right through the run. I never had to stop and wonder how will I deliver this speech, because you just knew how you stood with this man and it was there, so that was it. I understood this woman and her relationship to her husband, it came naturally to me. The residue from the emotion I experienced in the exercise was still there, so I didn't have to impose or colour the text too much myself; those sections where I referred to my husband just happened naturally. I loved when those scenes came up as you felt very secure in it, all you had to do was just tell the story, and you didn't have to impose or invest too much. Even today if I had to read that monologue I would remember the feeling. In that sense the exercises are great. If you have experienced it physically and emotionally, then the whole performance is much richer than if you have just worked it out in your head.

The other thing I remember was that Deirdre started at page one of the script and she had worked out how much time she was going to spend on each section. We came in with our lines learned for the particular section we were working on that day. We might do improvisations if we were having difficulty with the text. If you weren't sure about the dialogue when you came in, by the time you went home that evening I can assure you, you knew the script. Then we got a new section of text to work on for the next day and before we began work on the second section we ran the section we had worked on the previous day. The next day we ran through the first and second section before beginning work on the third and so on. She was very methodical about it, building up to a climax so she didn't do difficult sections of text until we had worked through the earlier bits. She had a very definite rehearsal plan. We teased out the script as we went along. If we were having difficulty she might do an improvisation or an acting exercise. The exercises were chosen to help solve a problem or build on something; if the text was working there was no need to do exercises.

When I think about Deirdre now I remember how, if you were acting, she treated you as a precious object and if people came in to the theatre while you were working she would say 'don't disturb the actors'. She was extraordinarily respectful and helpful to actors. The communication was wonderful. I remember her laughter. She was great fun at times. I can still hear her laughter...and the parties. But in a strange sort of way she was very retiring, she was very private. She never made herself very public outside the theatre or outside the people that she worked with.

Mary: Why do you think that was?

Margaret: Focus was very successful in the early days and I think there was talk about it becoming a bigger theatre. But I think at heart Deirdre was a teacher. She was an artist and a teacher and she said she knew she was a great communicator. She could only do the work she was interested in if Focus remained small. She loved having her studio and teaching people, and also acting and directing. She always said actors should be trained in a living theatre. It was a great privilege for an actor to be trained in Focus Theatre, to work backstage, on lighting, or front of house, sweeping the stage, working in the coffee shop and attending the classes, knowing how the whole theatre works. And I think Deirdre liked to teach that way, and she could only do that in a small space. She didn't appear to want to be a star; she liked the space she had created for herself to work in.

Mary: Can you tell me about your memories of acting with Deirdre in *The House of Bernarda Alba* by Federico Garcia Lorca directed by Focus actor and director Jayne Snow in 1999. Among the cast of ten women you played Poncia and Deirdre played Bernarda Alba.

Margaret: I remember seeing her script and it was marked in all different colours, sections in red, green, blue and I think the colours meant something to her about the different colours or emotions in the dialogue. I think she had marked her script in different colours to indicate changes in the dialogue. During rehearsals Deirdre took part in all the Stanislavski exercises we did with Jane including the 'character study' exercise. I remember one thing about her character study. At the end of the exercise she was on stage standing up straight with her two arms stretched out very wide on either side and she was distressed and I wondered why she was doing that, holding that stance with the arms stretched out wide and she also had an object, a silver cup that was significant and had belonged to her husband.

When we came to performance there is a point in the play where the daughters are fighting and Deirdre, as Bernarda, knows that things are breaking down. I was on stage with Deidre and all her daughters and she orders them all to leave saying 'I saw the storm coming but I didn't think it'd burst so soon. O what an avalanche of hate you've thrown on my heart! But I'm not old yet – I have five chains for you and this house my father built, so now even the weeds will know of my desolation. Out of here!' She sent them all away and I was left on stage with my back to Deirdre and she had a line saying 'I'll have to let them feel the weight of my hand! Bernarda, remember your duty'. At that point I turned round to see her after she spoke that line and whatever way she was sitting and whatever expression was on her face, she actually looked like someone who felt like she was being crucified, it was like she didn't wish to do this thing but it was her duty, she had this weight of crucifixion on her.

And then I remembered her stance from the character study exercise when she was standing with her arms out because there was a sense of crucifixion in that, she looked like a cross. I didn't understand when she was doing the actual exercise but now in the play there was that sense of crucifixion again, it was like the agony in the garden, it had a biblical connotation and I remembered the silver chalice: it had all come together in a biblical sense. It was her 'psychological gesture'. She saw Bernarda Alba as being crucified by her social position and society around her, that she had to behave that way. She had explored and experienced that in her character study exercise.

She was the only actor I ever saw playing Bernarda Alba who was strict, domineering and in charge yet had that huge vulnerability underneath it; she still maintained the femininity and sexuality while being domineering and you could still see her pain. You don't often see that.

She was lovely to play with, it was almost impossible to not have a response because what she gave was so clear, direct and engaged, she had that capacity to focus and deliver with such clarity. Every single night before the performance, you arrived in early to prepare and she would call you over to her corner in the dressing room and run lines. She never missed that.

Mary: Can you tell me about your work on creating public improvisations at Focus?

Margaret: One of the most exciting experiences I had in Focus – and you were part of it as well Mary – was when we did the improvisation play on a Sunday night for Deirdre's family who were gathered in Ireland for a genealogical get-together, people from America, Australia, New Zealand. They were hoping to see a play at Focus Theatre but there was no actual production on at the time so Deirdre decided we would do an improvisation play. To start the improvisation she gave us the dilemma and situation, she didn't give us a character. We were all working down the country in a large house where we were running a place, a sort of Rehabilitation Centre for young people who had been in trouble with the law. A farmer had provided the house on loan and apparently someone had gone out one night and killed some of his livestock and the farmer believed it was someone from our group. The farmer said the person responsible had to be found and sent away otherwise he would no longer give us the use of the house and the project would close. So that was the dilemma we had to solve amongst ourselves – were we idealists or were we prepared to compromise. In addition to the dilemma there were personal relationship problems that arose between the characters in the course of the improvisation. In rehearsal a lot of us wanted to keep the young person who had committed the crime and then as we rehearsed some people changed sides to achieve a better balance. We continued to rehearse, creating a shape to the improvisation. What worked well was ensuring that when two or three people were arguing out a point within the improvisation everybody else was to watch and listen. One person would raise an issue and that would be explored fully and others listened, then when that had climaxed, someone else would pick up a point and run with that and so on. At no given time would everybody on stage be talking at the same time.

We performed to a full house and it worked very well. The audience were enthralled and said they believed they were watching something real happening on stage. Obviously the performance was not a repetition of the run through we had. We had a sense of each other and we were clear on the dilemma, but it wasn't all about the dilemma. For example, if one actor said something that sparked off a personal dilemma we would end up with a personal conflict that was acted out within the wider conflict and of course there was plenty of comedy.

That was an amazing experience, to do a two-hour improvisation show and no script. Normally backstage you have the comfort of the script as you wait to go on but you didn't have that crutch, you just sat there with nothing and you went out on stage to a full house. When you were out there you had no idea where it is going to go. It was a very disciplined and structured performance, it was excellent.

Mary: What have you taken from Focus Theatre in relation to creating a performance on stage?

Margaret: When I get a script I read it a number of times. At first you get just an impression. Then you examine the script. You may hit moments that are more meaningful than others. So I might start there, why is that moment meaningful and then continue exploring through character studies or improvisations.

When the character study exercise works it carries you right through the performance particularly when you are in a long run. Sometimes during this exercise things come out that you have subconsciously absorbed from the script but may not be consciously aware of but are released through the physical playing out of the exercise. Improvisations are great for filling out what is implied in the script but not actually said. But you don't often get a chance to do that kind of work. I also enjoy doing impulse work, which I do with you Mary and I find that great, I like that.

Sometimes you get a part and you just instinctively understand the spirit of the person and you don't have to think about how you are going to play it, it just happens in rehearsal. When it clicks or is truthful, that is when you just 'get' the character, you get the woman or the spirit of the person, she starts to speak for you, through you.

Mary: What do you mean by the 'spirit' of the person?

Margaret: I suppose their energy; it comes from somewhere or it may be their voice, or a gesture that captures them. If the person jumps off the page it is easy. If that doesn't happen I might take the script and explore the physical behaviour or actions, what am I doing here, or the physical image of the person and see where that takes me, using abstract psychological sound or movement. I may also work on defining clear and specific objectives related to the other person and also explore what my 'need 'is (I want something but why do I want it?, what need is in me?) maybe for every line or paragraph. I work it out and then forget about it and try to work on instinct.

Generally speaking I learn the lines, I have to know them 200 per cent and then wait for the instinct to come but you always know if what you are doing is empty. You always know when you are just saying the lines and there isn't enough behind them or underneath them. You know when it is working and when it is not. A sense of truth is when the words have a depth that isn't on the page and when you find that depth you know you are hitting the right note. To get truth I find I have to have images in my head, really clarified and specific. They can be still images or moving. I try to visualize specifically all that is happening in the scene, fill in all the detail, rather than just generalizing, and to connect emotionally with the other person. I like to paint the pictures for myself; I like to work on images as I learn the script. You need to look for all the different colours that are in a character; nobody is just one colour; you need to find the different shades, and if the script is good the shades are in the script. In terms of different colour, exploring irony within the text can be good and I often read or re-read acting books to stimulate ideas. What I am looking for is to get underneath the script to the point where it really doesn't matter what words you say. The words are important because they give meaning but then you have to go for the emotion that is there and is found inside yourself. It is not so much the words you say that is important. What goes on between the characters is what is important. I think talking to create character is not the most helpful approach. I'm always looking for an action rather than to talk or write about it. The relationships and the choices you make as that character are such an important part of preparation for me.

Mary: To finish, what final word would you like to say about Focus Theatre and Deirdre's legacy?

Margaret: For me the exciting thing about Focus was that it did not matter whether you became an actor or not. Nobody came to Focus and went out the way they came in. Everybody left Focus different. Because, under Deirdre's direction, everybody was trained as an individual. She saw the strengths and weaknesses in different people and she built on them. She taught you to reflect on yourself and learn about yourself and move on. So even if people did not become actors, they left with more skills than when they first came in.

Mary: What kind of skills?

Margaret: They grew within themselves and got the confidence to be themselves and present themselves to the world as they were. You saw people develop. They left different because they had been given the freedom to explore. Deirdre saw the areas which they could develop. I think that was her special skill. She was so perceptive and had a great capacity to feed back what she had observed clearly, in a meaningful way to you. I thought that was fantastic.

Deirdre knew exactly what she was doing, her vision was very clear, she wanted a theatre and studio where she could train actors in a 'living theatre' and to present classics that maybe wouldn't see the light of day. She liked American and European classics, it was a kind of 'classic' theatre. She didn't do much experimental theatre. That's not to say she didn't like other kinds of theatre but that was for someone else to do. It seemed to me that she liked plays with stories, narratives, and rich relationships.

As for the future? Deirdre taught the Stanislavski system. She perfected that. She worked with a system she knew really well, and she specialized in it. It is a different Focus now, people work in other ways, styles of acting move on through the decades, and scripts are written with different demands. I don't know if the studio will stay rooted in Stanislavski. Focus may explore other methods but I hope it will always produce work that is truthful, spontaneous, brave and exciting. I wish the theatre the very best in the future.

6 | Focus at Fifty

Elizabeth Moynihan

At the bottom of a lane in the heart of Dublin at a time when actor training was confined to the Abbey School of Acting and college drama societies, Deirdre O'Connell went against the tide of emigration and left Hell's Kitchen, New York in the early 1960s to return to the land of our dispossessed forefathers. What possessed her? I remember asking her brother shortly after her passing. He was as nonplussed as I was. Who can explain the drive an artist like Deirdre O'Connell has to embrace the empty space? I mused over this will my fellow Focus members on many occasions in those intervening years leading up to her passing. And yet I never arrived at an answer. You would have to know this rare and incredible person to fully understand her drive and passion and none of us fully achieved that no matter how many hours we spent in her company.

At the time of her arrival in Dublin Deirdre was a young woman in her early twenties, with a genius needing to be shared beyond the United States, the country of her birth that never felt like home, not in the way Ireland had been for her parents who had emigrated from the midlands to New York in the 30's. Two of her siblings had already made the move back to Ireland in the 50's and so for Ellie, as she was known to her family, the call from the old country was so strong she returned to live in Dublin at the age of 21, leaving behind her training at The Actors' Studio. She was one of the youngest ever to be allowed the status of studio member at the studio founded by the world-renowned Lee Strasberg. The Godmother of contemporary dance Martha Graham trained her as a dancer and asked her to choose between Dance and theatre. As it turned out neither of these world-renowned pedagogues could hold on to this beautiful young maverick. The Gods of Art shouted

louder than either of her mentors ever could and Deirdre listened –
crossing the Atlantic to set up the first Actors' Studio outside Moscow
and New York in a converted garage at the bottom of Pembroke Lane,
Dublin.

Thirty years after Focus was founded I found myself back in Dublin,
tanned and directionless after a difficult year in Australia searching for
my inner comedian. I failed to find it. My agent suggested I go to see a
show at the Focus, 'The Balcony' by Jean Genet, directed by Alan
Gilsenan. It was artistic love at first sight. The intimacy of not only the
space but the work...I fell hard. It is a love and passion for the space and
company we call 'Focus' that reaches beyond the grave which sadly
claimed Deirdre 10 years ago. Several other company members who
shaped me, not only as an actor but as a writer should not be forgotten;
Jayne Snow, Robbie Doolan, Paul Keeley, all went long before I was
ready to lose them as fellow 'Comrades' in Art. So ten years ago when
not only beloved company members shuffled off this mortal coil, our
founder and mentor left us also. It seemed as if the pillars of Focus
theatre were crumbling and the doors of the theatre were in danger of
closing after forty years of creating theatre in that tiny magic space
when she passed away. How can an idea born out of one genius of a
woman's head survive after their death? Deirdre was Focus and she it.
Not mutually exclusive. And so a huge vacuum was created and those of
us left behind were devastated. Inert, not knowing what to do.

We were like starving dogs guarding a carcass. So we pulled
together, yelled, cried, fell out, made up and survived. It was
heartbreaking: the idea that what she started might not survive her
death. I almost lost my sanity trying to find a way forward but as a
collective we did. Like a republic born out of the ashes of a war we put
an end to the derision and opened the doors to the idea of a new Artistic
director, not one of us, but someone who would be mindful of our roots
and honour the memory of the woman who gave Focus life and
direction in the work and development of 'The Studio', which is the
life's blood of the company. Joe Devlin accepted the daunting task and
ten years on he is still there to keep the Focus doors open and the studio
vibrant with a new group of student actors emerging every year. Deirdre
referred to Studio members as 'The Savages' in the fondest way and that
is what we are I suppose; our desire to perform is savage, but it needs to
be guided and honed lest we scare ourselves and the punters who come
through the door 6 nights a week.

How to articulate this one woman's effect on me, and the company
of actors left behind, is overwhelming, but here goes: I remember

sitting in the darkened theatre week after week waiting patiently for my name to be called to the stage to become more than just an observer at the Saturday studio where DOC as we knew her, spent hours with us only stopping for a twenty minute break to sip a glass. I wanted to be part of this company so badly that I sat there for 40 Saturdays in a row never missing one, even though I was working in the Gate theatre at the time and was a fully paid up member of Equity. But the Saturday studio was different. You just wanted to train with Deirdre. She was just so inspiring.

The Stanislavski system is a demanding one and it required you to work for 5 hours on a Saturday. We worked for three hours then DOC would break the session. The Savages would breathe and she could sip a glass in Hourican's or Darby's on Leeson Street, and contemplate the work she had seen us attempt. 'This is not a performance!' was a favourite battle cry of hers. That is what was so invaluable. The Saturday Studio was an afternoon and evening of exploration under the brilliant guidance of a creative giant wrapped in layers of black cloth and head scarf, rain or shine. The lithe dancer's body, clip board in hand, guided us, developing our skills using the Stanislavski system and exercises without the pressure of performance. Delicate only in appearance. Tough and resilient when it came to dealing with her company of emerging actors.

If she gave you a nickname you knew you were in. She had a secret language that you soon learned and the thrill of speaking it made you feel you really belonged to her and she to you. Although her wit was acerbic it was never cruel. Her notes were tough and razor sharp. Deirdre O'Connell saw into your soul in a way no other person could, apart from your mother. I would often say when asked to describe her that I had two mothers, the one who gave birth to me and DOC. It felt like she had given birth to me in the artistic sense. I was an insecure, untrained mess before she got her hands on me, and although an actor never loses that overriding sense of insecurity about the work, she imparted to me a system that acted as a blanket of security around whatever talent I might have had. Ironing out the 'Little mannerisms' and revealing gently, when I felt overwhelmed by the job of being an actor, that it would always be a painful process, difficult, requiring mental strength and discipline, enabling me to go to a very dark place and come back intact.

I miss you every day DOC. You helped me to commit, reminding me during 'The justification of an action' or 'Room re-call' to 'Make a choice. Right or wrong you are right'. That note has served me well throughout the last 18 years: a simple and profound adage that can be applied to the creative process as well as to one's life beyond it.

Thank you DOC for sharing your vision, your love, your wit and the bop nights at your house on Dartmouth square. Anything I have achieved I owe to you. 'Every time we say goodbye I die a little...' That was your signature song and the lyrics evoke how we felt at the end of a tiring Saturday in studio. Spent, yet never wanting to leave that sacred space. My husband David Jordan would wait outside in the car for me and tease me that I always seemed a bit full of myself after studio and thinking back I suppose I was. DOC built up my confidence with each class, and I would come to need it. The job of being an actor is a sobering one at the best of times. Rejection on a weekly basis is hard to take for even the most self-possessed and I had at that time very little confidence or self belief. But for a few hours on a Saturday we at Focus were given a chance to feel that anything was possible. The Focus stage belonged to us and like Deirdre it felt as if we too had come home.

7 | The Tern: a Memoir

Mary Elizabeth Burke-Kennedy

I was watching the birds going about their evening business among the reeds at the edge of the lake. Suddenly a tern swooped over our heads and flew beside our boat as we puttered along. It was unmistakable in the evening light, its pointed wings, with their elusive black tips and the graceful trajectory of its flight. The bird was protesting at our noisy interruption, defending its territory with all its strength, and when we were safely out of the way, it flew back to its nest.

I remembered another summer night, as long ago as a fairytale. It was swelteringly hot in the theatre. The door of the dressing room was open into the poky, overgrown garden out the back, in a vain attempt to circulate some air. The occasion was a technical rehearsal, which in the early days of Focus, was always a gruelling marathon.

One reason for this was that no one operating the primitive, clunky technology of the time, was in a position to see what was actually happening on the stage. Once the lights had been hung by Declan, climbing endlessly up and down a perilously balanced and flimsy ladder (purchased with Green Shield Stamps), the lighting operator was dispatched up the same creaking ladder to the lighting control box above the stage. The ladder was then removed and the unfortunate operator was marooned with three temperamental Junior Eight dimmer boards, which had to be cajoled into action, occasionally with the use of a stick. From this eyrie the lighting operator, who could not see the performance, took all the lighting cues from the lines and faded in subtle effects by counting. The absence of soundproofing that made the cueing possible, also inevitably meant that the slightest noise from the light box could be heard on stage. Not only did the operator have to tame the Junior Eights, but this had to be done without moving, breathing, miscounting or dropping the stick, all of which generally started to happen around midnight.

The music and sound cues were run from an elliptical, reel to reel tape machine in the dressing room behind the stage. This meant that the sound operator had to open the door on to the stage and listen from behind the set for upcoming cues. During these interludes, life in the dressing room had to be suspended, a mute discipline, which also deserted most people as hours of repetition wore on and the only way to keep going was to make coffee and tell jokes.

Any sound of life going on elsewhere, provoked paroxysms of fury from those unfortunates trapped on stage, for whom life had stopped. As these endurance tests progressed, banter morphed into bad temper and finally into Beckettian fatalism.

The tech on this particular sultry night was for the production of *The Father,* by Strindberg. The set comprised three ten-foot, free-standing flats, each covered by magnificent sepia photographs of the protagonists of the play, taken by Fergus Bourke. On the stage right stood the photograph of Laura, played by Deirdre, willowy and radiant, and on the stage left, in proud military regalia, stood the Captain, played by Johnny Murphy. They were both smiling and gazing at the character of their infant daughter, depicted in the centre photograph by our one-year-old daughter, Ruth.

In front of this idealized family triptych, were the furnishings of a Victorian sitting room, in which was played out the vicious conflict between the father and the mother for ownership of the child, the fight to the death, which is the action of Strindberg's play. It was a drama that had moved us, incensed us, fired us with its modernity. But now, we were just tired. There was a table and some stiff-backed chairs, on which the Pastor, (Frank McDonald) and Doctor, (Tim McDonnell) were sprawled, waiting for the adjustment of a light, or death, whichever came first. There was a chaise longue, on which I sat, with Johnny Murphy, whom I as his faithful old nurse, had tied up in a straitjacket some hours before, and who now lay resignedly with his head in my lap, knowing that Declan would never be satisfied and would never let us out.

It was two o' clock in the morning and no one any longer had the energy to be frustrated. Deirdre stepped on to the stage from the auditorium, where she had been carefully watching every painstaking adjustment. She sat into a rocking chair and lay back wearily, wrapping Laura's shawl around her, her own black dress showing as flecks through the white crochet. Declan asked her to stay as she was while he made one more change. She groaned and dropped her head down to her shoulder.

'You look like a tern', he said.

She demanded to know what a tern was and Declan told her about the bird; its beauty, its fragility, its courage in protecting its young. She was fascinated by the image, connecting it at once to Laura.

'Did you all hear that? Declan says I look like a tern. A tern.'

She resumed her watching brief in the auditorium, smiling with pleasure.

And her delight in her discovery of the bird, refreshed us all.

8 | The Hen-Night Epiphany

Jimmy Murphy

There's an old theatre joke about an actor who wants to change lines in a new play that ends with the writer asking where the actor was when the pages were blank. And while some suggestions by actors are interesting and may even get onto the page, for the most part they're usually the dull, myopic ramblings of the second rate that have no place in professional theatre. And though feedback is helpful in developing a new play, there needs to be boundaries. In the urge to have a play accepted a playwright sometimes will bend over backwards and make any changes suggested if a production beckons at the end of it. With the result the playwright ends up writing a play he thinks pleases everyone but one far removed from his original idea. Therefore a safe environment is required where the playwright's play can be challenged, rigorously if needs be, but sensitively. Otherwise the whole endeavour ends up in a shouting match and nothing artistic is achieved.

For me it was a joy to discover such an environment existed in The Focus Theatre. Joe Devlin, in his time there, had, through the Stanislavski Method, created a sacred space for theatre artists. A second home; welcoming, hospitable and encouraging. There was an overwhelming generosity of spirit amongst the actors who willingly gave up their time for free so I might develop a play further, while all the time understanding there was a chance they may not make it into the final cast, should the play make it that far, and many of them didn't. And one of the things that struck me most about the Focus was the selflessness of the actor to put the work first, the commitment to the development of the theatre that had been built up over years by the wonderful Deirdre O' Connell.

My journey with *The Hen Night Epiphany* and the Focus Theatre took just under two years and looking back now, the achievement far outstripped any expectations. I had a play that I knew worked but was broken in parts, and no amount of rewriting could or would fix it. Sometimes plays are like that, they find themselves in dead ends. It's a horrible crossroads for a playwright, as they're faced with abandoning the two or three years work or finding it in themselves to write one last draft. The only other alternative is a reading, but very few theatres in Dublin offer the opportunity to have your work read out and discussed in a safe and creative place and over a prolonged period of time. These cost a great deal of time and resources not to mention money. And while the Focus had very little of the latter, it had an abundance of the former and was generous in the extreme to those who came in search of it.

The Focus Theatre had always been on my radar. It was a huge part of my theatrical growing up; from the mid 1980s I'd attended almost every play it produced. Its actors were heroes of mine. And it was fitting that the Focus held a special place in Dublin theatre, a place that separated it from everywhere else. But by the mid 2000s the theatre had closed down, funding was being cut gradually and the theatre was forced to operate in various small venues around the city so I never really considered it until one day I discovered Joe Devlin was still there.

I first encountered Joe back in the Abbey Theatre in the mid 90s when he was Associate Director under Patrick Mason. It was an extraordinary period for new Irish playwriting though no one seemed to realize it at the time. Garry Hynes had left the Abbey with a dazzling array of new plays by new playwrights, and Patrick Mason, her successor, wasted no time in building up on that inheritance by introducing a number of new directors to work with the new playwrights. The ensuing seven years resulted in some of the most wonderful plays and productions that Irish theatre has seen in a long time.

I contacted Joe, and he suggested I send him the play. Some months later he rang back to say the Focus had an in-house reading of it that went well and they were interested in working with me on it, in bringing it further. And so it began, over the next year and a half we had about 5 readings. Each would be followed by a short discussion, I would take notes and go off to consider the next draft and then get to work on it. It was a slow process, there was no rush, no deadline. We worked at my pace and when I had a new draft ready, I sent it in. Joe would arrange an in house reading of it, and so it went on until we both felt the play was ready for production and a date was set.

I felt very much at home throughout this process. I had what every playwright dreams of; a small theatre company, with it's own stage, a core of dedicated actors, willing to let you succeed and fail at your own pace. We didn't know it then, but it was to be the last full-length play produced in the Focus. The Arts Council, apparently, more interested in the monetary end of things than the creative, deemed the theatre not financially viable, and finally stopped funding, with the result that the Focus Theatre, a year shy of its 50th birthday, had to close its doors for good.

I had already begun work on another full-length play for Focus, and hoped to have it produced in the theatre during the 50th birthday celebrations, and no doubt other playwrights, actors and directors had plans for coming years too that have had to be shelved due to the Arts Councils' decision. And while Focus will continue to exist in name and perform wherever it can, it was that tiny, elegant stage and those few cramped rows of red velveted seats that was the heart of the theatre, and with that gone we are all now the poorer for it.

9 | A (partial) Return to the Irish Fold

Brian McAvera

Not long ago I attended a symposium on Shakespeare at Queens University Belfast where I was giving a paper which essentially looked at his work from the point of view of a contemporary working playwright. As a Northern Irish writer who had lived through The Troubles, I found a wide range of points of contact with the Elizabethan dramatist. He was from Warwickshire, I from County Down, so we were both rural men who had spent time in the city. Belfast and London were ports and just as Shakespeare obviously benefited from the wide range of people, sailors, travellers, businessmen, refugees and so forth who came through London so I benefited from the wide range of people who came to the North because of the conflict.

In both cases the times were extremely violent – public executions, bearbaiting, duelling and police spies in Elizabeth's time, in mine the Provos, the Shankill Butchers, continuous bombings, and shootings. Both of us were brought up Catholic but lived in a Protestant world so we both learnt to be cagey, diplomatic, guarded: 'Whatever you say, say nuthin'.' For Shakespeare, living in an authoritarian society, to be Catholic could mean torture and execution. For me it was running the gauntlet of the Reverend Ian Paisley's violently anti-Catholic rhetoric which stirred up the Loyalists and kept sectarianism in the forefront of everybody's mind's eye. The political dangers of the time for both of us were suppression and censorship – the possibility that one's religion and one's political party might be extirpated.

Because Shakespeare's father was well-off, Shakespeare was able to go to grammar school. Because of the 1948 Education Act, so was I. Shakespeare learnt the Latin and Greek classics. I learnt the English ones (though not the Irish ones). In Elizabeth's day, history was up for grabs: revisionism. In Northern Ireland, revisionism is happening as I write.

What interests me about Shakespeare has to do with him being a working playwright who was also an actor, a director, and a businessman. He was a practical man-of-the-theatre who knew what he was doing. He was lucky enough to live at a time when language was in a melting pot and he utilized a very wide range of different registers of language: Warwickshire dialect, city slang, Anglo-Saxon, the Latinate, and the French. It was a language which was flexible enough to be able to slide from classical allusion to legal terminology; from farmer's lore to poetic flights of fancy. It was also a dense language which was delivered swiftly to an audience which was actually composed of a very large number of smaller communities: the groundlings, the court, prostitutes, the underworld, tradesmen and apprentices, the emergent middle-class, townspeople, and country people.

Shakespeare, self-evidently, had a lot to say, and he said it under pressure: the pressure of densely-packed verse. Equally self-evidently, to get his work across, he needed actors who were capable of delivering what he wanted. He had a long apprenticeship, working in all kinds of theatres and theatre spaces, and with various different companies before he achieved every playwright's dream: a fixed company of actors for whom he could write. He could write to their strengths – and he could disguise their weaknesses. We know that the weaknesses included a tendency for the clowns to enjoy improvisation, a bit like today's stand-up comedians. But we also know that these actors were intensively trained. They had specific skills which (apart from speaking verse) included dancing, fencing, acrobatics, singing and wrestling. They frequently did up to twenty-six plays in a month with half of these being new plays, so their memories were prodigious. They rarely had more than two and a half days rehearsal for any one play, so they had to be quick on the uptake, with the playwright functioning as overall director. They also toured the length and breadth of the country, working in all kinds of spaces, so their vocal abilities as well as their physical ones, had to be superb. In a theatre like the Globe, they would be playing to between two and three thousand people, without a microphone. They had to be able to deal with hecklers, with those who were drinking and eating; they had to be able to appeal to those of limited intelligence as well as to those with the highest – and they had to entertain, otherwise the audience hissed, or mewed like a cat, or threw nuts at them. You had to know how to command attention.

At the same symposium an Irish academic Dr. Patrick Lonergan (University of Galway) gave a paper on 'Performing Shakespeare in Ireland' in which he said that Irish actors seemed to be largely incapable of handling Shakespeare. The obvious question to ask here is: why? And the obvious answer is: because the actors, by and large, were not and are not capable of handling Shakespearean verse. They have never had proper training – which is where the Focus Theatre comes in. But I anticipate...

Around 2006, Joe Devlin approached me and asked if the Focus could stage a number of the plays in my cycle of eight, *Picasso's Women*. I said 'No'. I was remembering when Radio Three had decided to do radio versions of four of these plays and, for political reasons, I was asked if I would mind them being done out of Belfast. Somewhat reluctantly I agreed. When I met the director Michael Quinn, in 1994, and he asked me about casting, I was delighted to find that he agreed with me when I stated, somewhat bluntly, that I didn't think there were any actresses in Ireland capable of doing them. We got Lindsay Duncan, Barbara Flynn, Josette Simon and Hannah Gordon, all classically trained actors who had worked with the Royal Shakespeare or the National Theatre in London. These were all actresses with remarkable vocal techniques, a wealth of experience and – a humbling experience for me – despite the fact that they were only being paid a pittance to come over to Belfast for a day's work, they had all researched the plays in detail. Barbara Flynn, for example, who played Olga, had not only read various biographies but, as her character was Russian, had gone to the Russian community in London and studied the accent. For me, Irish actors were technically inadequate, and lazy – the good ones all left!

Perhaps I need to justify this. Let me backtrack. I started directing plays when I was at university, doing medieval morality plays, Tudor interludes, Shakespeare, Ibsen, Chekhov and even Joe Orton. Shortly afterwards, when I was training to be a teacher, I continued to direct, winning the all-Ireland Amateur Drama Festival with a production of *She Stoops to Conquer*. The playwright John Arden was the adjudicator and at the festival he gave a reading of a play he was working on called *The Ballygombeen Bequest*. Egged on by my actors I suggested to him that we would like to stage the play in Belfast. To my horror he said 'Yes', and two weeks later a script thudded into the hall and a week after that the playwright and his wife arrived up to Belfast and we started rehearsals.

Because of this production John arranged for me to join the 7:84 Company who were going to do a new production and take the play to the Edinburgh Festival. I got to see a remarkable English theatre company at work (Stephen Rea was one of the group then) and also got to see a wide range of English companies including the Ken Campbell Roadshow, not to mention a raft of international companies at Edinburgh, including Japanese Noh theatre and Polish avant-garde theatre.

Under the influence of Arden I switched from writing poetry and short stories, which I had been publishing, and I started to write stage plays. In 1977 I was at the Young People's Festival at the Royal Court with my production of a play of mine called *Some Time Soon*, and was also seeing London theatre, both at the Court and in the West End. When shortly afterwards I went to Bangor, North Wales to do post-grad work, on John Arden as it happens, I found that the Theatre Gwynnedd did twice weekly rep. One week might have the Actors Company with Ian McKellen and company doing *An Inspector Calls* for the first half of the week and *Three Sisters* for the second half. Another week might have Theatre Cluyd under the direction of Michael Bogdanov. One began to realize that there was a serious acting tradition in England and Wales and Scotland – and it wasn't just 'from the neck up'.

Then I went back home: the shock was considerable. The histories will tell you that the Lyric Theatre delivered fine acting and fine productions. Not in my experience. I remembered sitting through Mary O'Malley's production of *Peer Gynt* and, three and three quarter hours into it, realizing that everyone else in my row was asleep. I remember actors like Louis Rolson (nice guy, awful actor) playing an Ulster Comedy one week and an Ibsen the next but always playing the same role: Louis Rolson. Frankly, the acting was terrible. Huffing and puffing, volume, all substituted for technique. No understanding of the emotional requirements of a great role. No understanding of basics like pace, rhythm and tone. It was a small theatre seating less than four hundred, but many of the actors couldn't be heard properly. And as for directors, the less said the better. I stayed working in the North until the end of the eighties. I had spent almost twenty years doing community theatre, school's theatre, Street Theatre, Youth Theatre, not to mention forming or co-forming various theatre companies including New Writers' Theatre, but enough was enough.

Mind you, the Abbey wasn't much better. Bigger: yes. A larger pool of actors: yes. Bigger sets: yes. But essentially the same problems. Directors moved actors around the stage in pretty patterns. Actors 'declaimed'. And as a number of essays in this book demonstrate, the average Abbey actor wasn't remotely interested in extending his or her stage ability through the good offices of the Focus Theatre and Deirdre. They kept apart. Training was for wimps.

This attitude, and this style of production, have not vanished. At the symposium mentioned earlier, we were all invited to go and see a new production of *Macbeth* at the Lyric Theatre in Belfast which was directed by Lynne Parker, an acclaimed director in Ireland. I left at the interval. The play was miscast. Most of the actors couldn't handle the verse. Neither Macbeth nor Lady Macbeth (nor for that matter anyone on the stage with the exception of Eleanor Methven who was playing one of the witches) could inhabit the character as opposed to playing it from the exterior. The set (which was dangerous: Macbeth tripped within the opening minute) didn't know whether to be abstract or figurative and ended up as a mismash. Every emotional moment was signalled by loud music telling you what to feel. The lighting was superb though.

Rubbish, like this production, is being peddled to schoolchildren and students as 'serious' – is it any wonder we have such a small audience? Instead of actors inhabiting their characters and emotionally taking us on a journey, we have director's theatre, signalled by emphatic lighting, emphatic sound and music, emphatic but confused sets, and plodding, boring acting. All of the things that I hate about a certain type of theatre...it *was* the theatre I grew up with, the theatre I reacted against, and it is still with us today, albeit with more of a technical gloss.

When you walk into a theatre, sit down and the play starts, you know within thirty seconds whether it is going 'to fly'. And it's not the set, not the lighting, not the sound-effects that grab you – or don't grab you – it's the actors. They are the ones who can take you on a journey. But when they are inadequately prepared, when they are inadequately trained, when they lack the vocal resources, the emotional resources, indeed at times the intellectual resources, the result is Dead Theatre – which brings me back to Deirdre and Joe.

Joe Devlin, being a Northerner like myself, and having some knowledge of what I went through, kept pursuing me. Finally he said: 'Look, why don't we do a reading of all eight plays with eight different Focus actresses. If you don't think we can get a cast out of them, then we'll go to England'. 'Great', I thought, 'I'm going to get an English cast'. Now I have to admit that, apart from the occasional trip to the Abbey or the like, I hadn't really kept abreast of theatre in the Republic of Ireland and, in particular, I didn't know the Focus theatre. It was just a name to me, and one that I never heard spoken of in professional theatre circles, so it was a real shock to the system when I arrived down for the readings. I simply was not prepared for the standard of acting, even as revealed in a reading. These actors were very different from the ones I was used to seeing in Ireland. They had energy and intelligence, they had robustness, but most of all, they had vocal attack: they had technique and they had emotional intelligence. I was entranced.

When you decide that it is no longer profitable to work in your own country, you need to keep your resolve. You need to be pretty sure of yourself. And you need to be open to new experiences. I was always interested in what an actor brought to the table. As a young university director my first productions (probably like those of everyone else) were meticulously planned out. I made little models of the set and little stick actors whom I moved around from scene to scene. I determined how a line should be said, even to the extent of giving line readings. By the time I had started to direct my third play I knew that this approach was wrong: that it closed down actors rather than opening them up; that it was over-determined. I decided to jettison the idea of a pre-prepared director's interpretation in favour of exploring the text with the actors and finding out what emerged. This approach demands nerves: you don't 'block' until the final week, maybe even the final few days, so that you leave maximum room for discovering the possibilities inherent in the text.

This taught me, in relation to my own texts, that even though I knew them better than anyone else, it was nevertheless a mistake to over determine a production, as with Beckett for example, or an English playwright like Nick Darke who even specifies the number of beats between lines. For me, this does not allow a text to breathe. Every production should be different.

When you watch your own plays in translation – and I have been lucky enough to be translated into over seventeen languages – and when you experience different acting traditions, you begin to realize the difference between acting and simply performing. In Italy I was lucky enough to work with actors (and a director) who had been trained by Giorgio Strehler (arguably the most influential director of the 20th century) at the Piccolo Theatre in Milan. Even when acting outdoors, at night, on an improvised stage, in the sculpture garden of the Guggenheim in Venice (no shortage of competition!) an actress like Milena Vukotic was not only crystal clear at the back of a packed garden, even when she was whispering, but she was also emotionally pitch perfect. She was also able to do three of the plays (all radically different in tone and structure), one after the other, something that no English actress would even attempt!

Will Van Kralingen, one of the key members of the Netherlands National Theatre, could do the same in a 750 seat theatre without seeming to so much as raise a bead of sweat. Technically, emotionally, vocally, physically, these actors are stunning in their ability to make the complex seem simple and easy, always the mark of the great professional. For most of the twentieth and twenty-first centuries, actors like these simply did not exist in Ireland. They did in England, though rarely with the same degree of physical ability. I remember watching Alec McCowan in *The Gospel According to Saint Mark*, and marvelling that he could do 16 lines of the biblical text on one breath without any sense of strain.

What Deirdre O'Connell, and then Joe Devlin, have brought to Irish theatre – even though Irish theatre refused to acknowledge the gift for so long – was the proper training of the actor, a training that acknowledges that the actor has to be constantly open to new experiences; a training that acknowledges that the road is harsh, often difficult, and that many will fail along the way; a training that realizes that unless the actor fully possesses technique, vocal and otherwise, then he or she will never scale the heights. And without comprehensively trained actors to work with, writers unconsciously 'write down' to the level that the actors are capable of giving.

If you ask yourself why complex writers of a non-naturalistic bent such as Denis Johnston (1930's onwards) made so little headway in Irish theatre, or why Shakespeare productions were so poor, one answer must be that there simply weren't the actors capable of delivering these texts. Indeed, if you ask yourself why, for the most part, the dominant 'bent' in Irish theatre is naturalism, the answer is obvious – it's the easiest! It's what actors naturally gravitate towards, an inclination heavily reinforced by British and Irish television soaps and serials. Naturalism however, is but a blip on the map of world theatre, having only appeared in the last quarter of the nineteenth century. Deirdre's claim to fame is that she was the first to deliver a prolonged and detailed actor-training, the importance of which is only now beginning to be appreciated.

10 | Writing as Politics, Politics as Writing: a Conversation with Brian McAvera

Steven Burch

[Brian McAvera has written more than twenty-five stage plays including the internationally acclaimed *Picasso's Women*, as well as *Yo! Picasso!*, and *Francis and Frances*. Most recently he has been working on the book adaptation of a musical version of the classic *The Irish RM*. He was asked to join Focus Theatre as an artistic advisor, and recently he became a Royal Literary Fellow at Queen's University in Belfast. He is also an art critic and historian, and a stage director, not only of his own works, as he also directed, amongst others, the world premiere of John Arden's *The Ballygombeen Bequest.*

In the summer of 2012 my wife Deborah and I visited Brian and his family on their farm in Downpatrick. Gray skies, some rain and an enjoyable walk around the farm (some of its buildings or ruins go back to Elizabethan times). I have known Brian since we met at the initial conference for the Irish Society for Theatre Research at Queen's in Belfast in 2007. I had just presented material from a book I was working on about a Scottish playwright and actor, Andrew P. Wilson and his work at the Abbey, work which had been consigned to history's dustbin due to a contretemps between Wilson and W.B. Yeats. In the process I managed to tweak the noses of a few Irish academics who had continued a cult of silence surrounding Wilson and it was apparent that the conference attendees took some delight in hearing some of their peers being shown up. I suspect that's what brought Brian to me, as Brian takes great delight in tweaking those in power.

In 2008 he offered me a residence at Stranmillis University College in Belfast. I came for a week in October, during which I presented a paper on American playwright Lee Blessing, assisted in interviewing some Polish performance artists, and listened as Brian pulled together a group of teaching colleagues and some students to give me a reading of an early draft of a stage adaptation I was working on of *Moby Dick*.

This is my first visit back since then and I have come to conduct a series of interviews, mostly in and around Dublin with actors, directors, writers, producers and designers from the Focus Theatre. Several were there at its legendary beginnings in 1963. Others, like Brian, have only recently become a part of its story.

As we walk and talk around the farm and at dinner, I see that Brian is a study in perpetual motion. It would be nigh impossible to imagine him getting all slug-like and putting his feet up and taking it easy. He is constantly working, on new plays and essays (usually about art history), in the kitchen preparing food with Una his wife, researching in his library (which I remember contained more than 20,000 books), completing chores on his farm and tending to a new batch of pigs and keeping a watchful eye on the horses that come into the yard and try to steal the pigs' food.

Finally we retreat to a cozy nook in his library and I ask him about having a theatre to write plays for and with.]

Brian: Well it's the first time in my life that I've actually had it. And you always know theoretically what it is like: looking at someone like O'Casey, for example. When he made it, he was supported; he got the first batch of plays out. Then, the next thing he knows he's out in the sticks, he's over in England, and he no longer has a regular company to work with. Although I happen to like a lot of later O'Casey I think it is self-evident that the plays would have been a hell of a lot better if he had actually had a regular company to work with. And in my case, with O'Casey, I think that was the first time I really became aware of the usefulness of a regular company. It was through directing that I got the bug to actually write plays as opposed to anything else and I would probably argue that even fairly early on, I was aware of what you could or could not do on a stage, purely from the basis of directing stuff. When directing you become aware of what you can or can't do with an actor, in relation to the capacity of the actors you are working with. Before I first got outside of Ireland for any extended time, I had been doing things like, you know, street theatre up and down the Falls Road, working in community theatres, and working in youth theatre. I was doing a lot of directing with the Colleges of Education as well as forming my own company. When I got out in 1977 to do post-grad work I remember thinking, when I went in to see *An Inspector Calls*, that it was a horrible chestnut of a play, and just being astonished at this production which was minutely naturalistic in terms of the acting – and rep was exactly the right way to do it as well. The point here was it made me very aware of the gap between the kind of acting I was used to in Ireland and particularly in Northern Ireland, and what I was seeing here, in North Wales, which was not exactly the centre of the world! This small community theatre only seated about 400, and this small theatre was getting this remarkable quality of work on a regular basis.

Before I went to Wales, in a way, for a very long time I had to get a hell of a lot out of very little in some respects. So there were particular experiences which I think in retrospect were extremely formative, and that was one of them: and a second one would have been working with AJTC who, long story, ended up commissioning *Yo! Picasso*! They said to me, 'why don't you come and work with us for a week, it might give you some ideas,' and I said, 'actually I don't work like that' (though I did!). I have to wait for the right moment to start writing a play, otherwise, halfway through the first act or something like that, I end up having no clue as to where the hell I am going. In that business of waiting for a play, a number of things cross-fertilize.

The playwrights John Arden and David Rudkin were also very formative in different ways. Rudkin was extremely informative from the point of view of saying 'if you're going to write a play from start to finish in 6 months you're writing journalism; anything of any value will be on your back burner for 5,6,7,8 or nine years. Learn to wait for the play, and do all of your research,' and that turned out to be extremely good advice. Arden writes plays backwards. Start at the last scene and work back. That I could never do: I can understand it, but it wouldn't be my ways of doing things, but he did teach me that you have to know the ending before you can really start the play. What he also taught me was to analyze and revise: I had done a number of early plays which he described as 'ok Brian, this is you in your intellectual mode, doing existentialist drama like Sartre, but you need to learn to write dialogue that actors can speak.' Quite right, too!

Going back to AJTC, that was interesting because normally I would not have written bits and pieces and kept things around beforehand. I actually found it a fruitful experience. Partly because I learned very quickly that they were two really quite remarkable actors (Mick Jasper and Iain Armstrong), and that I could push them and the ideas, intellectual ideas; that I could get out of them what I wanted an actor to be able to do. I could explore textual possibilities with them. For example what you get with *Picasso's Women* and you get in *Yo! Picasso*!

is what I call 'transparency' of the role, where you have Picasso himself playing one of the women in his life. You've got Picasso and you've got Sabartès, his secretary and friend. They are in some kind of limbo: you don't really know where. You know that there is some kind of tussle going on but you are not quite sure what. Part of the progress of the play is that Sabartès is actually trying to get Picasso to acknowledge the moral aspects in relation to the way he uses people for his own ends. And to do that he requires Picasso to go inside the heads of the various women. I didn't want impersonations. What I *did* want was the emotional truthfulness of the moment. When Picasso and Sabartès were going inside the heads of the women they had to feel that they were playing by the rules: this is what this person felt; this is what actually happened at this particularly point in time. So far so obvious, but then in terms of transparency my argument was, because Picasso was such a dominant person, he's automatically, instinctively, going to try and manipulate the material, not by altering the so called 'fact' but by altering the wit of the emotional element. I wanted to see, as in a chess game, how many Knight moves you could do, so that you could keep an audience guessing but not lose them. And as in that old game, Six degrees of Separation, I wanted to see how many degrees of separation I could get before you lost the audience. Working with AJTC just for that week was for me intense because I realized quite quickly that I could actually get two, three, maybe four degrees of separation without any real difficulty. The actual difficulty was: how do you sustain this over an entire play as opposed to bits and pieces of scenes here and there? So it was at that point that I realized, I suppose, the speed with which you can move if you're actually working with a group of people that you've got to know quite well.

So finally, about the Focus, it's the first time I was given a position in which someone said to me not only that they wanted to do the plays, but also that I could take my time! If I wanted to do readings, to rehearse, to do more readings, workshops, or whatever, there was no hurry. It could be one year, it could be four years, it was up to me. And that I found really quite liberating. I don't think it's an accident that even during the relatively short period, what is it, four years, that I have been working with Joe that *Francis and Frances* has been produced, I have written another play, unproduced, which is *An Evening with Dave (and Davy and Doreen)* and I've written two others within that period. I have been able to workshop and do rehearsed readings with my adaptation of *The Irish RM*. And I think you can do that because you have the confidence that you can get them all on stage eventually. For years, I was writing plays, stockpiling them. You know it is very difficult to keep going, in those kinds of circumstance, when no one is responding: there is so much untruth, for want of a better word, in relation to the history of both the Abbey, say, and the Lyric Theatre. You would think that this was a great period in Irish theatre but I would turn around and say, show me the new playwrights that they produced. Very few were produced at the Lyric, they may have eventually produced them, like Graham Reid after he'd had three plays on in London and Dublin. These theatres, especially the Lyric, sure as hell weren't interested in new drama; they certainly weren't interested in socio political theatre. For about 20 years, I sent stuff to the Lyric and never even got an acknowledgement, never mind anything else. The standard was appalling. And The Abbey wasn't, frankly, a lot different. You have occasional moments where a director of some substance or a younger writer of some substance got in and did something for a while. But what I remember is actors ranting, substituting volume for subtlety; and again, actors being interchangeable between plays; and direction which was more about moving people prettily around the stage than anything else, and frankly it bored me to tears. I hated that kind of theatre and most of the time I won't go any longer because I really do not want to be subjected to it. I've a very low boredom threshold.

Steve: Probably a feeling that life is too short to have to sit through these things again. Does it, well, does it rankle you that you're getting a space but that it's in Dublin, not up here in the north which is your home and your home base?

Brian: It used to, but I kind of reached a plateau. You should take a look at the last issue of *Theatre Ireland* which was in ninety two or ninety three, something like that, the only time to my knowledge that I was in it. The editor knew me very well. He had been at the Lyric, but he very carefully ignored me, both at his time at the Lyric and in his time at the magazine, but I think that he felt that in the final issue he really had to do something and so he asked me to write an article on my career so far. You know if I look back on it now it's interesting to see just how astonishingly negative it was: I opened up with a quotation from Henry Miller cursing everybody left, right, and centre. That was very much my mood then: I was very bitter at that point. Because effectively I was having to leave: to go outside. Now I suppose it's awful to say so but I don't care two shits any longer. While it'd be nice if something happened in the North, I'm certainly not going to go looking for it. And I don't actually think it's important any longer, in the sense that the only thing that is, finally, of value is that you find an audience and that the plays stay in print, as then you know that you will get further productions. And if I was being brutally honest, I would far rather sit in a theatre, whether it's in Holland or Italy or wherever, and have an appreciative audience who seem to actually like what they're seeing and are literate enough, because some of them will speak some English, to be able to come and talk to me afterwards. I don't get that kind of thing over here, and I'm not really interested in what I call the Abbey play or Lyric play. The staple up here is a kind of local version of Feydeau to put it crudely, you know, comic theatre but without the craft of Feydeau. I love comedy. There's comedy in everything I write, no matter how dark the piece is. But I don't like comedy which is just for passing the time. You, as a theatre historian, will know only too well that for every interesting play from the South there are several score which are just the same routine pot boilers. I've always been very antipathetic to them. Oddly enough, and I suppose this will be another strange element, when I went to grammar school I was taught English language, English geography, English history, and not Irish history or Irish Geography. It was only when I went to University, that what Arden always called The Matter of Ireland began to become of some importance and I began to read a bit in and around that. I was formed by that.

When I went to university you were given a reading list which started with Anglo-Saxon (which you had to learn!) and then you read right the way through. I'm amazed that these days you can go through university only studying four or five texts per year. We were given hundreds upon hundreds of texts, which we were expected to read, and which we did read. Right the way through. So I got a pretty good grounding from that point of view and I was always more interested in European stuff than I was in purely Irish material. So I suppose as a playwright, whether it's technique or subject matter, I'm much more influenced by British and European and to a degree American dramatics. And very little by the Irish. I like Friel, but I found Friel very suspect in certain areas, especially politically. It's not the language, it's the form. When he actually does experiment, as he did in early plays, Friel is superb; and I'd be interested in Tom Mac Intyre, or early playwrights like Denis Johnston, you know the ones who actually play around and experiment, but the general run of Irish theatre really doesn't get my juices going at all, I'm sorry to say.

Steve: What about Focus's actors? Has its training has been useful for you? Why this theatre as opposed to other places in terms of having a space for your plays to work in. Is Focus more attuned to experimentation?

Brian: I think with Joe Devlin, well, a number of things happened. Joe is from the North himself, and although obviously several generations younger than me he is very aware of where I am coming from in relation to the difficulties of producing work and of getting work done up here. Secondly because he did a lot of his training in Eastern Europe and in Russia I think he is attuned more to the stuff I write. And thirdly under his aegis there was a much stronger emphasis on making the Focus a centre for new writing and not just a theatre doing classics. For all of those reasons I think I certainly got a welcome that I would not have had previously.

In terms of the acting, that was really the key point for me, because Joe had come to me over a period of about a year and a half, saying that he wanted to do *Picasso's Women* and would I give him the rights? I said no and he kept asking why? I would say because, frankly, I don't have a very high opinion of Irish actors and these pieces are technically very difficult to do and I've watched some of the best in the world handle them and not always get it right. And he said to me, finally, probably out of desperation: 'I'll tell you what, we will do a reading. I will cast 8 actresses and we will read all 8 plays in one day and if you don't think we can get a cast to do three of them then we will go to England.' So I thought, well, great, I'll have three decent English actresses. What am I going to lose? Sure!

I can tell you now that when I went down I got the shock of my life. I really wasn't that familiar with the Focus, but I really couldn't believe what I was hearing. Any time I had gone down to see theatre, it would be to see something at the Abbey, with half of the actors really sleep-walking their way through the roles. I was always complaining to Joe about the acting abilities of Irish actors, because their technique is so often appalling. I went down and I saw this whole raft of relatively young actors. I mean I don't think one of them was over 40, and out of the 8 of them there were only about 3 who couldn't cut it. But the other 5 could. And that was the point where I thought, I could do something here. You know, if there is this kind of talent around, and they are willing to take risks and (incidentally) work for very little, maybe there is a way I can be useful.

For example, *Francis and Frances*. There is no way on God's earth I would have got that on in Ireland otherwise. I'll be very interested to see what you say when you watch the DVD, because it's a leap forward. The play was started, long before I went to the Focus, in 2004, and in the wake of AJTC experience. I was at some theatre conference in England and met an artistic director from Cambridge who ran the experimental festival held in March in Cambridge. He turned around to me and said, 'Nobody does plays about artists. I want somebody to do 20 minutes. 'Why don't you do me 20 minutes of a new play?' And again I said, 'I don't work like that.' He said, 'Why not? It's in two months: you've got the slot if you want it.' I thought, ooh...So, totally against the grain, I produced about 20-25 minutes of it, and in a weird and wonderful slot at Cambridge, at 10 o'clock at night. About 40 people came in, who must have been in their 70s. I thought, I'm dead! And then about another 20-30 came in who were about 15 years old, so young that I thought maybe they won't let them in the door. And it was quite weird: on at 10pm, the piece was finished by 10:25. Yet everyone didn't go out of the theatre until half past one because they just wanted to keep on talking about it. And I kind of knew I had hit upon something. I said to one very old woman who had been cackling away, that I was worried when I saw her come in. She said 'Why, dear?' I said, 'Well, it's a play about a very famous homosexual who is quite deviant, and the language reflects this.' She just turned around and said that it was funny. 'You let us into it through the humour.' Some of the younger ones said that they had no idea what was going on but were just intrigued, and I knew I was on to something, but I couldn't sit down and write it. I had to wait and let it percolate for a long time.

So when Joe heard me talking about this at some point, after we had done three of the *Picasso's Women* cycle, he kept nagging at me saying, 'Go on, do *Francis and Frances*.' So I finally said, 'Come on give me a workshop'. It had a very peculiar genesis because we got one actor who was interested but was quite dark and quite serious; then when we came to a second rehearsed reading we got another actor who was far too dark and again was overly serious for the piece. Then we did a third one where there was a very nice actor, but literally too 'light' for the role. So I was at that stage, actually quite worried. Now, this is the great thing about Joe, he really does give you enormous confidence; he just said, 'Look, we are going to do auditions and we will find the right people.' There were only two characters in the play, and halfway through day two I had about three options for each of them. I was quite happy and then literally the last two people, Cathal Quinn and Tara Breathnach arrived, and the moment the pair of them walked on the stage it was like *snap,* you just knew this was the combination. At this stage I really didn't know much about them. I didn't know he was a voice coach either. But they embodied absolute precision and fluency and risk taking in the voice. I needed someone who was not going simply to imitate the vocal mannerisms of Francis Bacon.

That's another thing that gets my goat, this need for literalism in theatre audiences, but more to the point with theatre critics down south! In an otherwise perceptive review of *Francis and Frances* in the Irish Theatre magazine the critic was still staying 'Oh no, the character was far too far away from the original Francis Bacon,' and you think, why would I want to do something that was simply a copy? I think it's my biggest single quarrel with Irish theatre that, irrespective of the kind of play that they are doing, they want to play it as naturalism. And the direction will be, by and large, naturalistically-orientated. When it's not, it's intensely literal. For example, there was a play on a couple years ago that starred an actor I really like, and it's essentially a parable about AIDS. But we had this direction where every time the actress is to be lachrymose, you get a giant blow-up of her in video at the back of the stage with, literally, tears streaming down her face, so it's just absolute repetitious literalism. Not even any kind of counter pointing: and somehow this passes for being avant-garde down there, and I don't really understand that at all. I suppose it is because it's supposedly very visually orientated. I would like to think I'm visually sophisticated. But I find most of what passes as visual theatre to be frequently very pretty but usually dramatically inert: no forward progression occurs. You stagger from one sequence of spectacular imagery to the next, and I don't see the point of that.

I did write one piece as a kind of critique of that style of production. Set in Poland. The last 25 minutes is actually a Performance, as in a Performance by a Performance artist, and it's done by a performance artist, or an actor played by a performance artist, in the piece. It is done in real time as well and it's called *Uncharted Waters* and on one level it's about places like Poland where critics under one regime are suddenly catapulted into another regime and don't know where they are; and it's also a play about cross-connections between Poland and Ireland in terms of Catholicism. It's essentially me trying to take the theatre form and fuse it with an actual piece of Performance theatre and make it work. I'm very interested in those kinds of hybrid experiments as long as it's not performance for performance's sake. That's where I part company. I always want things to tie in all the time. It's like me and doubling: unless there's a function to the doubling I don't see the point.

For example, in the adaptation I did of *The Irish RM*, I kind of take this to the point of ridiculousness to make a point but I hope I'm making a point that is funny at the same time. So in a couple of cases the actor will actually have to play two characters, who speak one after the other: you have a line of dialogue for Character A and the actor will literally have to switch over to Character B in the next line of dialogue, thus creating two distinct characters who talk to each other, even though there are three other characters on the stage. I like actually making a point about the theatrics and what you can do with the theatrics and I think you can not only be very funny using that kind of thing but more to the point you can access material you can't really access in any other way.

Steve: Let me ask you. With *The Irish RM*, you are still in the stages of polishing this: given the kind of theatrical celebration of theatrical elements you are so keen on, do you think that there will be a tension with the audience? I'm talking about an audience who come to see the show being so familiar with the original, as opposed to something like *Francis and Frances* where the audience, not having the familiarity, may be more inclined to go wherever the play is going and not be resistant to what this kind of theatre promises to do with any material. Do you think or sense that, due to such familiarity, there will be a reluctance for an audience to go with you on that journey in that particular instance?

Brian: Oddly enough, no. There was a TV series in the 80s with Peter Bowles, co-produced by RTÉ, and what they did was they filleted the stories: removed the politics, removed the entire context in many ways, and they made the stories into nice, sweet, very English versions of the Irish. Now part of the fun of the original book is that it was written by two Anglo-Irish ladies who were extremely literate and who were, to a degree, sending up not only the Irish but also the English and in particular the Anglo-Irish land owners. And there was, if you remember, the Land League at that time, people were being killed on the lands that Somerville and Ross (the authors of *The Irish RM*) owned. And all of that, while not prominent, is in the book. So what I was looking to do was to pull in the generation that probably watched the television series and give them something they weren't expecting; and to pull in a younger audience who might have been put off, not only by the language, but also by the fact that they didn't know or care what an *Irish RM* was. So I reframed the stories, introducing the characters one by one, each having their (Victorian) photograph taken with magnesium flash, and recreating the stories as if they are coming from the future with the characters suddenly finding themselves back in this Victorian persona with memories of the future. You have this frame that effectively tells you who everybody is, and what the RM did. Then I treated it very much as what John McGrath in the 70s would have called a good night out in the theatre. I worked with 7:84 after I directed some of Arden's plays and I found that a very interesting experience because McGrath was interested absolutely in communicating to a broad working class audience. The paradox was that he was as middle class as they come, with all the middle class attributes and aspirations, but with a practical point of view. I wanted to do this piece of very physical theatre in which you had five actors who were then required to play 14 or 15 characters. I said earlier on that I'm not interested in doubling for the sake of doubling. You have to embed doubling in the entire fabric of the play. I loved the notion that the actors, as in so much of my stuff, would be talking directly to the audience, even in the middle of a sentence, as well as to themselves. But it is astonishing how many actors do not like doing that! That's a nice thing again about the Focus. There is a kind of fearlessness about a lot of the actors: they are quite prepared, and they trust you. And they will jump in and take risks. Cathal, when I said 'we are going to play this with the lights up', said, 'Me in underwear doing a striptease! You are joking!' and I said no. But he did it and he played with it and you can't create those moments unless you've actually got actors who are going to try to follow what it is you want to do.

Steve: You said earlier that you were not largely aware of the Focus during its glory days in the 1960s-'70s and you only really became aware of it during the end of Deirdre's life. And yet, Focus has become a home for you. When did that come about?'

Brian: It was at the point when *Picasso's Women* was first done at the Focus. Joe asked if I would become co-artistic advisor. What that really means is that I'm at the end of a telephone. Anything from advice on how to handle the Arts Council to advice on scripts. He often asks me what I think of a particular script; do I think the writer is worth bothering about; or occasionally, as quite recently, when things had not been going particularly well and when it came to the dress rehearsal, he wanted me to go down, and basically see the show at that point, advise, and give notes. So it could be from a very hands-on situation to something which is more political in intent.

Steve: It also sounds a little bit like an official dramaturg but without the particular title.

Brian: Yeah, if you like. I think the advantage of someone like me is that I've just been around for so long. You know, there's not a lot that will faze me, and whether it's on the quality of the acting or the directing or it's about the script or about the politics of how we might move forward, I'm reasonably able to contribute something useful.

Steve: Do you, as an advisor, see your role as essentially being reactive if not passive? Or maybe not just going to bat for Joe's choices, but giving him options, some script material from other writers. Do you see this as you having put your own imprint on Focus and on what it's doing, what it's about, what its future might be?

Brian: Only within certain, very limited areas. I would see it very much as trying to enable Joe to take the theatre in the direction that it's currently going in, which is very much in the direction of new writing – number one – which is very much about supporting Joe in terms of the political battle. Then the Arts Council, after Joe had just done a season in which they did 15 new works, withdrew funding entirely. I mean, entirely: nothing. So Joe was supporting things with his own money: with a bit of teaching money that he gets. So, one of the things I said to Joe at the time was, first, use the freedom of information act and get the background on these Arts Council decisions, which was very interesting indeed because it began to show up the politics of it. You actually had a situation where there was a direct conflict of interest revealed...

Steve: Is there somebody you can appeal such decisions to? Are you stuck unless you go public?'

Brian: A number of things happened. I wrote a number of letters to the press on behalf of the Focus. But essentially we've gone down a slightly different route. Joe's very much like me: proactive in the sense that we want to get things done. Joe was determined one way or another to continue. Part of my job was to enable him to do that. Part of it, in terms of Joe getting a new board and a new chair together, was enthusing people, contributing ideas, and suggesting ways in which we might develop in the future. And that so far seems to be beginning to happen. The political route was the other aspect. We were lucky in one sense that within six months of the funding being cut, the President of Ireland and his wife referred on television to the good work being done at the Focus. That very much became a part of the thinking: we were going to utilize that, so we had a day at Áras an Uachtaráin (the official residence of the President of Ireland) where we had basically everyone who had been at the Focus who was available, as a celebration, carefully dovetailed with Bloomsday. One half of it was us reading our bits out of *Ulysses* or whatever and the second half was a series of reminiscences. In the wake of that, Joe had a meeting with one of the ministers of state, and that seemed to be a much more intelligent approach. Anyway, it's all about who you know and how you control things. While neither myself nor Joe would be particularly keen on that state of affairs, it's the way things work, so I think you've got to be pragmatic. You know that the book and the plays would be part of the strategy of pushing the Focus back into public esteem, building on the fact that so many people had been through it. What's happening at the moment is that a minister is advising Joe to apply for European money and saying that he or his officials will help him through the maze of form filling, which makes quite a lot of sense because then, if that does happen, it basically enables a European wing to be created whereby we take stuff out and we bring stuff in. And that would be an ideal step forward. If we could do it.

The problem with all of these things is that Joe has been unpaid for the past year and a half and he wasn't getting a particularly large salary anyway. The Focus relies so much on people who want to do something. My sense around the Focus – and I certainly wouldn't get it around the Lyric or anywhere like that – is that there are a lot of the younger ones who can see the value of what has been happening, and actors who want to take chances. If nothing else, I see it as a very good training ground. That seems to me to be where the energy is, to put it very crudely.

Steve: Thinking down the line, what should Focus's role be? Continue what it's doing? Is there a necessity for expanding it? I'm thinking that the only parallel theatre I can think of in the States might be Joseph Papp's...is that a role that Focus might want to emulate?

Brian: First of all, yes, the Focus should expand, and in the kinds of ways we have been talking about. This becomes political in terms of funding and the way you access funding. It needs to be all Ireland, so it needs a northern access which, if things develop, will go through me, I suppose. It needs a European dimension which means we need a couple of European partners, because that way you can start to access European funding. As I was saying earlier on, it starts becoming a Focus theatre which actually gets not only new productions of classics, but gets new writers out into Europe in a direct line, bypassing the rest of the theatrical establishment, and then equally bringing in new work from Europe to here, and again, effectively bypassing the theatrical establishment. It's also demonstrating that you can do that cheaply and efficiently.

Now if we go down the route of fund raising and getting a new theatre, it still needs to be a relatively small one. We would be thinking 250, 300, maybe maximum 400 because nobody wants to get into the business of running a large-scale theatre, because then all your energies are tied up having that. Having a 50 seater as a kind of tryout, effectively a studio theatre, is, I think, still viable and still needs to be done. But you would need to develop and the problem is that, as a financial model, it's impossible to survive on a 40, 50, 60 seater. It's got to be at least a couple of hundred just to break even, which is all anybody wants to do. So, I think the emphasis will increasingly be All-Ireland and Europe.

But ideally, it should be much more proactive and much more regular. You can't do it if you don't have funding. I think the emphasis on new writing and on cross-fertilizing the basic Stanislavski techniques with new developments, as well as with other directorial patterns that emerge elsewhere, is a good one. Myself and Joe would both be interested in Eastern Europe but that would be by no means the only area. It's cross-fertilization I think that's quite crucial. The way I read Irish theatre, the problem is that cross-fertilization doesn't tend to happen that much, and when it does happen, it's with individuals who often don't have any way to do anything about it and so end up like O'Casey, having to attempt to develop elsewhere. John Arden is a very instructive example here, John Arden and Margaretta D'Arcy. Arden had an Irish wife, they went back to Ireland in the late 60s, and here you have a man who had had a whole raft of plays, not just at the Royal Court but in the States, and right throughout Europe, who even by the early 70s had umpteen PhD theses and half a dozen books written on them. They come to Ireland to live in Ireland. What happens? Not one single, solitary professional theatre anywhere in Ireland would put on an Arden play. *The Non-Stop Connolly Show* was done with the Trade Union movement. All of the others were done with amateur groups, or groups that they put together. Now that seems to me to say something fairly radically negative about the world of Irish theatre. If you cannot take someone who is regarded as a world talent, irrespective of what you personally think of him/her or their relationship, or some of the individual works, there's something wrong. Surely to God one of the major theatres here should have been able to forge a relationship with them. And every now and then people will tell you that Arden was extremely difficult to work with. As someone who directed two of his plays, I'm here to say he was no difficulty at all. He was a very astute man. I learnt something interesting from him, when we were doing *Ballygombeen Bequest*. What had happened was, I was working with joint teacher training colleges in Belfast and we took our production of *School for Scandal* to the All-Ireland Amateur Drama festival. This was in 1972, and we won it. Arden was adjudicating. I directed the piece. Arden gave a reading of a play in progress called *The Ballygombeen*

Bequest. We all went, and my lot were going, 'go on Brian, tell him you want to do it' and I was going 'I can't do that!' My group just egged me on. I finally went up and said 'we would like to direct this in Belfast' and he said 'ok I'll be up in a fortnight.' I just looked at him. The next thing I know I've got a script in my hand and we have an arrangement to meet.

Now the point about this was, first meeting, everybody came up to Belfast, and again remember, I'm very young, very naive, very callow, absolutely wet behind the ears, to use every cliche that we can come up with. I turned to him and said, I think it was scene 13 from memory, I said, 'I don't think that scene works.' Now, today, I wouldn't dream of saying that even to a young apprentice writer. But the interesting thing about him was he said 'why' and I sat down and gave him a little lecture for 20 minutes on why I thought things didn't add up. And he said there and then, hand on chin thinking about it, 'I think you're right' and took out his portable typewriter and he started a new scene which he finished a couple of hours later and that's the scene we actually used. When I look back on it, I couldn't believe I actually said that to the man, but what I thought much more interesting in retrospect was the fact that he said, 'tell me why it's not working,' and because I could, he immediately rewrote the scene. And that's the principle I've been working on ever since. Any time someone says to me 'no there is something wrong here' I say tell me why, demonstrate why it won't work. And if they can demonstrate, then I change; if they can't then I say no. But that's what I mean about Arden: he was an absolutely practical man of the theatre.

Steve: Sum something up for yourself and Focus. At this stage, and given all the real and potential negatives that are out there, you know, pot holes for the Focus, where do you see the Focus in the next ten years. Do you see Focus in the next ten years?

Brian: Well I would like to see the Focus in the next ten years actually having a circuit set up. Joe has always wanted to have a circuit, not necessarily to the major theatres, but to a number of the smaller ones, doing all the art centres which have theatres, so that the plays we do could go out on tour. And I'd like to see that happen North and South, and with the European axis open. That's where I would see us in ten years. And if we don't achieve that, then we probably won't survive. That would be the crude and harsh truth of it all, because you can only keep going for so long, and someone like Joe can only keep going if you can actually overcome the negativity of the circumstances. To do that, you have to be able to do the work. And get it out. Once the thing becomes a closed circuit, it always ends up being self-defeating.

I'm a veteran of the kind of policy that always happened in Northern Ireland, with the Arts Council: what they would do would be if someone wanted to set up a theatre company they would give them a very small amount of money. And they'd say, OK, what's your budget for the next two productions? You would give them the budget and they'd say, OK, we will pay you when you've done them. You would do them and they would then give you half of the money. And that's what happened to us at New Writers Theatre in the early eighties, and it happened to an awful lot of other theatre groups. We would be playing back to back with the Lyric and the like at the time, in terms of using their actors and so forth. So inevitably with companies like that, you run for two or three years, you do an awful lot of work inside a very short period, and then you turn around and you say to yourself, why am I doing this? Other people are being reasonably well paid: you are being shafted. Nobody cares, and you stop. And the history of Northern Ireland and, for that matter down South, but in particular in the North, is littered with companies who for two or three years really did interesting work and then just couldn't survive because no proper funding was ever going to be put in place. And Joe is in that position now. There is no funding at all and he is surviving but he is only surviving because he is doing a phenomenal amount of work. And he can't keep going on like that. And neither can anyone else. So if we are lucky and if the political dispensations seem to be coming our way, and they actually happen, and if the new chair gets his act together and the fund raising starts and this book and all the rest get out, then yes, I would be optimistic. But inevitably, there is always that little bit in the back of your head saying, it might not. And I suppose that, at that point, I would probably have to, very reluctantly, say that the Irish chapter of my career is closed.

Steve: Theatre has in many ways become irrelevant to peoples' lives.

Brian: Actually I wouldn't disagree with that. Remember I told you beforehand, about a tiny little village in Poland, maybe 400 to 500 people, and there was a Performance Festival going on. A group of Irish artists had come over, so it was half Irish, half Polish. So I assumed, in my ignorance, that 5 or 10 people might turn up. Instead the entire village turned out for every single event. And even at the Performance Artists' events the villagers were going through the streets at midnight! There was this real sense of involvement that you got pre the falling of the Berlin Wall. You got it in Romania, in East Germany, you got it in Poland. Art actually spoke directly to the people. Politically, art was the code by which they could learn what was happening and it could express what they felt. What was both striking and horrifying was the speed with which that collapsed, after the wall collapsed. I remember being in Bucharest in 1991. The people I was staying with couldn't afford to live there. They were university lecturers but living on a pittance. But there were guys out on the street selling Coca-Cola for the equivalent of a week's wages. I remember artists in Poland telling me that they suddenly found that the only thing that mattered to the general populace was 'cocoa-cola and pornography.' There is this real sense that they and we have lost contact with their and our audience. But I personally believe that we have lost contact because we are not doing what theatre *can* do. Why do theatre which apes what the movies can do better? Visual theatre in any shape or form. Why would you want to go to a piece of bad visual art theatre when you can see *The Dark Knight* or whatever, which, whatever you think of it, is at least very well crafted, has narrative drive, and takes you outside of yourself. This is part of my logic about the kind of theatre that I write. It seems to me that theatre actually has to focus on its strengths and its strengths are the fact that it is live, not that you are watching a screen. Its strengths are that you are going to establish all kinds of relationships quite directly with an audience. And its strengths are also that you can do this irrespective of your subject matter, which is what I have learned the hard way. You can talk directly to them about almost anything.

When I wrote *Picasso's Women* I was told point blank by a very respected director 'you will never get this done. A play about bloody artists. This is art house stuff'. It turned out to be the biggest hit I ever had across the board, because essentially, the play's themes are the themes of airport fiction. It's about sex, it's about relationships, it's about the people who wield power, it's about the harm that men can do to women. And what I learned in terms of the politics, shifting from the position of being a very political playwright, was I could say what I wanted to, within limits, and I could say what I wanted to through any form. Therefore my logic is: why use naturalism, which is the staple of television, and to a large extent, the staple of the movies, the staple of the mainstream. They do it much better than the theatre can. And they can do it with an intimacy, in terms of the small screen, that theatre really can't match.

So my argument, therefore, is that non-naturalistic theatre, which is actually the main root of theatre from the year dot right the way through, has to be the form. The second bit is that all of those people who are forever saying, when you give them language that is more complex than the kind of mundane affair that they can get on a soap,

'Oh this is literary!' as if that actually means anything. Yet even with extremely young audiences who may not follow in any kind of detail what's happening, they love the verve of the language. And they come back to it because they want to find out more. And the third element is how you tell the story. You know, if you are again going to be bound by naturalistic confines and just tell things in a simple linear, A to Z manner, you bore a theatre audience, because a theatre audience is much more alert than the passive audience for television, so in actual fact the more you engage that audience, the more you make them think. Brecht was, I think, perfectly correct in that area. The more they become one with, and want to become one with, what is happening of the stage, the more they engage, and the more they are taken out of themselves.

Figure 1 Before Focus
(Photo by Burke-Kennedy Doyle Architects)

Figure 2 Front of Theatre (Deirdre O'Connell's archive
Photographer unknown)

Figure 3 Dressing rooms
(Photo by Burke-Kennedy Doyle Architects
from Geraldine O'Connell's private photo archive)

Figure 4 Early Focus actors, left to right: Tom Hickey,
Tim McDonnell, Sabina Coyne, Michael Campion.
Front: Declan Burke-Kennedy (Photo by Fergus Bourke)

Figure 5 *Play with a Tiger* poster
(Deirdre O'Connell's archive.
Photo by Fergus Bourke)

Figure 6 *Miss Julie* with Mary Elizabeth Burke-Kennedy and Tim McDonnell
(Photo by Fergus Bourke)

Figure 7 *The Vice* with Deirdre O'Connell and Kevin O'Brien
(Photographer unknown)

Figure 8 *John Gabriel Borkmann* by Ibsen from 1974. Front: Deirdre
O'Connell and Frank McDonald. Back: Rebecca Schull
(Photo by Fergus Bourke)

Figure 9 Tim McDonnell in *Diary of a Madman*
(Photo by Cyril Byrne)

Figure 10 *A Month in the Country* with Joan Bergin,
Johnny Murphy, Gabriel Byrne and Olwen Fouéré
(Photo by Fergus Bourke)

Figure 11 *A Delicate Balance* with Ena May and Deirdre Donnelly
(Photo by Ros Kavanagh)

Figure 12 *Hen Night Epiphany* Deborah Wiseman, Lisa Harding,
Sinead Hackett
(Photo by Karl McCaughey)

Figure 13 *Hen Night Epiphany* Set, designer Sonia Haccius
(Photo by Sonia Haccius)

Figure 14 *The Kiss* with Tom Hickey (Photo by Karl Mc Caughey)

Figure 15 *Picasso's Women Olga*, by Brian McAvera with
with Cathy White (Photo by Alex McCullagh)

Figure 16 *Mother Teresa is Dead* Elizabeth Moynihan
and Gabeen Kane
(Photo by Alex McCullagh)

Figure 17 Brian McAvera (Photo by Deborah Parker)

Figure 18 Focus Theatre auditorium technical rehearsal on the last show *Hollywood Valhalla* at Pembroke Place April 2012 (Photo by Karl Mc Caughey)

Figure 19 Joe Devlin standing in front of portrait of Deirdre O'Connell. Painting by Brian Bourke (Photo by Karl Mc Caughey)

Figure 20 *Bankers* by Brian McAvera, opening May 2013 on the 50th anniversary of the opening of the Stanislavski Studio. Actors are Evelyn Lockley, Tara Breathnach, Michael Bates (Photo by Colm Mc Dermott)

Figure 21 Founder members of Focus Theatre with the President. Back row: Joe Devlin, Joan Bergin, Michael D. Higgins (President of Ireland), Declan Burke-Kennedy, Mary Elizabeth Burke-Kennedy. Seated front row: Sabina Coyne Higgins (First Lady of Ireland), Tom Hickey, Tim McDonnell (Photo by Karl Mc Caughey)

Figure 22 *Miss Julie* with Tom Hickey and Deirdre O'Connell
(Photo by Fergus Bourke)

11 | Focus is the Voice of its People: a collection of interviews with past and present members

Steven Burch

When I came to Dublin in the summer of 2012, my aim was to interview as many of the present and former Focus Theatre members as were available to me within my admittedly brief window of opportunity. The larger question, beyond availability, was their willingness to talk to a stranger about their time at Focus. I knew that I would hear to some degree the official stories that have been told and re-told over the years. What I hoped for was not a revelation of personal secrets, but an openness about their time with this remarkable theatre company and its founder and visionary.

Well, seek and ye shall find. For that is pretty much what I got. I am grateful beyond words to know that people seemed to understand I was not here to hunt for dirt or scalps, that my interest in them and their time with Focus and Deirdre and Joe was/is genuine. Each of the interviewees trusted me with their feelings and memories and sensed that I would not betray them.

When interviewing people, one is always treading a difficult line with leaving all the syntactical idiosyncrasies intact or rewriting and cleaning up the comments, so that the thread of intent isn't lost in a maze of guttural pauses and repetitions. At the same time, wanting to preserve the verbal individuality and colour of phrasing makes the task a tad unnerving at times. The sub-chapters were chosen to provide a grounding in the experiences of these artists, but were not included in our conversations. They were chosen afterwards, knowing that there would be some overlap.

There were many people I did not get to speak to, for a variety of reasons (mainly availability) and in one case I used an essay by Cathal

Quinn, written for my co-editor, within these verbal memories because it was so revelatory about the Focus experience. My thanks to him and to those who spoke to me, including, in no particular order, Geraldine Cusack, Mary Moynihan, Tim McDonnell, Ena May, Sabina Coyne Higgins, Mary Elizabeth Burke-Kennedy, Elizabeth Moynihan, Ronan O'Leary, and Joe Devlin.

In his wonderful trilogy, *USA*, John Dos Passos wrote that 'USA is the voice of its people.' Well, I feel that way about what I have learned about this most important theatre company, and experiment, in the second half of the twentieth century in Ireland. The core of what I know and feel about this theatre comes from these interviews. Focus Theatre is the voice of its people.

AUDITIONS

When Deirdre first set up the studio, the word on her audition process and the class activities became a local legend, as testified by Tim McDonnell and others. It wasn't 'acting' as her competition sniffed. And yet it appealed (and still does to this day) to those with a creative spirit. Former President of Ireland Mary Robinson once remembered taking a class when she was in law school. Deirdre assigned her class to think of a personal object and to become that object in class. As a law student, all Mary Robinson could think of was her briefcase, so that was what she attempted to become.

Tim McDonnell

Tim: One day I was walking around Stephen's Green. It was a half school day. I lived with my grandparents and my uncle. It wasn't an uncommon thing to grow up with your grandparents in the 40s-50s, you know, particularly if you were from a rather poor working-class family, but who were nevertheless extremely decent and passionate about education. You know: Jewish, and particularly, my uncle. So I was walking around Stephen's Green to see if my uncle was there in his taxi, and I got in this afternoon in April 1963, and he had the *Irish Press*, the newspaper. I picked it up and opened the page and saw this one page in particular, given over completely to a large photograph of Deirdre O'Connell. The Method comes to Dublin. That's a fact. The Method comes to Dublin.

They talked about this *On the Waterfront* movie, and my uncle said, 'No I haven't seen it but your grandfather has and he always talks about the Docker; the guy who played the docker.' It was a docker, so I said

Jeez, I gotta see this movie. So fortunately it was on in the Stephen's Green Cinema, literally a block around the Green, and it was on that week. And I went and saw it. I looked at it. I have never been so deeply moved or touched emotionally or imaginatively in my life. Now, I couldn't have intellectualized or verbalized that at that point in time as a young boy. But I knew that something very profound had affected my spirit, very profound, the fragility, the almost inarticulate kind of groping for an understanding of his condition, while gathered within a group of people who are everything opposite to him. With regard to sensibility, I couldn't have mentioned that when I was 17, you know, and I thought, my God Almighty!

So I saw the movie, I went back to the article, and I thought to myself if anything, in terms of acting or performance, is capable of moving me to this level, there is something profoundly vocational and almost spiritual in the craft and or art of acting, depending on your gift. Do you know what I'm saying? And I was immediately compelled when I went back to my uncle's car, to read the newspaper. I ran down to the Pocket Theatre looking for Deirdre O'Connell. She wasn't there that day but she would be seeing people the following day. I ran back down, stayed the following day and I saw her, and made an appointment for an audition. I think myself, Tom Hickey, and Sabina Coyne were the first three people to audition for Deirdre. Didn't audition with anything! What you had to do was open three doors, and each door had something more horrendous and horrific behind it than the one previously. And, obviously, what she wanted to see was how we would behave or what one's response would be to this imaginative reality. Well, I don't know how I did, but I can imagine it was bullshit. Imaginative bullshit! I believed in it completely.

And then the other one she gave us, which would be worthy of a painter in an academy, an arts academy, was the transposition of the object, or objects. She would put several objects down on the stage, any number of things, usually no more than three. I heard that from other people who auditioned. You had to explore the objects sensorially and imaginatively. And out of the sensorial and imaginative exploration you were to try and, not so much figure out, but somehow or another to enlighten as to what the objects might be, other than what they are. And how they might be used in their new being, for want of a better word. That was the second audition. It was wonderful to do. It was so liberating.

I remember the objects, there was a candelabra, there was a glass, the other object was one of the old-fashioned telephone extensions, and the glass became the thing you talked into. You know how one behaves between the two. And other objects, oh yeah, a deck of cards. You had to relate it all together. I think my least successful was the deck of cards because I had to use the telephone to tell the guy at the end of the phone that he owed me money for a game of poker from a week ago, and I still had the goddamn hand that allowed me to win. And then I flicked it around as a fan on the floor while talking. I made it into a fan. And I said, if this fan that I'm making on the floor at the moment was any harder, I'd beat the living shit out of you. Candelabra, the glass, and the cards. And that was the beginning of what I can only consider to be an extraordinary education in the imaginative process of the actor beginning to probe their own interior.

I didn't know that at the time. I couldn't have in any way articulated that. But as time went on, and the exercises essentially one followed the other, (in Stanislavski the actors work on self for the first section), that was the beginning of an extraordinary education which allowed me to begin to understand that my particular kind of imagination was absolutely made for this particular kind of small home that was going to eventually educate me intellectually, imaginatively, sensorily. There were about 10 in that first group.

Steve: Did they stay?

Tim: Six stayed. Well, I'd say about 12 auditioned, but I can't be certain about that; it seems like 12. The beginning studio, the first studio, was Sabina, Tom Hickey, Johnny Murphy, Eddie Clark.

Mary Elizabeth Burke-Kennedy

Declan and I met each other in University College, Dublin. We were both involved in the dramatic society there. Both interested in theatre. We heard about Focus from a mutual friend, Dick Callanan, who had been to the studio, The Stanislavski studio, and he said 'you guys come along here, this is for you', and that's how we found out about it. And that's how we met Deirdre, and that studio was in a basement in Fitzwilliam square.

Steve: Were you doing plays at that point?

Mary Elizabeth: Yes, Declan had been directing, and in fact he had directed a production in college that I played in, and at that time he was directing *Antony and Cleopatra*. I played Cleopatra. I think it was the production that bankrupted the drama society. For about five years after we left, they weren't able to afford to do anything else. So that was kind of our history, and apart from that I had been writing plays through my childhood, and in order to get them done I was giving all the good roles to my friends to play, so the play would actually happen. I'd been at that for a long time. Anyhow, we went along and we observed our first couple of classes in the studio. And I was absolutely terrified. I thought it was the most bizarre carry-on that I have ever seen in my life. Eventually, I was persuaded to try it out and I became more and more fascinated and interested in it.

Steve: What sort of bothered you?

Mary Elizabeth: The warm-up exercises. Sitting on a stage, making noises that weren't, as I could see, structured, or connected to any meaning. It just seemed, abandonment of control, and also because, I suppose, you've noticed this about Ireland, people are very verbose and word-orientated. And in these exercises we weren't using words. And were told specifically not to use words. I found that discomforting. I wasn't able to define things in the usual way that I could define them and the way I could control and master them. And this kind of 'noise' terrified me. And Deirdre, she didn't make it easy, you know.

Steve: Did you audition?

Mary Elizabeth: I didn't audition. We didn't audition. We came along and we observed and we tried it out and I think she figured 'yeah' we could do it.

Steve: How long did you observe?

Mary Elizabeth: I think it probably would have been a long time for me before I got up on the stage, because I would go along, and the next week I wouldn't go, I'd kind of lose my nerve. So, it was a question of going and running away. By the time I stopped running away, I think, I got on. That's probably the easiest way to put it.

Ena May

It was 1972, and at the Abbey it was suggested to me that I had talent and that I should go over to the Focus. I had to watch other students do exercises for about two weeks. And I took to it like a duck to water, and took it seriously to find about more about myself. There was no audition. It was up to Deirdre if she responded; if my exercises meant anything to her.

My first play at Focus was *To Clothe the Naked*, with Sabina [Coyne], Tim [McDonnell], and Frank McDonald. I was the Maid. I studied for ten sessions on Sunday nights after that small part. The second role was Maxine in *Night of the Iguana*.

Elizabeth Moynihan

How I came to know Deirdre is an artistic love story, I suppose. She saved me really.

Yeah, she did. I dropped out of drama school. I was involved in another group in the UK at the time called Theatre Praxis which was very difficult. It was inspired by *Theatre of the Oppressed*, that book by Augusto Boal. And at the time, my intellect was uh, sluggish, to say the least. I was a lazy, lazy student, and I didn't really, 'get it', although I knew how to work it, but I didn't know how it worked or why it worked. And I found it all a little too intense and too based on the intellect and not enough on the execution of the work.

Steve: You know, I find that so true about a lot of theatre: you read Artaud, these others, who have these great visions, although they can't come up with how do we get there.

Elizabeth: I know, it becomes too intellectualized, and performance isn't intellectual for me. It's visceral, it's more dirty and human than that.

Steve: Which I think is what gives plays more power. I mean, plays have to be about us. They have to be about the human condition, no matter what style you're doing, even musical comedy...

Elizabeth: You're really telling a story no matter what way you...

Steve: Absolutely, and audiences aren't looking at themes, they are looking at characters, the actors. Either representing things they recognize in themselves or others, or things they would like to see in themselves.

Elizabeth: I'm not really interested in theatre becoming performance art. I think it's a very different medium to what I do. Or what those of us at Focus Theatre did. We're interested in telling a story. That's the primary object of the exercise.

Steve: Since you straddle the Deirdre era and the Joe era, let's be chronological and start with the Deirdre era. How did you join the theatre? What was it that brought you to the class first?

Elizabeth: Well, I'd been working in England as an actor and it was in the early nineties, or late 80s, and my then agent's husband came to see me in a show in London, and afterwards he said 'Elizabeth, come on away back home. What are you doing here? You're going to only ever play these parts. Irish roles. You need to be coming away home'. So I bit the bullet and did. And my agent Ann Curtis took me to see a show at the Focus theatre called *The Balcony* by Jean Genet with Deirdre in it. And it was a turning point really in my, I suppose, creative life. And I just knew this is the kind of work I want to do. This is the kind of place I want to train in. To hang out in. And be a part of. And so I was. I was introduced to her in the pub afterwards and I said 'look I've been studying with Theatre Praxis in the UK' and she said 'I've never heard of that.' And then I told her about Boal's book and she said, 'Why don't you come down to studio on Saturday?' So I remember going down to the studio, really early, and it's typical for me, almost half an hour early for everything. Anyway I was in the coffee room in the back of the theatre. At the time you had to cross the stage to get to the coffee room and there was a woman there and I said 'I'm here for the studio.' And she said, 'Fine, ok.' So I sat down, and she said 'You can't wait here, you have to go outside until Deirdre arrives.' So I had to go outside the theatre, sit outside, and bit by bit the other students arrived, the other theatre members arrived, and eventually Deirdre arrived. It was a beautifully sunny day in the summer. And she arrived swathed in black clothes with her clipboards and her bag of scripts and teetering down the lane way: she walks like a dancer. And she had these teeny little feet and she'd just teeter on down the lane. I see the woman coming towards us and she's just greeting everybody and she ignored me, and that was her, her way you know. She didn't speak to you. Didn't acknowledge you until she was ready, if you were a stranger, and sometimes even if she knew you: that was just her way. Anyway, I sat in the studio and I sat there every Saturday. Sat there and sat there and sat there. And then I got a job, a part at the Gate, and still I continued to go to the studio on Saturdays.

Eventually, 12 months into the process, she said to me 'I want you to meet me here on Wednesday at 2 o'clock,' and she was there with her clipboard interviewing people in the dressing room for the next studio. When she heard that I had an Equity card and I was working at the Gate she was kind of, I think, shocked. Because she didn't realize I was already a working actor. But still I was willing to sit there every Saturday quietly because I was so scared. Even though I was getting a salary as an actor, I was still overwhelmed by what I saw and what I was learning. I thought, 'I'm not ready to go up there yet, I'm not ready to go up and do this work because it's so deep and it's exposing and it's very, I think, it's designed to shed you of your inhibitions. And yeah, so, I went up there and she gave me one word; you had to do the prepared work. I don't know if you know about Stanislavski's system, you get prepared work to do, and she said 'Ok, it's going to be the justification of an action. And, your word is disguise.' So I went away and for a week, I thought, what could I do that's going to be interesting. You know, if I don't say anything...if I just sit there and...? So anyway, I decided I was a journalist during the Kuwait conflict, and I sat up there for about 15 minutes, and I was writing in my notebook, and then eventually I picked up loads of this black fabric that I had, and I wrapped myself in it, so I covered up, and I thought, she's going to love this. Job done, 15 minutes. She made me sit there for another, I'm not exaggerating, 40 minutes. I sat up on that stage, and at the end of it all, you know, the end of the prepared work, you're not alone, it's not just you, it's three other actors doing their prepared work all at the same time, and she said, 'So Elizabeth how was that?' And I said, 'well, you know, I thought you'd call hold after 15 minutes, I mean, it seems ridiculous that I sat there doing nothing for all that time.' And she said, 'that's where the best work is done. When you're sitting there, inhabiting the space. That's what it's about. There is nothing more interesting than watching an actor just being in the space. It's not about clever improvised lines.' So that was my first lesson. Stanislavski's system and Deirdre's ability: to just let you let the exercise run and run and run and run as long as it needs to run. She had incredible concentration...

Steve: Everything I've heard makes me regret I didn't experience it. One thing you said I find interesting because in so many acting classes it is sort of forbidden, it's that someone could sit in and watch the actor's work.

Elizabeth: I've never experienced that. You had to be invited to be a guest, and you had to have I suppose a certain experience or passion for the craft. You didn't just randomly show up and observe like an audience member. Definitely it wasn't about that, it was about observing with a view to being a part of the studio. It was the first level. You get in at guest level, and then you get on to the stage. I mean, she's brought people on that stage to be a part of the studio after two weeks. She let me sit there for 12 months. Maybe I needed it.

Steve: How long were you studying before being cast in a show?

Elizabeth: Pretty quickly. I think it was probably...three months. And I do remember the show, *Strawberry Fields* [by Stephen Poliakoff], but you see, I was so impatient, and I suppose a bit arrogant, I was sick of waiting to be cast. Because I thought 'I'm an actor already. You know, I work around town, in other theatres, this is ridiculous.' The arrogance. And I decided to start my own theatre company. And I said, 'Oh can I rent this space from you, Deirdre@, and she said, 'You don't rent this space. We're not a bloody playhouse. This is Focus Theatre. We have artistic criteria.' And I said, 'Oh, ok if it's all other Focus actors,' which it was. And we did *An Actor's Nightmare* [by Christopher

Durang] at lunchtime and it was really at quiet time, pre-Christmas, and nobody you know, no one was coming to lunchtime theatre in the dead of winter, and so anyway, we did that. Rather successfully actually. I think after that she realized, yeah, let's give her a small role in a play. And she gave me a really beautiful role and she directed it herself, and then, then I was off. She just gave me one fantastic role after another there, and I had the privilege of playing Catherine to her Aunt Violet in *Suddenly Last Summer* which I remember even thinking at the time, 'Oh my god, this is just – kill me now – this is my dream come true.'

FOCUS VS THE DUBLIN THEATRE ESTABLISHMENT

Mary Elizabeth Burke-Kennedy

Steve: *A Doll's House* played for five months to packed houses and toured?

Mary Elizabeth: Yes, and don't forget packed houses meant 70 people a night.

Steve: That's true. Better to have 70 in a packed house than 70 in a theatre that seats 300.

Mary Elizabeth: Absolutely. I think they could have got more people to see *Doll's House*. The success of the production highlighted the problems that we had, with the infrastructure of theatre in the country at the time. The Abbey theatre had a director called Hugh Hunt who was quite an enlightened man. And see, the Abbey weren't doing modern classics. They concentrated on Irish plays. Those kinds of plays, Chekhov, Ibsen, Strindberg, that we were doing had been the plays that were previously done at the Gate Theatre. But they hadn't been done for years. So there was a great interest in them when we did them, like we were introducing a whole new audience to them. And the Abbey had this policy where they would invite companies into the Peacock to display their wares. I think the present director is doing the same thing now. So we asked if we would bring in *A Doll's House* to showcase it in the Peacock. So we were all set to do this and it would have been a huge thing for us, but Equity, the actors' union, vetoed it. Because we weren't members of Equity. In order to become a member of Equity you had to work in an Equity company for two productions and blah blah blah, so there was no way that we, as a repertory company, could do that. We asked if they would take us on as a repertory company and give us membership while we were members of the rep, and they wouldn't do it. So eventually that kind of contributed to a feeling of being outside, beyond the Pale, in many ways, for us. A feeling of being just the outsiders, which I've already talked to you about, in terms of people's attitude towards training, you know?

STANISLAVSKI TRAINING

In the United States Stanislavski's training is called The Method, especially as popularized by the training at the Actors Studio in New York, which is where Deirdre trained. It was run by the legendary Lee Strasberg with a roster of students in the 1950s (Paul Newman, Geraldine Page, Rip Torn, Kim Stanley, James Dean, Shirley Knight, Eli Wallach) who charted a new course of acting and who brought a freshness and a new sense of realism to their art. In Russia, Stanislavski called his training The System and he evolved his System frequently, discarding some of his techniques in favour of others, with some acting teachers offering training in the techniques developed later in Stanislavski's life. Others, like Strasberg, adhered more to the early writings, fixing them as immutable. Deirdre, though trained by Strasberg, was much more fluid in her teaching, sometimes separating herself from her teacher in this way.

Mary Moynihan

I imagine anyone who works through the Stanislavski system probably puts his or her own slant on it. Stanislavski himself said to create your own system, not to 'depend slavishly on mine,' to take what works for you and to 'keep breaking traditions.'

Well, you mentioned Stella Adler earlier, she had a particular approach to the Stanislavski system that focused on imagination while others such as Lee Strasberg perhaps emphasized areas such as emotional or affective memory. Deirdre was unique in that she had immense talent as an actor, director, and teacher as well as having an instinctive understanding of acting, and her aim was to create a sense of truth in performance, that sense of 'moment-to-moment aliveness' on stage. It is important to give time to intuit the process and to find out what works for you in the moment; to continuously develop and grow, an ongoing process of discovery and learning. Stanislavski himself understood that and his whole system changed from what it was in the beginning to what it was in the end.

Steve: How much was Deirdre's background, an intellectual attitude?...

Mary: Deirdre had a unique gift of understanding the human condition and understanding human relationships and she was a great communicator. That made her unique as a teacher. I did ask her once if she preferred to be an actor rather than director or a teacher, and she said her preference was actor, and director and then teacher but she was equally gifted in all three, which is an unusual combination. Deirdre was excellent at passing on the knowledge of Stanislavski, which she excelled in. She had a very keen gift in being able to spot what an actor needed and how to develop the actor in a very supportive way, which I think is a unique gift as a director and teacher. That combined with her knowledge of Stanislavski. She trained with Erwin Piscator, Saul Colin, and Allan Miller amongst others, with Lee Strasberg at the Actors' Studio in New York and she had that unique combination of an intellectual understanding and, more importantly, an instinctive understanding of what the work is about. It gets back to that idea of the Stanislavski approach being a system as opposed to, you know, a particular style of acting or a set of exercises that you slavishly follow. It's more organic and intuitive.

Well, you have to understand it's what works for you in the moment. And it's not to follow slavishly what he said, it is a system, and it is going to continuously develop and grow.

Steve: I didn't get the impression that Deirdre was a Lee Strasberg acolyte...was that in fact the case? Or did she have her own take on Stanislavski?

Mary: Like many Stanislavski practitioners Deirdre had her own focus which tended towards what she referred to as the Eastern Stanislavski 'system' as opposed to the 'Method' which may be associated with a Westernized approach. Deirdre placed an emphasis on action and objective, and on sensory work, developing the actor's sensory apparatus in order to create or lead to emotion in performance as well as work on relationships. While we did do emotional memory work in the studio, there was not the same emphasis that perhaps Strasberg took, in terms of his focus on 'affective memory.' Work in studio consisted of one-person character studies or justifications, or the personal object sense memory, or room recall exercises and various improvisations. Even with [Michael] Chekhov – Deirdre would have been aware of him and used some of the Chekhov exercises, particularly the Psychological Gesture – but she wouldn't have gone as far with the work on impulses or sensations or the grotesque as Chekhov, although we did do a lot of physical work in Focus. Deirdre's objective was similar to Stanislavski and Chekhov in terms of seeking truth, depth and spontaneity in performance. I do think there was a huge common ground between Stanislavski and Chekhov, and Stanislavski himself was always developing his system, moving away from a very strong emphasis on the emotional memory work towards an emphasis on physical action in order to stimulate emotional depth and truth, similar to Chekhov.

Tim McDonnell

The way, in my understanding, the Focus extended that, was in allowing the emotional reality or the inner life reality that one creates imaginatively as a result of reading a play, whatever that emotional, imaginative reality may be. How to harness that for the purposes and the objective of not only the scene at hand, but the objective of what the play is trying to state imaginatively. Because there is also a playwright who has to be taken into serious account, you know, so it was also there to be sure you worked within the loop of what the demands of the play were; or the scene was that you were doing. That you were able to fill richly with your own imaginative take on what was going on, that allowed you the freedom then to express that in a way that was uniquely yours, but with the help of a director and/or teacher to make sure that you didn't go outside of the parameter of what was demanded by the actual play itself. Very important, you know, terribly, terribly important. How can I put it, I talked to Joe [Devlin] about this, because he knows my fondness for music, and Deirdre was a great educator that way. It would be like, for example, that Simon Rattle went to the Berlin Philharmonic and produced an extraordinarily loose interpretation of Bruckner's great Eighth Symphony. And suddenly, adding a jingle there and a jangle there, a little bit of whatever here, well you know what would happen? He would never work again with the Berlin Philharmonic and it's unlikely he would anywhere else. And that kind of reality was grounded into you: that the respect for the author's work at a given period in time, in Ibsen's or Strindberg's completely puritanical society, is very different in NY in the 1930s.

Steve: If we switched to technique for a moment, how concerned was she with...

Tim: Oh, very deeply concerned about that. As she said during our first or second class, 'I don't teach voice and I don't teach dance or movement. So I am enrolling you in the Royal Irish Academy of Music for the voice classes and voice production classes with Mrs. White-Lennon, and you'll go to modern dance class with Evelyn Burchill,' who had an old Georgian house in Stephen's Green. And that's where Tom Hickey and myself used to go on a Tuesday night. On the bar and on the floor: we did all of that, and she insisted that you do that, and jump improvisational work, effective memory work, justification of the action, any of those exercises. There is a myriad of them in the first year, the actors work on their own self, you know, she made sure that was balanced by, and rigidly balanced by, the other reality. So she was very concerned with, say, for example, effective memory, which is not an exercise I particularly like as a teacher. And not an exercise I particularly liked as a student because I much preferred the Stella Adler of the imaginative 'ifs', the 'as if', dramatic action, searching for, trying to reach an objective, already chosen. And of course it has to be dealt with on the moment with the other actor. Whereas I found, myself, with the effective memory, that a lot of the time the actors were just working at their god-damn navels and you could get no response from what was going on, and I think Stella Adler had it. I think she nailed it. She was absolutely instinctively right, and she went to see Stanislavski in Paris. I don't know how she got there, boat or whatever, and don't forget she was born in Odessa so she spoke fluent Russian: a lot of people forget that, and she told him, 'Jesus you are ruining the actor's acting craft.' She actually had quite a staunch and confrontational argument with him about that particular exercise, after which he said, 'Well I'll have to think about that again.' I mean he was always open to that kind of thing you know.

Deirdre was up against a phenomenal amount. And she was abused, verbally, and terribly, you know, in pubs and wherever people would actually go and drink and chat about the theatre. I remember a well-known actor and his going on about her. 'Who is this one coming over from New York telling us how to act. Who the hell! Who the fuck is she coming over to this country to tell us how to act. Nonsense. Go back home.' Now that's the kind of thing you heard regularly, and these are from people who never even bothered their ass to go down to the studio and have a look at what the process was about; the detail of the process. They never read a book by Stanislavski, Meyerhold or anybody else. They were profoundly, in relation to this particular process, ignorant in the extreme. And everybody used to say, 'Well, but they do great naturalism, you know, it's great naturalism.' And Deirdre said one day, 'There is a huge difference between copying life's reality, á la naturalism, without having any imaginative psychological depths.' So she was very much in the camp of Strindberg, if you know what I mean, a playwright she adored and admired. She revered Strindberg for the profoundness and rawness of his capacity for emotional reality: do you know what I am saying?

Steve: Were all of you students aligned with her on this; did you have any arguments?

Tim: Well afterwards we all got an opportunity to criticize each other. That was a terribly important part of the studio: understanding the language. We got an opportunity to say, 'Well I think that it was his privilege to pick that choice in relation to trying to accomplish this objective with this actor, but I think his work on the moment to moment wasn't allowing him enough time to change gear and seek another way...' She allowed that kind of criticism all the time and encouraged it. She did not in any way deride or degrade people like [Laurence] Olivier [did]. She thought such criticism had its own relevance, its own particular deep cultural foundation, and it was to be respected as such.

Steve: How long in the process before Deirdre had you doing scene work?

Tim: I'd say it took us a year and a half going through improv, situation improvs, the word exercise, personalizing the word and bringing it into movement and sound with another actor opposite you. Then at a certain point she would ring the bell, and the other actor had to take it on board and run with it. 'I don't know what the fuck you're talking about, were you that drunk last night?' You know whatever it was, and then that would lead on and on. We did quite a bit of this. I believe this is somewhat related to the Meisner technique in some degree. And she also had us do exercises from Michael Chekhov and stuff like that. Somebody I never warmed to. I always found that working with an actor as a director, for example, improvising before the text, that suddenly as you find yourself instinctively searching for an objective with another fellow actor, that somebody might do this [Tim put his head down in his palm] and you'd say that's it! That is the psychological gesture. His brain is literally peeling out of his head. So you don't have to intellectually choose to do it. It has happened in the improv, you will remember the imaginative experience in the improv that led to it, ergo use it when we get to the text. So I was always a bit puzzled by Chekhov and that sense he always found in working with colour. Now this is my problem, it may not be anybody else's. I always found work with colour, like green and orange, all very fine, but I found that for me it lacked specificity. What are the specifics that I needed, not the generalization, but the specifics that each actor needs in any given set of circumstances?

So we walked through quite a bit of that in the 18 months before we actually got a scene. And I remember the first scene I ever did was from

Death of a Salesman, and I did Happy to Tom Hickey's Biff. And that was the very first one, and I'll never forget it. It was just, you know, we made it a dog's dinner, but at least we were getting on there. And the other one I remember with great, great warmth was with Michael Campion, who is also one of the early founder members of the theatre. It was *The Long Goodbye* by Tennessee Williams. I played the guy who wanted to move and do all of that, he was the guy who was a little more stagnant, a little more insecure about the move. And we had this prop I brought on the stage which I got in a shop, it's a German thing. You light all these candles on the top of the bar. You have all these little animals, horses, and what have you. And then the candles move around and make a certain sound. I did it for imaginative purposes because I was attracted to them. But by extension it also had a kind of a metaphorical reality with regard to which way anything was going to go. You know what I mean? And people were talking about this metaphor, and I was saying 'Did we achieve the relationship?' For Christ sake, that's what we are trying to do here man. And we did. Mary Elizabeth [Burke-Kennedy] remembers it to this day. Because that was the studio Deirdre started. Do I need to say any more?

Mary Elizabeth Burke-Kennedy

Steve: When Focus came into being, you were an actor. So you were in *Miss Julie*?

Mary Elizabeth: That's right, I played one of the dancers.

Steve: And Declan directed that?

Mary Elizabeth: Yes, Tom and Deirdre were John and Miss Julie. Tim was one of the dancers as well.

Steve: Was that your first Focus performance?

Mary Elizabeth: Yes, it was. *Miss Julie* and *The Wedding*, I think they were done together, and I was the bride in *The Wedding*. I can remember the rehearsals for that because we were absolutely dogmatically religious about pursuing our process, what we had learned in the studio. I found this was one of the most difficult occasions, actually, in my whole experience of the transition between the theoretical, the studio work, the open-ended studio work, the transition between that and performance I found very difficult to bridge. And there was this guy playing the groom who was the most charming, wonderful fellow, but I didn't understand why the Bride agreed to marry him. And we improvised and improvised and improvised until the rest of the cast would turn and scream 'just fucking kiss him and be done with it!' But I didn't understand, you know, like Dustin Hoffman and the playing with the tomato in the salad in *Tootsie*. That was the kind of actor I was. So, you know, I ran up against the theory. I hadn't made the bridges that were necessary there. My sense of truth was predominant, and to do with me and my ethic. I couldn't really see around that. And I think it's a kind of egotism that a lot of young actors experience. I had to find my own way eventually.

Steve: Was Deirdre along with the cast telling you to kiss him, or was she willing to allow the improvs?

Mary Elizabeth: I don't think she was involved in those rehearsals, one way or the other.

Steve: Let me ask you then, in terms of production, was there an emphasis, a stress on the process, or was the end product becoming more central?

Mary Elizabeth: The process was pretty crucial. Because it was the process which created the main difference between what we were doing and what anybody else was doing. And of course the process created the sense of ensemble, the sense of a life lived on the stage, which you didn't get in other productions. So we knew that what we were doing before the production was what gave it its quality, and gave it its dimension that the audience was seeing, and causing them to say 'There's something different going on here.' Right? However, that's not to say that we didn't want to finish the production properly and give it a professional gloss. But there was a sense of handmade-ness about our productions, I suppose. Declan's mother would gasp when any opening night arrived and she saw half her furniture on the stage. Especially if it was a Chekhov play or an Ibsen play. She had a lot of Victorian furniture and it would inevitably end up on the Focus stage. So it was that kind of handmade-ness, you know.

Steve: So process is still central as opposed to result. Is that something as a director that you find that you still pursue; that you still stress process with your actors and try to find ways for them to progress and fully understand their characters?

Mary Elizabeth: Oh, absolutely. Although in Focus in those days, we are talking about the 70s now, early 80s, we were a semi-professional company, so we had a very long rehearsal period, which other theatre companies didn't have.

Steve: Was there an average length to rehearsal?

Mary Elizabeth: Oh, six weeks, absolutely minimum in Focus. When I later established Storytellers (my own theatre company), I used to fight with my financial controller to get a four week rehearsal period, when small, independent companies were often reduced to three weeks rehearsal. So, you know, that obviously curtails the process. So actors would get very jittery and they would want to get on to the text pretty quickly, and get the blocking done and the thing would be to resist their inclination to adopt postures and just to keep them open minded and keep them exploring for as long as possible. And some of them are just nervous about improvising, people that haven't done it, haven't training in it, find it quite terrifying. But I certainly use it and, yes, I would use exercises. We followed quite religiously, as I say, at the beginning, the text of *An Actor Prepares* and *Building a Character* and that kind of stuff. We started off with the open first reading and then we did character studies and then we did improvisations off the text. Then we did improvisations on the text, step by step. Nobody can afford that now. So, I mean, very few actors that I know would have the training to do a character study. So, as I say, I devised exercises appropriate to the actors to help them into roles. In fact, I would have used Charles Marowitz's ideas more than Stanislavski's.

Steve: Over the years have you found that more and more actors are fully prepared, in terms of working, through Stanislavski methods?

Mary Elizabeth: Yes, of course. Because when we started off in the studio in the 70s, there was one other training school for actors which told you how to walk onto a stage and how to sit down and stand up, how to make an entrance, an exit. You know it was purely technical, rather than developing a technique. And, the attitude – I'm sure the other people you have spoken to have said this to you – the predominant attitude in Ireland was acting is a talent, a gift from God. You either have it or you haven't, and you don't interfere with it. And what we were doing down the lane, or in the basement, with this mysterious red-haired woman all dressed in black was regarded as almost a cult. I mean it was regarded as certainly self-indulgent and real actors didn't do that kind of carrying on. Now there are two training schools, The Gaiety School of Acting and then Trinity, which had a hiccup and closed down and is now open again, but those training schools would introduce students to Stanislavski, and to rigorous training, to develop a technique.

Sabina Coyne Higgins

We had to be flexible as other things were required. We were recommended by her to be doing things, so, for example, we did dancing with Evelyn Burchill, a kind of a modern dance which was really good. She had a dancing school so we used to go there, and we did fencing. We were also doing voice production. In the theatre at the time, there was no notion that you would be teaching a kind of a system – there was I suppose a dismissive attitude toward this 23 year old upstart, coming and teaching Ireland to learn to act! We already had the Great Tradition and you learned from that. The talent that came out of that. So there was never a kind of 'let's see', even early on. Some of the main critics never came to shows. They were part of the establishment and we were not.

What Deirdre brought for the first time was teaching...That wasn't really happening as I know at the time. It spread into the arts. To actually be studying life for yourself and reproducing it, that was what she was giving us! She was getting us in touch with our creativity, and showing us that it was only in the *doing* that you could discover this. Then there was the quality of life. I mean those were some of the most wonderful times to be onstage; when you improvise and explore the revelations that come from that. There was also the freedom of thinking for yourself and, of course, the freedom from the restraints we have in normal life. They are not the same things. All these conformities that people live...When they are removed on stage, and one has the freedom of expression, then one discovers a lot and sees the other person so differently: you're seeing people at a very intimate level. Very often it is seeing *into* them. They are exposing themselves, and you are exposing yourself and it is a fantastic communication that you do. And that's how the repertory company or ensemble theatre was built up. It had such a sense of 'the other person' and of the freedom: you were doing it but you were doing it in this creative space, so when the performance is over that was it: you had expressed everything. And it was something new.

Steve: Was improv more fun than the scripted text?

Sabina: No, they were both wonderful, but the improv was quite a sophisticated thing and so wonderful: you were creating new plays; doing them alongside. When we toured, for example with *A Doll's House*, around the country, because it was a terrific success, to major cities such as Cork and Galway, we would do an improvisation on an afternoon as well, which was great for people who hadn't seen improvisation, and was also wonderful fun. There was also a kind of a community: scenes were being explored, so in a way it was letting people see that this is also theatre.

Steve: There's quite an adrenaline rush doing improvs.

Sabina: Well, it's very different. It is probably very dramatic. You are always inside. You have all the restrictions you would have in a play. We would break down a play: analyzing, bringing it down to the super objective; where was the climax in each act? What was the climax of the play? And then, with each individual scene, what is the objective and what were all the minor objectives of other characters? But it all had to be feeding into each other area so there was a discipline in that when you're doing it. You have to find your own way: what all of these little branches were leading into. And it was exactly the same in an improvisation: when you did one you would have those restrictions, yet you would know that you were in control. You had set up your own controls.

We would do improvisations on the play that would be very similar. We would improvise the play: you would have the freedom to do so, and a longer time. When you are doing a play proper, an act might be thirty minutes long, but when doing an improvisation on that act, it could last as long as you wanted it to, so you could really explore what it was the character might be striving for. So you try this or you try that, and then, as you're doing it, you begin to question the logic of one thing or another, and then you begin to know what the character would be about. And that you have it! It becomes organic, so that when you do a play every night, reproducing it is always new. You are doing the same things, but the great thing about the Stanislavski system is that you are able to go into the depths.

Even though the Abbey theatre would have been a very, very good theatre, it would never have been able to go into the depths, the emotional depths, that a Focus production could have brought up, nor could it have gone into the truthfulness. You know *at the time of doing it* that this is the truth. That is the great thing. You know for certain and you only know it because you have gone so much into your being, being fed by such authenticity. You know that it's not a scripted thing that would come out every night, but it would emerge *out of it*. It goes on forever for anyone who is trained in the system. As all these years and years went by, we became more and more able to use and understand the creativity of the human being. We understood how the process works: how to acquire from the conscious things; the breaking down of the textures, the smells, putting them together again, recreating them. Really, after years you can see that more and more. There's never only one night. The next night is something new; they are not just repeating last night; they are alive...

DIRECTING

There were many directors at the Focus, including, primarily, Deirdre herself, and later Tim McDonnell. I spoke with Mary Elizabeth Burke-Kennedy, one of the more acclaimed of Focus's directors, and Cathal Quinn offered his reminiscence of directing some Samuel Beckett pieces at Focus.

Mary Elizabeth Burke-Kennedy

Steve: What was the first play you directed?

Mary Elizabeth: *John Gabriel Borkman*, believe it or not. It was huge. I was absolutely terrified.

Steve: Did you decide to do the play?

Mary Elizabeth: Yes, the play was offered to me. Declan was designing it. He did a wonderful design. Rebecca Schull was in it. She subsequently had a huge television success in America in the sitcom *Wings*. Rebecca played Mrs Borkman, Deirdre played Ella, and Frank McDonald played John Gabriel.

Steve: Getting back to Focus. You mentioned a change...did it abandon its principles?

Mary Elizabeth: In the early days it was the group's ambition to form a repertory company. It gradually became clear that that was not going to happen, because, financially, the space was unviable and also because of the troubles we had with Equity. In order to become full-time professional actors people had to leave Focus and get work elsewhere. So then it really kind of boiled down to the only people that were working full-time in the theatre were Deirdre and myself.

Steve: You had a second company?

Mary Elizabeth: I had a second studio and was doing different kinds of work. We were going along in tandem very well together. Deirdre recognized that what I was doing had come through the studio, even though, as I say, it wasn't necessarily her artistic preference, but she felt that the theatre could accommodate the two things and could see the advantage of the theatre that had an alternative vision. So I mean that was fine. We would bring back core members to work with us any opportunity that we could get when they were free. But it became the fact when we wanted for example Johnny Murphy for a play, we kind of had to work it around his schedule, his professional schedule. And Deirdre was always very anxious not to push members of the studio ahead of where they were able to be in terms of performance. So we couldn't just hike people out of the studio, so we had to go elsewhere for casting.

I did a production of *Alice in Wonderland* which moved into Project Theatre. That was the first time we moved from the home base, apart from touring. That was also a first for Focus in terms of content of the play, the nature of the play. Suddenly Focus was doing a) something for young people, and b) something fantastical and surreal, non-naturalistic and funny. So it was quite a big change. And it was the first production that I did that took me off in a different direction, which is another story.

Steve: I want to ask about your work with Masks.

Mary Elizabeth: I didn't really work with masks like Yeats or, you know, studying Japanese theatre. I used masks in my plays.

Steve: Outside of Yeats was there a use of masks since his time?

Mary Elizabeth: Well there was a wonderful mask-maker who I happened to know and he gave me the masks for *Alice*, there were a few of them. And I asked him again to make some masks when I did a production of two of Lorca's puppet plays. They were the only times I used masks at Focus. The other time I used them significantly was in a production for Storytellers of Oscar Wilde's fairy stories, *The Selfish Giant*, *The Happy Prince*, and *The Star Child*. Anyway, there was wonderful, real mask work in that, and puppet work. But that was very much at the instigation of the director, who's Bairbre Ní Chaoimh, who is another Focus person. If you wanted to ask her about Stanislavski and masks, she is the mask person. That production was quite astonishing, with the use of mask and puppets and shadow puppets.

Steve: Let's go back to *Alice* for a moment. You were taking a break from a typical Focus play. Did you find resistance from Deirdre or other members in terms of this break from the naturalism?

Mary Elizabeth: Deirdre wasn't that keen. But she didn't interfere.

Steve: You also did the Soviet play (*He Who Gets Slapped by Leonid Andreyev*) which certainly is not a naturalistic play, either.

Mary Elizabeth: No but it was by, you know, a Russian, from the classic canon. And Deirdre was more inclined towards that than she was to *Alice*. It was just something that was in me: that I enjoy exaggeration. And I enjoy it in literature; I love Dickens, for example. I remember at one time doing a character study of Betsy Trotwood, from *David Copperfield*, and having cotton wool in my ears, you know sticking out, it's more than exaggeration, it's parody, it's a mask in itself, you know? And Deirdre couldn't understand why. She kept saying, 'What do you want to do that sort of stuff for?' And I couldn't really explain it to her. It was just I thought it was great fun and had its own truth and I had a feeling for it. So I decided to do *Alice*, the set by the artist John McNulty was basically an adventure playground. It was beautifully coloured, and it was all made from wood and was a very lovely thing to look at. It had a staircase, a chute the actors would come down. Had a swing, all kinds of levels for them to play on. So you know, that was the first break from what the audience had come to anticipate. When they came into the theatre, there was no curtain. And then the lights were free-standing on the stage, and when the actors were not in a scene they would change the lights and re-focus them and do that kind of thing. And I think that Deirdre felt that I was smashing the 4th wall, smashing everything. It took her a long time to become reconciled to it.

The thing was, at that stage I had a studio of my own. The actors who were in *Alice* were from my studio. We focused on, for a lot of the work, the legends and Irish mythological material, on abstract ideas and abstract exercises in Stanislavski. The stuff that had frightened me at the beginning, right. Somebody like Donal O'Kelly, he is a remarkable actor. He found a great deal of inspiration from those exercises. And so that's how we approached it, with psychological gestures, you know. We approached this kind of fairy tale work, legends work, stories like *The Nose* by Gogol. I was the resident director in the theatre and was the administrator, and you know Deirdre said, 'OK if that's what you want to do, you do it.' And then we would do a naturalistic production, something more to her inclination. I maybe had one show a year. But, you know, that's not to say that Deirdre was hostile to this. For example, one of the things she loved which we did, was a production called *Lovers of Viorne* by Marguerite Duras which is based on this extraordinary murder case where pieces of the body were being discovered all over France in freight trains. They were the same body. North, south, east, west, all over the place. They discovered when they looked at the map of the railways there was one place where all these trains converged. A railway bridge where they all passed under, so they figured that someone was lobbing these body parts off the bridge into different trains as they passed. And they went and they discovered the killers. It was this ancient, sedate married couple and they had murdered his cousin who had been working for them and the story is an analysis of why. And it's not a naturalistic play. The Interrogator and Claire Lannes are in the first act and in the second act there is an interrogator and Pierre. And they tell the story. Deirdre adored that play. She was nominated, won an award for her performance. So she wasn't really hung up on the stuff of naturalism. It's just that the kind of material that I was working on would not have fired her.

Cathal Quinn

Mouth on Fire Theatre company was set up to perform the works of the Nobel Laureate, Samuel Beckett. Its co-founders both have Masters degrees in Beckett, and Melissa Nolan, also our principle actress, is researching a Doctorate concerning the female roles in his plays. We were looking to perform in conventional and unconventional spaces, to make Beckett accessible to all, and to be innovative in our approach to his work. Mouth on Fire acknowledges the many fine productions of Beckett's plays at Focus over the years, and is proud to follow in their tradition.

Mouth on Fire had its first theatrical performances in a Music Festival and an art gallery, but neither time was lighting subtle or fully under our control. Performing next in a lecture theatre and then a church, both within the grounds of a psychiatric hospital – which hadn't had a theatre performance for over forty years – we sought to perform at Focus, to settle in an atmospheric theatre which had a history of Beckett performances. Beckett himself knew his work would be best in a chamber setting, writing 'my work is for small theatres' in a letter to the director Alan Schneider in 1958, (Dilks, Portraits of Beckett as famous Writer, p 167 IUPress, JML vol 29, no 4) which is especially appropriate with regard to his later, shorter plays.

The cold, black, thick walls of Focus lent itself to the plays chosen for 'Silence and Darkness', Beckett x4, performed at Focus for two weeks in April 2011. The programme consisted of *Rockaby, Catastrophe, A Piece of Monologue* and *Play*, the evening beginning with *Late Poem* ('One Dead of Night...') interpreted by Colm O'Brien, who also played the Protagonist in *Catastrophe* and operated the spotlight in *Play*. Melissa Nolan produced and played V and W in *Rockaby* and W1 in *Play*. Jennifer Laverty was the Assistant in *Catastrophe* and W2 in *Play*; I played the Director (!) in *Catastrophe* and M in *Play*, whilst directing each show. John Cullen played Luke in *Catastrophe* and was ASM for all other shows. Stage Manager was Sophie and the lighting design was by Becky Gardiner. Marcus Lamb was Speaker in *A Piece of Monologue*. The one that excited most comment was Marcus Lamb's fine interpretation of the aged Speaker, waiting for death, when Marcus himself was at the tender age of 31; his physical presence enhanced by a wig, made especially by Val Sherlock. His spellbinding stillness and precision with the text made Emer O'Kelly of the Sunday Independent comment that he had a very bright future in interpreting Beckett, and others to liken him to a young Barry McGovern, perhaps the most celebrated performer of Beckett alive today. Sarah Jane Scaife, a leading exponent of Beckett's shorter plays worldwide, came into the dressing room after the first preview and told Marcus not to sniff up the mucus that was dripping out of his nose in his thirty minutes of stillness and staring out into space, and to let it become part of his characterization, which he did, making the Speaker even more human, pathetic, incapable of the most basic human functions.

The Artistic Director of Focus very generously allowed the cast to rehearse twice in the space prior to the performances which helped all the actors and the director to ground themselves and the plays, prior to the technical and dress rehearsals, and to fill the space physically and vocally, which, despite being very intimate, still needed breath support and sufficient resonance to reach the back wall.

Contrary to popular opinion one cannot 'project' the voice; it is light that projects; sound resonates. As Glenn Close told an audience in Dublin recently, actors should not just think about projecting voices: 'they need to project their thoughts'.

When a theatre of any size has an audience the bodies absorb sound, so the actors must make the effort to articulate excellently and to resonate the dense, brief and minimalist words of Beckett's short plays at whatever speed is demanded, as well as to project the fragmented thoughts which are constantly being honed and redefined. Another challenge is to speak with little inflection in the voice but to retain vocal energy. Beckett was always asking his actors to deliver his lines with less colour. Most Southern Irish accents tend to go down for stresses, very useful for delivering Beckett, but we still had to counter the tendency to lift the first part of any sentence which gives one vocal presence. Ultimately we found that energetic toneless delivery; and the modulations were subtle but present, enabling us to find various shades of grey. It was in the Focus that the voices had the time to settle and consistently deliver the colourless tones, identified by Billie Whitelaw as the withdrawn voice of her niece with whom she spoke on the telephone the day before she committed suicide.

On the first preview of 'Silence and Darkness 'all had been going swimmingly until the final show of the evening: *Play*. Three characters in urns side by side, very tightly lit by a single spotlight – an external force exerted upon them – dictating when each character was to speak.

During the chorus which began each segment there are supposed to be three separate spots to illuminate all three characters' heads at the same time.

Looking through Beckett's Theatrical Notebook IV, I noticed he had been keen to find a way to make this more effective, and for one light to incorporate all three heads.

We managed to solve that problem by moving our one light rapidly from side to side during each chorus which gave the effect of a search light to those who had seen films or who had actual memories of the Second World War during blackouts due to air raids, with a light splitting the sky in search of enemy aeroplanes. In the intimate environs of the Focus, mounting a tripod for the light seemed too intrusive, so it was decided to reserve a seat in the middle of the front row each night and place the light under that seat during the interval, the actor who operated the light, hooded, slipping in after *A Piece of Monologue* and operating it from his lap. However, on that ill-fated first preview, this one light blew during the first chorus, and the actor operating it had left his back-up (tiny bicycle light) in the dressing room. Unabashed, he proceeded to gesture very strongly with outstretched arm towards each character trapped in an urn in the dark with impassive face covered in grey face mask, who was then prompted to speak his or her lines without colour and at breakneck speed.

The Stage Manager, thinking her job now done for the evening, and the light in the hands of the actor in the front row, was looking down and failed to notice this rather inconvenient technical hitch, but the lighting designer was present and sitting near the back. She silently alerted the SM, gestured to her to put up a new spotlight and climbed up onto the back of a seat to manipulate this new spot according to the gestures made by the hooded actor in the front row.

This could have worked...indeed the play proceeded on at its blistering pace, the actors trapped in the urns all facing out and witnessing the chaos but remaining as impassive as possible.

Unfortunately, the lighting designer decided that the one light she was operating was too faint on the actors, so frantically gestured for the stage manager to put up another spot, and to stand beside her on the back of another seat, the pair of them swinging their lamps in accordance with the semaphore continuing from the actor in the front row!

This was all too much for the sanity of the actress playing W2,whose grip on the play began to unravel, and she found herself, as the cue approached for her to say, 'Then she came in licking her lips, etc' unable to utter anything more than 'Then she came...she came...'

In such a tight and speedy show, keeping to the rhythm is vital, and one tiny break in the continuous flow of the three interwoven monologues, apart from the silences written into the piece, disturbs all four of the players and more mistakes are bound to follow, until one of them hauls the others back on track.

The director, being integrally involved in the show and having performed the play on five previous occasions, had informed the actor usually operating the light – in a moment of hubris – should anyone dry or lose their thread to put the light on to himself and he would re-establish the play's rhythm.

Of course, with all the shenanigans in front of him and with no cue as such to work with, when the conductor unexpectedly gestured towards him and the two spotlights followed his lead, he too succumbed like a rabbit in the headlights and dribbled out an echo of 'she came...'

It was left to the other actress, W1 just that bit further away from the panic stricken others to her right, to reclaim the actual play and moments later all proceeded on with no more extra drama.

The next night, the show commenced at approximately ten minutes past eight (as there was, notoriously, only one toilet for cast, crew and audience, so a show very rarely started on time). During the first line of the brief poem prior to the first play, *Rockaby*, there was a knocking on the locked front door of the theatre. After a Beckettian pause, the poem continued... and so did the knocking, growing louder each time.

As the poem finished the knock reached its peak of volume, so the stage manager, with eight plays at Focus under her belt, stopped the show, left the auditorium and told the stranger at the gate in no uncertain terms to go away, before returning and resuming the show where she had left off.

I do happen to know who the culprit was, but have never revealed his identity. I knew he was coming that night, but it was his first visit to Focus, he couldn't find the theatre and of course he had no idea of the proximity of the front door to the performance space.

No other problems occurred from first night (13th of April, Beckett's birthday) to last, isn't that what previews are for? Some of the actors were convinced that Deirdre visited us in the dressing room. Every time we tried to quietly open or close the dressing room door it squeaked mercilessly, but it used to open itself once a night without a squeak, causing even the most cynical of actors to whisper 'Hello Deirdre'.

Mouth on Fire's next Beckett show, in November 2011, required a different setting altogether.

It was entitled 'Tyranny in Beckett'. A radio piece onstage, a short prose piece and two plays, one of which we had already performed in 'Silence and Darkness'. The intense blackout of Focus would have helped the atmosphere, but we were also interested in the possibilities offered by the architecture of The Boys' School, Smock Alley. It reminded one of Orson Welles's film version of Kafka's *The Trial*, which we exploited as best we could, the audience on many levels, the performances on every level available, sometimes simultaneously, the lights employing the gothic arches to great effect during *Rough for Radio II* that the Beckett Estate allowed us to stage, only if we did it in the dark. We compromised by dimly lighting an old radio, and a red hue lit up the arches whenever the torture victim was beaten into speaking or screaming.

None of this was available to us in Focus, and as the architecture was of prime importance for the piece we chose our venue carefully to be site-specific, as apart from one small box and a wicker chair this unique space was also the set.

We returned to Focus in April 2012 with 'Before Vanishing...' four Beckett plays none of which we had ever done before, plus a World Premiere: *Come and Go* in Irish, translated as *Teacht Is Imeacht* by Gabriel Rosenstock.[54] Nick Devlin and Colm O'Brien alternated each night as Reader and Listener for *Ohio Impromptu*, Melissa Nolan and Geraldine Plunkett were May and V in *Footfalls*, Marcus Lamb was in *That Time* and Jennifer Laverty joined the other two women for *Come and Go* and *Teacht Is Imeacht*. John Cullen was ASM, Becky Gardiner lighting designer and stage manager, all under my direction.

The sound system had not been working prior to our show but with three voices shifting between three speakers for *That Time* we had to hire a sound mixer and three reliable speakers at considerable cost, and a haze machine to add extra atmosphere to the magnificent lighting of at least two of the shows.

The haze machine proved impossible to use in a theatre of this size, it was noisy, it needed to be put on fifteen minutes prior to being used

---

[54] We have since found out that Declan Kiberd translated it in his student days at Trinity College, asking Beckett himself for permission. He received a card stating, 'Me in Irish? You're mad!' And permission had been granted for the student show. Ours was still the World Premiere of the show professionally.

and worst of all, when put in the cramped dressing room to reduce the noise, it set off the smoke alarms.

The first day of the technical for these ambitious shows went gloriously, not a frayed temper, the shows filling the space, the actors growing more and more comfortable. On the day of the dress rehearsal, however, extra costumes that had not been worn previously took time to adjust to; the floor, having been painted the night before, became irritatingly noisy for *Footfalls*, its stickiness rendering each step painful to the ear. It was remedied by putting stockings over the shoes and the faint shuffling that ensued had the desired effect ('I must hear the feet however faint they fall').[55]

Lights started to misbehave. A subtle spot that had been set at a low level, suddenly decided to be ultra bright even when brought up to the same low level, and once fixed, defiantly repeated the stunt again and again. Was the ghost of Deirdre O'Connell deciding not to be upstaged by the spectral May of *Footfalls*? Or was it that theatre lights need to be serviced every three months, and it has been a very long time since those at Focus had been given that amount of attention!

That light was replaced. Half an hour to go prior to first preview... and the sound stopped working. An integral part of *That Time*, the show cannot run without it, a computer that we had brought in to manage the complexities of *That Time* would no longer accept the sound jack in its socket.

Focus being situated in a lane, our trainee knocked on the door of a house opposite and asked them whether we could borrow a computer. As they went looking for one, a rat bounded along Pembroke Place and disappeared under their garage door, as if for the hundredth time. Not only had complete strangers pestered them about borrowing an expensive piece of machinery but they were then informed by the same strangers that they had another unwelcome visitor!

The preview began thirty minutes late but went very well indeed. No problems on the opening night: Friday the 13th of April, Beckett's birthday!

However, at the start of the second week the lighting board decided to lose memory of all the lights programmed into it, so the operator had to go through every setting to find which one would pinpoint Marcus Lamb's head (and nothing else) as he stood ten feet tall on a box, to give

---

[55] Gerry Dukes, friend and a biographer of Beckett, who came on the first night, commented that the pacing of May was 'mercifully quiet.'

the illusion of looking at him from below for the duration of *That Time*, and she had to guess again which light would illuminate all three women sitting on a bench in *Come and Go* and *Teacht Is Imeacht*. All subtlety gone, once the *Come and Go* light was found, it was re-used for the next play instead of adding a sepia tone to distinguish visually between the English and Irish versions.

Despite all these technical glitches 'Before Vanishing...' received a five star review, a theatre packed to bursting point, and was a fitting end to Beckett's plays returning to Focus, the penultimate show prior to the theatre closing. As it has closed we will look for equally atmospheric spaces, but there are precious few that can match the utter darkness, the openness of the stage, the way a pause can be felt and registered so acutely by every single member of the audience. Micro emotions, subtly varied grey tones, frosted breath, all were possible within Focus's thick cold walls.[56]

BUSINESS

The business of running a school and a theatre is daunting in the best of times, and Deirdre then (and Joe now) must have struggled every day with the full weight of responsibilities and obligations. Sabina and Elizabeth brought this out (and Sabina brought in the larger question of how we need to start with children's education to create an appreciation for the arts in the country).

Sabina Coyne Higgins

We couldn't become a professional theatre because we couldn't get Actors' Equity. And you could only get an AE card if you were working in an Equity house. A theatre could give an AE, but only an Equity theatre which is paying Equity rates. There were hardly any theatres doing that. We were just dividing up what we had got from the week. We continued to pay into the studio which meant that we would have classes. And all of that really went towards funding the rent and the rates.

Steve: Would Deirdre let students stay if they couldn't pay?

Sabina: She would, yes, mostly people would pay what they could. There were some very interesting students. Deirdre was very good to

---

[56] 'Before Vanishing...' has been invited to the Galway Festival to play in Druid Lane, to the New Theatre in Temple Bar, and to Theater XCai in Tokyo.

people who were talented. We had a great puppet theatre person, and Deirdre met him because she could see how talented he was, so she said 'come along.' He wouldn't have had much money, and when he came along she was doing 'objects to play with.' You pick up whatever you want from the selection of objects. He picked up a piece of velvet and he was playing away with it, and he put his hand through it and he started doing all kinds of things and through that he told a big part of his own biography. Deirdre said, 'I don't know what you're doing, whatever it is, keep doing it.' He became a great puppeteer, and he was just brilliant. He made all these wonderful, creative, fabulous puppets. Then he became a street performer, working with all of these puppets, and playing piano. He was just so gifted: his puppets are, I think, in a museum. He described working in the theatre, coming in and discovering Stanislavski, as 'I thought I'd died and gone to paradise'!

People also became writers: they discovered their creativity there. They discovered a new medium. And that's really what people felt: this sudden freedom, this creative thing that's in everyone: suddenly discovering oneself, expressing oneself, being motivated to say and do things. It should be so much a part of education.

There was this American girl with us all the time. Her granny was one of the first people who went to the first environment conference, Friends of the Earth. I think it was in Norway and she went as the United Nations representative. She came over and she was part of the theatre. She was wonderful and she did stage management. Her grandmother gave us a car to travel around with the theatre. I directed different things such as community theatre and city pantomime such as *The Prince and the Princess.* Children loved them because they so readily believe!

I also did musicals, and I worked with social groups and organizations, but I was very much involved in education and in arts, and in making arts in education, because again, there was such resistance to that! I remember seeing it at school. We should have the arts: children should have dancing and yet there is such a resistance. That's how you would have everyone discovering their creativity. It might be music or whatever that would bring that creativity into it and then you would discover that also you have an audience...there would be a huge pool of great talents, and a pool of people to appreciate them. There's nobody better than children for *seeing.* And they are completely generous, but they can actually see; they develop their appreciation; they can see what's beautiful. If only everybody was doing music, and dance, and drama...

PRODUCTIONS

Old guard and new guard, what were some of their best and brightest achievements and how did they come about?

Tim McDonnell

Steve: I'm curious. Were you, the class, aware that she wanted to start actually doing full productions?

Tim: Oh yes.

Steve: Did she talk about the choice of material? Did you all have input? Were there roles promised? Had she looked at you in terms of casting, either in parts, or in other things in the production that you could do? I've read nothing about how that came about from the studio.

Tim: Yeah, she very definitely did from the very beginning. And we knew this from, oh after three years, and the studio went on in a functioning, learning capacity, in that kind of process, at least four years before this theatre started. But she very, very definitely wanted a group of actors knowing the same language. She very definitely wanted an ensemble company. The Focus Theatre was to be an ensemble company and the only thing that would stop her from using the young students who are now actors in the company would be a matter of age. If they really needed to be 70, she would look for a really good 70-year-old actor who could fill the part. She wasn't in any way elitist about that kind of thing. But she did not refrain from casting younger actors as older characters in the first production or the second, but by the time we got to the third which was *Evening Without Angels*, there were three plays. And by the time we got to that, we were all of us connected, choosing the productions. We were reading all of the plays, we were then making our positions clear as to why we liked x, y, or z. And she would work very democratically, obviously with her own particular likes and dislikes involved. She would very definitely choose the one that had actually taken the day, as it were. And that's the way the theatre functioned all the time. All of the time, even after I was injured and coming back, she was calling me in New York, every week: you know I was in rehab. Once every week she'd call me to tell me the theatre was there for me, she was there for me, that in time I would be able to get back to being a working actor, which at the time I could hardly understand. You know, it was, inconceivable.

Mary Elizabeth Burke-Kennedy

Most of my work in Focus was as a director and as a writer. I stopped acting, well I stood in for Rebecca when I was twenty-nine and she was playing Agnes in *A Delicate Balance* and I was asked to take over for her: she went back to NY. It was Hell on earth. Do you know that play? Oh, it's superb, but I was far too young for Agnes, barely had time to learn the lines. The first sentence is a page long, it's all subordinate clauses. And then I was playing Deirdre's mother in it. And Ena May was my younger sister. Both of them are older than me. Tim was playing Tobias. Of course he wasn't injured at that stage. I had to die my hair gray. I could have done it now! I was putting all these lines on my face and I was so nervous, and my pores were just opening up and the grease paint was all just disappearing and they were saying to me in the dressing room 'Put more lines on your face, you look ridiculous!' and by the time the last act would come along I would be fighting for my life to remember the lines. That was the last time I acted in Focus. I wonder why...haha...but after that I concentrated on directing and writing. Really the other reason that I concentrated on directing was that once the play had opened I didn't have to be there and I had two small children, so that was it.

Steve: I also heard Deirdre was a singer? I did hear that Focus would have people singing Sunday nights or something. And one night I guess Luke and the other Dubliners were there and singing their usual songs and Deirdre got up and sang a traditional Irish song. And people in the audience started heckling. Because it wasn't, I guess, the rebel songs they wanted and Ronnie Drew started heckling the hecklers in the audience.

Mary Elizabeth: I don't remember that. But we did have Sunday night at Focus where we had improvisations every Sunday night. That was quite an event. You didn't have any regrets when you were in a play, if you made a bags of something, you could sort it out for the next performance. In improvs there was no opportunity to retrieve anything and the actors would be beating themselves up all week if they messed up on a Sunday night. There was no chance of redress. But it was great. Marvellous fun. They were well attended. They built up quite a regular following. Same people would come back every Sunday night.

Steve: Same performers?

Mary Elizabeth: Yes. Tom, even though he wasn't performing in plays was part of the improv company. Frank, Tom, Joan, Declan, Ena, Sabina, myself. Deirdre didn't do it. She managed it. Very seldom participated. She ran the whole thing. But you know, it's funny, it struck me when I said Focus was our family. Sabina is now married to the President of Ireland, and Tom, Johnny, Ena, Joan, Declan, myself, we have a bond that comes from having spent our youth together. It is very much a family bond.

Sabina Coyne Higgins

Steve: What was the favorite play that you did?

Sabina: I loved *Uncle Vanya* and, of course, *Hedda Gabler*. I was so much involved and I see it as the life in the theatre when you are so much an ensemble. *Antigone* was terrific: that was very important at the time. It very much spoke to what was going on at the time. The *Uncle Vanya* was very much Astov, the environmental aspect. Because of doing the improvisations we were very socially conscious, as we were always in the improvisations dealing with social themes. But also with *Antigone* and *A Doll's House*, it was just when the women's movement started, and I remember when we started having people speaking, coming on Friday nights and having discussions after the play. There was a lot of chauvinism at the time. I remember somebody got up at a discussion, saying 'you wouldn't be here if there was any man who wanted to ask you out tonight.' There was such resentment of women's rights and of Nora, about her choosing to go out and find herself.

Steve: It was popular...you were obviously striking a nerve in your audiences.

Sabina: Yeah, it was even before any contraception was available, through the 70s and 80s, before any breakthrough, and not even having information available in shops about any kind of family planning. You know that the state of Ireland Deirdre came over to was very conservative.

Cathal Quinn

Whilst still performing in 'Silence and Darkness' I was asked to audition for Brian McAvera's new play *Francis and Frances*. Having a passing resemblance to Francis Bacon and a proclivity for heightened text, I auditioned with energy, partnered with Tara Breathnach, whom I had met briefly before as I had taught her in a Voice class many years previously. Brian and Joe Devlin immediately sensed chemistry between Tara and me, and we were offered the roles later that day. I had to ask for approval from my wife, having two young daughters, a full-time job teaching and a paper to write for the Beckett Working Group meeting as part of the International Federation of Theatre Research in Osaka, the deadline looming.

Maria, my wife, consented, but I neglected to tell her that it involved being whipped, a striptease down to fishnets, a leopard-skin basque and matching knickers, she only found that out when she came to see it. To the delight of my nephew and my wife's brother, *The Irish Times* decided to publish the picture of Tara and myself clad identically in Penney's finest leopard print in their 'We are curious about...' column, and he still shows strangers a close up of that picture to this day, saying 'Have you met my brother-in- law?' I also – very briefly – became a gay icon, my face plastered on the front page of a gay monthly magazine.

Like Peter Falk in *Colombo* I wore my own (leather) coat, having previously used it to portray the devil in *Tam O'Shanter* and an evil Baron in a tango ballet, and underneath it a suit that I had had hand-made at Sam's tailors in Hong Kong for my wedding day, and had only worn since on our anniversaries; underneath all that: the basque, knickers and fishnets.

Tara had advised me to wear smaller black knickers inside the leopard-skin ones – just in case anything slipped out – and how to put on tights without laddering them (I hadn't worn stockings since playing John Keats twenty years previously); but she had neglected to pass on the wisdom of pulling up one's gusset; if you look closely at the publicity shots you will notice it hanging down embarrassingly low!

The show was a delight to perform, beginning with a fifteen minute monologue which Brian insisted be performed with the houselights up, which was most unnerving as in the Focus you see every single member of the audience! When Peter O'Toole performed *Jeffrey Bernard is Unwell* in London's West End he insisted that when he addressed the audience the lights were so strong that he could see no-one...no such leeway with our director.

Indeed I went into the audience on at least three occasions, to strip (depositing my expensive shirt over the head of the nearest unfortunate male audience member), to fall down into them (and then be helped up and proceed to sit on the kind person's lap) and to go in search of a fellow artist in the house; all great fun for me and to the rest of the audience, all apart from the poor man who had to wear my sweaty shirt, bear my weight or have his ego ruffled .

Vocally I filled the space and far more with this flamboyant character and ladled colour and a size to the vocal performance that was a direct antithesis to the Beckett, and a foil to Tara's thankfully slightly more understated feminine side of the same character.

Francis and Frances had a two week run in May and June 2011. Brilliantly designed on a shoestring budget, the fractured mirrors on every wall echoed one of the London clubs that Bacon would frequent and they showed distortions of the actors rather like some of Bacon's malformations, and the space looked twice its actual size.

After opening night Tom Hickey knocked on the dressing room door and told us it was 'like Focus in the old days', no more fitting tribute to all the collaborative powers of director, designer, lighting designer, stage manager, author and actors working so hard to bring a heightened text fully to life. On the last night we were given a standing ovation, the author/director's intentions fully realized as all had fully committed themselves.

MEMORIES OF DEIRDRE

[This was without doubt the richest and most fruitful of all the topics I covered with my interviewees. All had memories, some short and piquant, such as Ena May's image of Deirdre dancing on her tiny feet, and some, such as Tim McDonnell's memories, are fairly involved. But the love that poured forth from each of them felt genuine and was remarkable, eleven years after her death. Here, perhaps more than any other of the sections, I wish I could have just printed a transcript instead of excerpting from their stories. Without any doubt Deirdre O'Connell emerges as an extraordinary figure, and not just in the Dublin theatre scene.]

Mary Moynihan

Steve: How much was Deirdre's background an intellectual attitude?

Mary: It's probably a combination, but definitely it was. I rarely say people are geniuses, I wouldn't say that too easily, but I do think that Deirdre had a unique gift of understanding the human condition and understanding human relationships. That made her unique as a teacher. How to get to the heart. I will tell you that I did ask her once if she preferred to be an actor rather than a director or a teacher, but she was equally gifted in all three which is an unusual combination. Usually you have a great actor, who may not be as good at passing on the knowledge, but Deirdre was excellent at passing on the knowledge. She had a very keen gift to be able to spot what an actor needed and to develop the actor without making them feel they did something wrong, which I think is a unique gift as a director and teacher. So that is something she had in herself. That combined with her knowledge of Stanislavski. You know, I can't remember Deirdre's academics. I know she trained with various teachers. But she certainly had an understanding which I think is what Stanislavski was talking about anyway. It gets back to that idea of it being a system as opposed to a set of exercises that you slavishly follow; it's more organic.

Steve: Did Deirdre choose the play, the season?

Mary: Well there was a very strong artistic policy at Focus. And every play had to fit in to that. She was very, very, conscientious about that. And once it fitted into that, then it was a combination of plays which she would bring forward and which people would bring to her. She was very open to ideas so people would come to her. She would read them, if she liked them. If it fitted, those were chosen. To be fair, there would be a committee decision. She was open to listening to people and people would always bring suggestions. But like any artistic director I suppose you are the one who gets the final say.

Sabina Coyne Higgins

Steve: What was Deirdre like as a director?

Sabina: When she sat in the theatre she was just the same as when she was being a teacher. She was never cross. She really taught us all to love. Every one changed who went there. There was nobody who went there for whom this wasn't an enormous element in their lives. Everyone recognized that and we were all part of the family as well. We knew what was important. That was her quality. No sentimentality; no preaching. She never seemed to open her mouth. Then it would come to the criticism, and it was all revelatory to the people then discovering it, and she would be saying 'yes, that was right, you did that right' or 'Maybe the first was the one to go with'. That kind of directing would be the gentlest directing.

She never in her life raised her voice, or said anything that wasn't good. She never used the word 'bad'. She was so extraordinarily gentle in her treatment of every human being. She would just not say anything hurtful to anyone, ever. Everyone would go on stage. They would just be like us, even people doing ordinary exercises. We were always in the audience, even during a class, just giving them all our attention and seeing how wonderful they were as human beings. That was how she would treat everybody: every exercise, every production, everything.

She was, for me, a Christian, someone Christ-like. Inside, it was the family you saw the great love for. But this was for everyone: the beggar in the streets would be given whatever was necessary. It was just amazing; she was just quite a genius. Everyone that comes here now feels her presence around still, because she was so influential. Some became directors: Mary Elizabeth set up her own theatre, after doing it there, and wrote a lot. People brought her spirit into education. A lot of the artists when they taught class, as at the Project Theatre, they came in with us early on as well.

Tim McDonnell

Steve: Reading this material on Focus and your association with it really struck me as pretty remarkable. Was *Zoo Story* your idea?

Tim: I said it to Deirdre. She would visit me once a week when I was back in the apartment I'm in now. I was married then, and my ex-wife Elizabeth was wonderful encouragement because I was reading plays, but I was going around thinking 'well maybe I could be a macrobiotic counsellor, or maybe I could get into acupuncture and help heal people.' And Elizabeth came in one day and she said, and you know she wasn't a woman to swear, but she said 'For fuck's sake, would you stop imagining all these nonsensical things. You're an actor. You were born an actor. Get back to being an actor'. Bingo. And it was Elizabeth that nailed me down, like that. Got me to take down the *Zoo Story*. I read it within three quarters of an hour. I called Deirdre up, she said, 'Yes Tim, is there something that you want to do?' and I said, Yes, there is something that I very definitely want to do. I want to play Jerry in the wheelchair. She said 'I'll call you back in an hour'. She did. She said 'Tim, ten legs or no legs, you were born to play this part' and I said, 'don't you think that the wheelchair, without even being mentioned, would actually heighten the sense of alienation, the sense of loss. The bereftness of the man. The inability to relate?' I said, 'Don't you think that?' 'She said absolutely! When do we start?' I said, 'As soon as possible.' And we started the following Monday.

Now, you must remember this was 1985-86. I just want to make this point because it wouldn't be understood unless I made the point. Out of every hundred people who are injured and end up in a wheelchair with a spinal cord injury, only four percent of them ever get back to work. Sometimes five in the United States. The country that has the most is Switzerland, because they create jobs especially for people who become disabled. That's what makes them have that kind of high level. But the thing is, Deirdre didn't even think of the wheelchair as an obstacle. It was always going to be another way of manifesting one's imaginative expression.

She'd get annoyed with me at times about this. I often think it was that kind of nuts and bolts, native New York thing that made her absolutely oblivious to the fact that a wheelchair could be an impediment. When in point of fact she was seeing it in the opposite direction. And it could be something that could enlighten and heighten the reality of what one was doing in this particular piece of work. So, I mean, that was exceptional. I think I was the first professional working actor who became injured in New York, while living there, trying to work as an actor, who was employed again as a professional actor, while working from the wheelchair. Now, that's not only true of Dublin, and this happened out of this small 70 seat theatre. I don't think, before me, anybody in the NY theatre who was able-bodied, and who had become disabled, and got back to working again in the professional theatre, ultimately ended up receiving an Obie Award for outstanding achievement in the NY theatre! Now, that's why I wanted her there so much in NY with me, because I knew we had a good thing going. I just knew it was the bee's knees and the cat's meow.

Steve: There is such a strong, symbiotic relationship...

Tim: Absolutely. I wanted her to be there. And I remember the announcement of the presentation was made by a wonderful New York Yiddish actor called Fyvush Finkel. He called out my name after giving a speech about the poignancy. And I'm kind of still dazed, because I don't quite believe it. My publicist and her colleague were there, and Fyvush Finkel was sitting on my right, and Fyvush said, 'Excuse me while I go up and make this speech for the next recipient.' I said, Go ahead', and up he goes, and he mentions all I've said, and suddenly a guy comes from behind, puts my breaks off, and ZOOM, wheels me up, totally wheelchair accessible, right all the way up to the stage...Whereas when I received the award in Dublin for best actor for *Diary of a Madman*, I couldn't get up on the stage, I had to make my acceptance speech on the ground, with a microphone in front of me, and Deirdre was five rows back, weeping her heart out. Not because of me being on the floor, but because I was receiving it. That's why I knew if we hit the day in New York it would be such a joy for her. And it would expand Focus as an entity. And what Focus had done in the role of disability. So, anyway, the terrible, sad irony of getting the award was that it was handed to me by Christopher Reeve, and he made the speech in relation to giving it to me, and we chatted afterwards, after the whole gig was over, as it were. We chatted for about a half an hour, and he was one of the most delightful, charming, humble kinds of human beings you could talk to. And he was asking me how it was possible to get back on stage after all of this. And dear Jesus, eight years later he can't even move a finger. There is something very strange in all of that. So to get back to your original question, about a year and a half before we started doing scenes, and about six months later, we were doing plays.

One of the things I want to say about Deirdre as an educator is that I mentioned my background, and although I had been brought to art galleries as a kid by my grandfather, and eventually my uncle, the first book I got on art ever, the first book I was ever given, was a book on Modigliani and the first piece of classical music I was given was Sibelius's *Symphony number 1* with the Bournemouth Symphony Orchestra. And that was given to me by Deirdre, who told me when she gave it to me, 'Enjoy Elvis and The Beatles, enjoy all the Rock 'N Roll, relish it all, but stretch your imagination into other areas of music.' And I'll tell you, that has saved my life, Steve, I swear to God, between Sibelius, Bruckner, Shostakovich, those three people in particular, and there's many Americans as well. But those three in particular, in moments of despair, have come and have actually given me salvation. And that is all due to the fact that this woman wanted to stretch my imagination, and she also loved me as a person and as a student, she wanted to see me grow. That's very important. Very, very important. True lady. But with great heart and meaningfulness.

Steve: Would you talk more about Deirdre as director?

Tim: I don't know how, we had gone into character studies, we had gone into all that work on scenes, done many plays there, and the wonderful thing about Deirdre was that sometimes she would cast. And certainly you wouldn't be old enough for the part, but she knew that with a little make-up, which was still, you know, something that people did in the theatre, you could make the leap. She cast me in *A Delicate Balance* playing Tobias. I couldn't believe it. Jesus. She said, 'You'll be all right.' So I went down and had my hair dyed. I adored that play, more than all the plays that I did in Focus, apart from *Diary of a Madman*.

In the bed, in *Diary of a Madman*, you are using each part of the stage, as if different characters came in to either haunt or help or berate. And behind the bed, which only occurs twice – Deirdre was a believer in things like that – he thinks he hears something behind him, and there's nobody there at all. It's just his mind beginning to collapse, and I remember her saying that during rehearsals, because she did rehearse that for seven months. Three days, every three days. We were talking one day: we'd broken the play down into beats and units and what have you. We wanted to make sure it had dramatic shape, that it wasn't just a narrative story; that it had to have a dramatic narrative shape. I said to her, I'm not sure about the kind of heightened level he's at in the beginning of the play. On the other hand, it's paramount to our understanding, although it might seem a little heightened and theatrical, it actually is paramount in importance to the fact that this man lives a life, totally and utterly without any sort of real carnal, sensual experience. At all. In fact the only thing he experiences in work is being mocked. Somebody said one time, no wonder somebody goes mad when you're living in a mad society. I remember us saying, we agreed on this together, and I said the more possessed he becomes (I never use the word mad, interestingly), the more possessed he becomes by the spirit of this woman, the more the delusion actually begins to make him conversationally more human, because in his mind it's a real experience, but still retaining the dramatic transition points for the heightening and development of the theatrical experience, which couldn't be forgotten.

We weren't doing a kind of whisper-in-your-ear sort of thing: it had to be understood, and she said, 'Yes I agree with that, and I wouldn't worry, it's not too heightened at the moment, and as we go along in it, [we will find] that point of transition, particularly when he becomes the king of Spain. That makes him free in his own mind and spirit to do anything. He's capable of doing anything, being anything. He's got it all.' It's the only time actually that Deirdre has ever appeared on film, with the exception of, *Hold the Passion*. But the only time she had been on film as an actor, and I twisted her arm. She is the one who comes in and kisses him and folds him up in a straight-jacket. I said, 'You have got to play her.' She said she was very nervous. And I said, 'Look , if you don't appear in this with me ..., I'm your ex pupil. I'm also a colleague and a fellow actor, and I've also been your director in several plays, so please do me the favour, otherwise I'll divorce you. I want you to be in this film.' She said to let her think about it. Movies weren't in her soul, although she loved movies. There is no doubt about it. She said, 'I'll do it for you.' I thanked and gave her a big hug. And she held me like that after [putting me in] the jacket, and the director kept saying to her, 'It's too long, Deirdre, it's only supposed to be 10 seconds at the most.' So then he said, 'Oh don't worry, I'll cut it out later in the editing room.' So she held me for about 15 seconds in the bed, and she was weeping like a child, and kissed me on the eyes, it was a beautiful moment. So, afterwards she said to me at a particular party, or whatever it was, 'I'm so glad I did that.' I said, 'You know something, so am I.'

Mary Elizabeth Burke-Kennedy

Declan took to it more easily than I did, in a way. But he never wanted to be an actor. His interest was always in direction. But he figured that we were twenty years old and wanted to find out about everything. As what Deirdre was teaching became clear to us, and as we began to understand what the value was of what she was saying, it just opened up incredible creativity. Much, much more so than anything we were learning in University, which was just nothing in comparison. It was by far the most enriching education, apart from some of the teachers I would have had in my secondary school. Certainly, no teachers in the university compared to Deirdre, in terms of her insights and her vocabulary and her way of elucidating things and drawing us out. This was the magic, you see, in terms of what we were doing. That she was giving us this opportunity. At University, we were reading Wordsworth, and somebody was telling us about Wordsworth. And our own creativity was not involved in any measure.

Steve: In terms of casting, what was the process? Did you talk to her, consult with her about roles you wanted to be considered for? Did you audition?

Mary Elizabeth: Not in those early days, no. I know when we were considering doing *A Doll's House*, Declan said 'I think Mary Eliz should play Nora' and then she said 'ok'. And Tom [Hickey] in *Uncle Vanya* was far too young. And he was superb.

I have to say to you that at one stage, after I did *Alice in Wonderland*, I went to the festival of Avignon. The Department of Foreign Affairs had a cultural wing, and they had decided to send some people out to attend. This was 1980...and they asked Deirdre to go and she wouldn't. She hated travelling and she didn't want to be far away from Pembroke Place. She was in her nest and didn't want to leave it. And she really didn't speak French and had no wish to go to see plays in French. So I was dispatched instead, and I stayed overnight in Paris with a friend called Mary Wilson who had also trained in Focus. While there I went to see a production, *The Simple Heart* by Flaubert, about a servant lady. It completely blew my mind the way they did it, because they had three different people playing her, for a start. They narrated the story bang out through the fourth wall. It was completely abstract. She would come down out of the flies and she would lie in it and disappear. It was wonderful. The first thing I saw in Avignon was Peter Brook's production of *Conference of the Birds* and it completely changed my way of looking at theatre. Completely. And while I didn't abandon Stanislavski by any means as a method of approaching a text or helping actors, I certainly was less interested from then on in naturalistic theatre. So, you know, it was subsequently that I started doing the *Legends* and *Currigh the Shape Shifter*, *Women in Arms*, those sorts of plays, and I didn't do them in a naturalistic way. The encounters between the characters were presented in all their psychological complexity. But the audience was always conscious they were watching a play. So that was the way that I was thinking, and so it really had diverged from where Deirdre was going, not that we were at loggerheads or anything. It was just becoming more difficult. Separation by 1984.

Steve: I personally have never found Stanislavski really at odds with a less naturalistic theatre. It always struck me that every actor has to come in, rooted in a truth that allows them to behave...creating a world. All the tools are still in place. But they are also in a theatre...

Mary Elizabeth: The other thing that I found liberating about Peter Brook's work was that you could take on bigger stories. I did adaptations of *The Mayor of Casterbridge* [1999] and *Emma* [1995]: you can cover distances in time and space that you can't if you are trying to do it in a naturalistic sort of way. Television does that better. I found that was very influential in terms of my thinking. From what I could discover about Deirdre, I wasn't involved in her class or anything over the final years, but it seems she became extremely fixed in her attitude towards Stanislavski and wasn't prepared to undertake any other theoretician, like Robert Lewis. Pure Stanislavski. I think she became very dogmatic and dictatorial about how Stanislavski should be presented as she got older, but I don't know. The last time I saw her acting was in *The House of Bernarda Alba*.

Steve: The last things I saw you directing at Focus are the Tennessee Williams one-acts. Just moving on into the next stage or...? I'm not trying to dig for gossip, just curious. You were there from 1968-84, so I'm just curious...

Mary Elizabeth: Undoubtedly Deirdre had genius in her. And a very powerful charisma. But at that stage I think I wanted to go elsewhere. I mean, the thing is that I was offered work elsewhere and I thought, yeah, why not? And I should also add that by 1984 there was a limited amount of funds and I felt, I think we both felt, that there were only so many plays that could be done in any one year. The answer for somebody like me, headstrong, running off in a different direction, was: let me go. And let Deirdre do what she wanted to do with the money that was there.

Steve: Was 1984 the year Luke died?

Mary Elizabeth: He died in 1985 and that was a terrible blow.

Steve: I'm sure it was. The marriage and their separation, a blow. Although my understanding is that they still professed a profound love or friendship.

Mary Elizabeth: They were the love of each other's lives. No doubt about that. And then he died.

Ena May

My favourite memory? At a party she always swished up her skirt and danced around on her size 3 feet. So full of life! Good times together and laughs. She was very charismatic.

She enjoyed other people's success, and wasn't threatened by other people's talent. I had written some stories, *A Close Shave with the Devil* and she encouraged me to do a one-woman show with three of the stories.

Geraldine O'Connell Cusack

Steve: Was Focus ever thought of as openly political? The choice of plays to be performed there seems not.

Geraldine: Deirdre wasn't political with a big 'p'. The plays always had to do with the human condition, yes, but the human is political. For Deirdre, she went with the artistic statement which was the human condition.

Elizabeth Moynihan

Steve: What are some of the other memories, of working with Deirdre before...

Elizabeth: Well, when she asked me to produce a season of new Irish writing, lunchtime plays, she allowed me to take that over. So, I started reading scripts, and she handed me 50 scripts and said 'pick three...or ten.' So I'd pick 10 and then we whittled it down to three or four and that was so exciting for me, you know. It was a huge opportunity to see how young, emerging playwrights write, and to help to choose the ones that we felt had talent to go on further and be developed by not only us but other theatres.

Steve: Were scripts chosen on the basis of what Focus and the company could bring to them? Specific roles called for...?

Elizabeth: Yes, and that was how she chose every play that went on there. That was the defining thing about each play. That's why I think she did so many American classics like Miller, Williams, Odets, Albee. You know the Theatre of the Absurd, she was really interested in that.

Steve: I was going to ask about the sort of Anti-naturalistic theatre that a lot of people would automatically think could be applied to...

Elizabeth: Chekhov is the great Stanislavski exponent, if you like, and vice-versa, and you see it got its name as a theatre of realism, and it was Turgenev who really spearheaded it, and yet we see it as very classical, as having rigid pieces. But now, to modern audiences, it worked brilliantly, using the system, which eventually evolved into the Method with Strasberg, or probably before that. Uta Hagen, sort of brought it to America.

Steve: Basically all involved in the Group Theatre: Strasberg, Adler, Meisner, and several others.

Elizabeth: But, it pains me to say this, Deirdre's method is not the method they developed in America. It was very much 'I teach the Stanislavski system as it was originally developed by Stanislavski in Russia'.

Steve: I picked up on that, she made a distinction between the training she received in NY and her understanding of Stanislavski. I picked up on commentary, of actors working in the method...

Elizabeth: She didn't want it to be a cult either. Some people at Focus theatre tend to give it a cult status; that's not interesting or useful. It's just a tool. It's not the Holy Grail. Stanislavski would have been the first person to say 'if the exercise doesn't work, throw it out.' Those exercises we know today evolved over time through actors using them, working them, owning, redefining them. It's not the bible. Not the word of God's, it's...taught and learnt.

Steve: I don't think there is an acting teacher in the world who can make a talented actor. But an acting teacher can help a talented actor master techniques.

Elizabeth: Agreed. You can't give someone talent. I'm never going to paint as brilliantly as Kandinksy because I just don't have that gift. And no teacher in the world is going to help me do that.

Steve: Although interestingly, all great actors going back to the Greeks, what they are striving for is emotional truth and however they can find it.

Elizabeth: Yeah, but only some people are given the gift of being able to access that effortlessly, organically effortlessly, and I guess that's the trick. But that organic talent has to be there.

Steve: When you began writing plays, was this still when Deirdre was alive, or after?

Elizabeth: Just around that time, she was actually still alive when I came up with the idea. I'm trying to get the chronological order. Yeah, she was still alive. It happened on the day of 9/11, I was on tour with a show in Tipperary. It was called *Chastitute* by John B. Keane. And we were standing in our costumes in the dressing room. I've told this anecdote many times, because it's true. We didn't know whether we were going to go home that night or not, because you know how so many of the Irish are overly empathetic with the Americans; with everything that goes on in America, because there were so many of us emigrating now, and...there are more Irish in America than there are in Ireland, so yeah, when 9/11 happened, we all went into mourning. That day, I'll never forget it. It was the most horrific. We saw the second plane hit the tower live on television at lunchtime. You know, actors are hanging around during the day. When you're in a small town like Tipperary there's not a lot to do you know. You spend lots of time in the hotel rooms, anyway. All of us were traumatized. One of the actors in the cast: her son was in NY running a bar. Couldn't get him on the phone: we were all really scared. And a friend of mine was reporting live for the radio from NY, so I was listening to all the radio reports. And, we're sitting there...we are waiting for the producers to tell us whether we are going on or not; whether there's going to be an audience. And I start telling an anecdote about my childhood, as you do. I was brought up in a pub, and anyway one of the actresses said 'that could be a play' and I said 'well I'm not a playwright.' And she said, 'you know what Elizabeth, you should just write up the monologues, the inner monologue.' She's Stanislavski-trained. She was a Focus Studio member as well. 'Write the inner monologue of each character. We'll workshop it from the day. I'll direct the workshop.' And true to her word she did. And that play went on to be a two-part radio play which won a best radio award.

Steve: I have heard from some people that towards the end of Deirdre's life, there was diminished work, or a deterioration in her skills and so forth. That must have been gruelling and heart-breaking...

Elizabeth: Well, when someone's unwell, it can be very divisive. Deirdre was the boss. Deirdre was the artistic director. She was our teacher. She was our mentor. We worshipped her. She would be embarrassed if she's listening now; she would be so annoyed at me saying that. But we worshipped her. It was effortless on our part to feel that. I mean my mother was jealous of her, because she was so good to us. She was so caring, she was involved in our personal lives, advising us, listening to our tales of woe. So to answer your question, because you have a person like that, we don't want her to be vulnerable to illness. We don't want her sad. Or sick. And we did everything we could to help her.

But Deirdre was a very single-minded person, and when someone feels that they want to go in a certain direction, you can't interfere with that. And she was still very vibrant right up until the last, although impaired by her illness. You know, her sight wasn't great. But she still had a razor sharp intellect. She still performed. I was in *House of Bernarda Alba* with her and I knew: I felt in my heart that that was going to be her last performance. She was very frail. She went over her script, it was the most heavily marked script. And I actually work exactly the same way: every beat is marked. She would use several different highlighter pens. She would sit in the corner every night and study her script. And you would get notes at the end of the performance. During *Bernarda Alba*, she called me aside and said 'Elizabeth, never tread on my moment'. And I was, 'when did I...?' 'You don't cry until Bernarda Alba cries. Bernarda Alba cries first then you cry'. And she's right: it's technique, it wasn't ego. It's actually technique. It's about craft as you said earlier. You know, it's boom, boom, boom boom, like an orchestra, a piece of music, it's not just bleh.

Steve: In her role as boss, was she able to be on good terms, friendly, one of the guys, or did she need to maintain a distance so her authority would remain intact?

Elizabeth: You know what? Her aura was such that she wouldn't have to try and assert her authority. I sound like I'm mythologizing the woman, but I'm not the only person who's going to say this stuff about her. You're gonna have this from lots of other people you speak to. It's just one of those rare things. She invoked a sense of respect, in all of us. And she was a natural loner, but she was a very loving aunt to her nieces. And a very loving family member, devoted to her family. She loved them very much, and was devoted to each one of us in turn, but at the same time, she maintained her privacy. I don't know how she managed to do all that but she did. She could be really motherly, like she was always telling me to cover up my chest, because I have a perpetual cough, and she used to get really worried about that. And she was always wanting me to have scarves...she was very maternal. She was making sure that you ate, although she never ate anything herself except miso soup, like it was some sort of elixir, you know. A complete meal in a cup.

Steve: So when she died, it was not unexpected?

Elizabeth: No, she had been ill for some time. And it was no less of a shock, but it wasn't unexpected.

THE TRANSITION FROM DEIRDRE TO JOE

[After founding, running and developing her vision of theatre for thirty-eight years, Deirdre passed away in 2001. It wasn't sudden, her health had been declining. Yet it was still a shock as her company had to search their souls and their resources and determine what the next step was to be – and even if there would be a next step.]

Elizabeth Moynihan

Steve: When that happened, was there a sense of 'what happens now?'

Elizabeth: Yep there was that. And there were a lot of people who rushed into the vacuum to fill the vacuum; I mean none of us could. It's not possible. A person like that comes along once in a hundred years. There are very few great artistic revolutionaries in my lifetime. And she was one of those, and yeah it was very difficult, but I was like a little Rottweiler. I thought 'I'm damned if this theatre is going to close. No, we have to mind her legacy. We have to move forward. We have to do something. I went in, in a very concerted way, trying to bring people together, and at the same time I didn't want to be or feel like I was a successor, even though I was very close to her and had been helping to run the theatre along with a couple of other people. But there was a coterie of people around her so, it was a very, very difficult and traumatic time after she died. I went back on the board and I also became our co-acting artistic director, and that was a very traumatic and tricky time for me, and the worst 12 months I've had in a long time. You know it was just not comfortable. You know, when somebody like Deirdre passes on, people are jostling to take over, and we all felt that none of us were qualified. A few really wanted to do the job, but I always felt that it was best to get somebody new in. And so I said to Kevin O'Brien, who was the chairman at the time, that I was willing to throw my hat into the ring and be there for the duration until we did the hand over to somebody new, but I was not interested nor was I qualified, as I said, to do the job. So, Paul and I held the rings.

Steve: Did you interview potential Artistic Directors, did you find Joe?

Elizabeth: I had nothing to do with it. They put out a public notice to that effect. They advertised for a new Artistic Director and the timing was very good, so we were able to attract a strong group of people to pitch for the job, not to audition, but to interview for the job. And yeah, they chose Joe.

Joe Devlin

Tim McDonnell told me that the word on the grapevine in the 1970s was that Tomás Mac Anna, the then Artistic Director of the Abbey, was rumoured to have said that 'the Focus Theatre was the biggest threat to the Abbey'.

The Focus had had 39 years of creativity before Deirdre passed over. She had pretty much a 30 year career of brilliance, working with an artistic pool of people like Mary Elizabeth Burke-Kennedy who was doing really cutting edge work with mythology and mask work, having first trained in Stanislavski at the Studio. Deirdre's tenure was never properly funded.

When I came in, Tim and I agreed that in order to get the Focus to where it had been artistically, we had to re-audition people. There were a lot of people around the theatre. Many of them we felt were not able to meet international standards of practice. They had to leave if they did not measure up. Deirdre did that in the early days. If people weren't moving forward she would quietly say, 'I don't think this is for you.' I think in her last days she wasn't able to apply that, in the same way that she had done as a younger woman. That takes a lot of energy to do. It's tough to do that. So Tim and I agreed that we had to do this and we created a new pool. We had to let a lot of people go. It was hard. But it's what it's about...work. And within 12 months, we got it back up again. We were creating work with really small budgets. And in my naivety I thought, I'll go get funded now! No, if anything, more doors were slammed, because, again, we were delivering very high-quality work on a budget of peanuts. So I just had to get on with it. When it became apparent that we could not be stopped, I was then contacted by certain people who said that they would help us with the funding if they were allowed to tell me who I could cast in a play, who I could work with; and if they could come into my rehearsal room and have an input into working with the new writers. The same people had already gone into other people's rehearsal rooms, and from what I was told from eye witnesses they had only created problems. It was really inappropriate. So I just didn't go there. I pretended that I didn't hear what was on offer and just moved on. I thought things would be ok but even more doors were slammed in my face. Make your own assessment of that as you will. That was what was going on in the 2000s. No amount of money is worth compromising your freedom of creativity for. That is the reason why we are artists. We would have liked to have been properly funded but the compromise would have been to defeat the purpose of our work.

So we just got on with it. To dwell on it was a waste of time and energy. We knew what we were doing. We had been successfully doing it for 40 odd years and didn't need interference. And you have to trust that the artist knows what he is doing. Just because you have administrative or P.R. experience and have seen a few shows, doesn't mean you know more than the artist. I understand now why, when I first started working at Focus, I was encouraged by a close advisor just to 'do your own thing and focus on the work'. In the end that is really what you should do as an artist, and ignore everything else.

Steve: You were talking [earlier] about clearing the debts when you took over Focus. Getting back to what it was. Do you see that now...or try to take Focus to follow your vision, not necessarily Deirdre's vision?

Joe: I basically worked within the parameters of Deirdre O'Connell's template for the first two or three years. Put simply, I had to demonstrate that I could do what Deirdre had set out. I was bringing to the table stronger production values and a uniformity of cast. This is what Tim [McDonnell] and other associated people had told me after my first big show. I was also told that Deirdre would sometimes have taken a play and put novices on stage to give them work experience. I came from a different point of view where you don't do that, because it actually weakens a production. But that's about her generosity. Sometimes you can get away with that in a small venue, but that depends on the context of the production, as to whether it is a student production or a professional actors' production. Once, I did allow that to happen which resulted in an uneven production. Never again. I also have a visual arts background, so I pushed the visual arts design aspects of set, lighting, and staging. I had to prove myself within the established parameters because I was being scrutinized, which is absolutely appropriate. I knew that my first show wouldn't have been received well if I did something too radical, as there was a tradition of style in the theatre. My own hunger for the creative process won't stay still, in one genre.

And then I have to challenge myself, too. Once I have nailed something I have to do other things. Opening up the venue to the Fringe Festival was a new avenue as it allowed the integration of the theatre into the theatre community, and then showcased other ways of presenting and doing things. And that then gave me access to do unusual work – translations of Eastern European work and integrating Viewpointing, from Anne Bogart, with Stanislavski-based performance. I was working with choreography at that point. I got away with it during the Fringe, but when the experimentation started to be demonstrated in the designs for other higher profile productions it was very controversial because we were teaching naturalism, and teaching working with domestic objects to reveal something about the inner experience. When we started maybe pushing things to a more abstract design, people fell out with me saying, 'that's not what we teach!' I was also getting poison-pen letters. It is hard to believe that now. Thankfully that is all behind us.

There is a very important point to be made about our identity as an organization. Are we a theatre or are we a school? We are a theatre first. We need to start separating out the teaching from the artistic goals, in terms of live, public performance. We can do classic naturalism in our sleep but we also have to push the envelope, to commit our own creative process and imagination into lots of different areas, as with the Moscow Art Theatre. They were doing very experimental design work and very avant-garde movement-based work. It gave me enormous confidence when I came back from Russia. Our work should be more eclectic. But the classic Stanislavski training which I teach shouldn't stop. That's the primary colours of a performance. We can do the classic work from time to time but it shouldn't be the only work that we do, otherwise you stop being relevant and you become a museum theatre. I mean there is also an alternative argument which Tim will probably make, as he is very much about the classic, dramatic action of drama, which I love too, but I also like other things.

If you consider Aristotelian *Poetics*, there are certain, eternal structures that do work. Some plays are made in a specific way, because certain structures work. Arnold Fanning's debut play *Those Powerful Machines* was so accomplished that we went with a more experimental second full-length from him. In this production the writer was deliberately breaking with form. He had already proved himself as a writer for the stage with his previous full-length play, so we supported the experimental nature of his next piece of work. However, once we had it on the floor and in the space, it did not fully work. There was just too much going on for actors to have clear through-lines, and too busy stylistically for audiences to fully connect with. I still stand by it as a worthwhile creative experience and as an experimental piece of work. You can take those risks within the context of a small arthouse production. It is vitally important to create a platform for writers to do that from to time. With certain dramatic shapes, there's also poetics in terms of drama; in terms of counter-pointing ideas from a central idea. All of those are eternal structures which do work, which I do accept, but it's also good to try other things. And so Ibsen, Chekhov, Strindberg, Miller, and Williams, all these great master playwrights, do adhere to doing what is Aristotelian *Poetics* in dramatic form – the general shape of tragedy, moving towards a point of drama on a revelation – what we call dramatic action. Plays that contain dramatic action would be the central work of the Focus. Our improvisational training is anchored in that dramatic structure and helps open up the actor's facility when it's applied over a three year period. Then you imaginatively work with a location, props, period costume, etc. That's a late 19th century/20th century model for most drama. It helps us all to reveal and reflect our vulnerability and humanity back to ourselves. Dramatic action does have an eternal quality because it deals with the emotional centre. This is the central point of classical Greek theatre. If performed well, it is timeless. The big question that we will always ask ourselves is, how can we create new forms and still keep what is the most important aspect of what we do – the emotional centre. That is, the area that crosses language, class, and cultures, and is the heart of live theatre. The wonderful thing about the creative process is that it will be a continual one that needs to move forward, but in dialogue with what has already been achieved. So, the vision brought to Ireland 50 years ago by Deirdre does inform what we do now, but it has manifested itself in different genres and styles and will continue to grow and develop. An ensemble company versed in a broad multi-disciplined vocabulary which encapsulates the emotional and imaginative creative centre will be at the heart of the work as we evolve over the next 50 years.

THE JOE DEVLIN YEARS

[So, things change. New administration comes in, makes some sweeping changes, and finds itself negotiating the break with the past along with its veneration: a very tricky manoeuvre. I turned to someone who has worked with both administrations.]

Elizabeth Moynihan

Steve: So, Focus in the Joe years...obviously he is not Deirdre. How do you feel that the theatre has changed artistically? He's been there ten years.

Elizabeth: He's doing something right.

Steve: Has it become more of a writer's theatre? There is a whole core of new writers he is bringing in.

Elizabeth: Joe had that skill already: he was already working with emerging writers and had debuted writers in Northern Ireland, so he was already bringing that skill to Focus. He also had a background in European theatre. He'd been to Romania; he was a very, rounded theatre practitioner. He'd studied Viewpoints, so he was interested, which is what I love. He opened the doors and let the light in. It wasn't just about the Stanislavski system. Of course that's the core of our teaching and that's the foundation of the Focus theatre. We are a Stanislavski studio theatre. But at the same time he allowed the students to become interested in other disciplines which I thought was fantastic. He set up workshops with the commedia [dell'arte] theatre. And they came over and it was the real deal! A commedia company teaching us mask work. They had an opera singer come in and do vocal stuff with us, teaching us all to sing, and it was fantastic. We also had Mishe Mokeev, a professor at Moscow Art Theatre, to come and do a week-long workshop with us. So we had young energetic people coming in and that's new blood and it's exciting. And it's how it has to be, it's what makes the theatre continue to have a fresh approach. The roots. Keeping our feet firmly in the roots of our discipline.

Steve: How did the old guard react to Joe? Was there a tension? Some who weren't ready?

Elizabeth: There was a suspicion, you know. The new guard always brings about some dissent, that's the way it is. People are naturally fearful of change, and Focus and Deirdre's legacy became this very distilled, precious thing after her death.

Steve: What do people feel?

Elizabeth: If we could use the metaphor of our country. You know, the irony of it all was that the man from the Six Counties came down and opened the doors of Focus to a wider theatrical discipline, and brought, in addition, new young actors, and revived a studio, and really he was focusing on building a talent base. To nurture talent.

Steve: Have some of those divisions abated, or have some people stormed off and said...?

Elizabeth: Well you know, Joe opened his arms. Went, 'I'm here. I'm here to learn. I want to know more. I mean I have certain disciplines that I'm bringing to the table, that's why I got the job, and I want to learn,' and he threw himself whole-heartedly into the system. And he and Tim McDonnell even went on holiday together, and talked the system the entire time. And Joe was doing everything in his power to be the best he could possibly be, and to make the theatre a very serious contender in a wider theatrical community, in the country, not just in Dublin. We weren't taking our place in a wider theatrical sense in Dublin. He was interested in cross-border work, working with theatres up there, making ties with Russia again, reviving those ties. Ties with New York. He had a huge task on his hands.

Steve: Indeed. Let me ask you, was it devastating to lose Pembroke Place?

Elizabeth: Absolutely devastating. I don't have any children and for me, it was my artistic home. It was like my home had been taken away from me. Deirdre was my artistic mother. It was my family, it was. I mean her family referred to it as Focus family and I don't know if people are going to get this, it's so hard to articulate it, but my husband passed away seventeen years ago and the last phone call I had with him was on the pay phone in that building. I lost my wedding ring in that building. I lost my mother's eternity ring in that building. I lost a Mexican crucifix that my husband gave me in that building. My plays have been done on that stage. I played Catherine in *Suddenly Last Summer* on that stage. I debuted writers on that stage. I had fights, I've worked with lovers on that stage. Your heart and soul is in the paint of those walls. The director that became a really dear friend of mine was dying of cancer as she was directing *The House of Bernarda Alba*. She gave us notes from her hospital bed. There are memories in the walls, in the carpet, in the seating. It's more than a building. And yet, it's just a building. You know?

And that's what we had to come back to (the people) but because Deirdre and her husband Luke Kelly built that between them and her friends, it becomes more than a building. President Michael D. Higgins, our President, and former patron of Focus Theatre, spoke on the last night of Focus theatre: he stood on the little stage there and that was an extraordinary experience for us all. Although we had shaken hands and had had drinks with Michael D. Higgins on that stage before, now he was the President, and Sabina was the first lady. I grabbed her and hugged her and then I thought: this is so inappropriate! I said, 'I'm really sorry, Sabina' and she's like, 'What are you talking about? I think you've put on a bit of weight, it suits you'. She's so the same, you know. But anyway, Michael D. said we are all but minstrels in time. And those words just stuck with me because everything is transient, including us. In a hundred years we are not going to be here but we always feel that a building is a legacy.

Steve: Yeah, but there is something, I don't know if it's holy, but there is something on this spot, even if the building itself doesn't exist.

Elizabeth: Yeah, I know. You see this is what's so sad...and I think it's such a travesty that the building is gone. In years to come, future generations may turn around and go 'why was the Focus theatre allowed to close, why?!' You know when they read your book, see *Hold the Passion*, and they will be saying, 'Why?', because I remember as a child my mother would say, 'Oh, I remember the Academy and I remember this theatre and that,' and I'd say, 'Mommy, why is it not there anymore?' 'Well, developers tore it down and put up that ugly building instead.' I'd say, 'Why did you let that happen?' She said, 'Well we tried to stop it but nobody listened.' And it just still happens.

Steve: Well, two years ago we were in Greece, in Athens, and went to Theatre Dionysus. It's not the same theatre as when Euripides and Sophocles were there. It was built a hundred years later. And I wonder if people asked 'where is the original space?' But there is something very holy in that space, because it wasn't about the stones, it was about what had gone on in that space: the truthful behaviour, the intimacy, the experiencing of art as a community. It's the memory.

Elizabeth: It's as you said. It's the company. Focus theatre is the company. But it's a very different company now, a very new company, and there are very few of the original members still involved and still working.

Steve: Is there a play subject there?

Elizabeth: Yeah, maybe. Maybe. Yeah I write about families anyway, so why not? Why not?

Mary Elizabeth Burke-Kennedy

Steve: How do you see where Focus...I guess what changes do you feel?...Are you happy with the work Joe has been making?

Mary Elizabeth: I don't know actually. Well, certainly the last thing I saw was the production of *Hollywood Valhalla*. I thought it was done with tremendous integrity and I thought I recognized that from the past. Just that absolute honesty and commitment to what they were doing.

The last play I remember seeing that I was impressed by at Focus was the story about the mathematician? *Proof.* That was very well done. That seemed to me very much from the old tradition of Focus. It held up very well. The cast did it very well.

12 | Focus Theatre and Deirdre O'Connell

Kevin O'Brien

I joined Focus Theatre in 1985 and started attending the Introductory Actors Studio run by Deirdre O'Connell, its founder and life force. Focus Theatre was Deirdre. Her entire life revolved around it and her boundless commitment to her beloved Theatre and everyone involved with it was obvious to all.

The place was full of energy, anarchy and general fun coupled with lots of hard work and commitment. Deirdre was a very rigorous but extremely generous teacher and minded us and scolded her students in equal measure. At the beginning of a new Studio everyone was under her surveillance. She was quickly able to weed out those who were not suitable and very gently guide them to the exit. Those who were left in the Studio were expected to give it 'their all'. Payment was not a problem. Deirdre had absolutely no interest in money whatsoever. For those who had money there was a modest fee and for those who did not, Deirdre simply overlooked it. The unspoken arrangement was that if you didn't have any money you were expected to help with productions by giving of your time. It was an arrangement which worked out very well because we were gaining additional experience helping out on the various productions.

Deirdre didn't care much for rules and regulations. She was a rebel and loved nothing more than the challenge of mounting a production against all the odds. When the Theatre was 'dark' the place could look pretty drab and uncomfortable. But once a production was in rehearsal everything changed. By opening night, Deirdre would have woven her magic and her little Theatre would sparkle like a gem under the stage lights. It really was quite extraordinary how she managed to do this time after time.

Of course to keep the Theatre going on little or no funding took its toll on her over the years. I remember one time we did two One Act plays by Luigi Pirandello, *The Man with the Flower in his Mouth* with Tim McDonnell and Frank McDonald, and also *The Vice* with Deirdre, Maurice O'Donoghue and myself. Deirdre played the heroine, Maurice played her husband and I played her lover.

At around this time, the Moscow Art Theatre were celebrating their centenary and as part of the celebrations in Moscow the Moscow Art Theatre were very keen to have Stanislavski practitioners from all over the world attend, and Deirdre was duly invited to Moscow. The Russian Ambassador was also involved in the process. Preparations were put in place for the great event which coincided with the rehearsal of our two Pirandello plays.

Issues arose during rehearsals and I remember we had a meeting in the Theatre one very wet and very cold Monday morning. I remember sitting huddled into the Theatre in my overcoat watching the rain running down the back wall of the stage through a leak in the roof and wondering what the hell I was doing there, putting myself through all of this stress and angst. Deirdre was holding forth on the current problems which we were experiencing in our rehearsals when the phone rang in the Green Room which was at the back of the Theatre. The job of Stage Manager for the Production had been bestowed upon the wonderful Paul Keeley who, sadly, is no longer with us. When the phone rang Deirdre asked Paul to answer it and Paul duly went to the back of the Theatre and we could hear him talking on the phone. Just then, there was a loud knock on the front door and Deirdre herself duly opened it to be confronted by an elderly gentleman with a flat cap and well-battered leather bag. Deirdre invited him into the Theatre where we were all sitting and enquired most politely as to the nature of his business. The gentleman gave a mumbled reply which none of us heard and Deirdre looked at us for some assistance. We blankly returned her gaze whereupon she said to the gentleman 'my dear, could I please ask you to speak up'. The man duly roared, 'I am the gas man and I am here to cut off the gas because you haven't paid your bill'.

While all this was going on Paul Keeley, who was still on the telephone, was calling through to Deirdre that there was someone urgently looking for her on the phone. Deirdre, feeling she was in something of a fix, shouted back to Paul, 'Who is it?', whereupon Paul replied, 'It's the Moscow Art Theatre looking for you Deirdre, they are enquiring as to when you are going to arrive in Moscow for their celebrations'. Deirdre, who was now beginning to feel a little perplexed, shouted back, 'Tell them I can't speak to them now'. Paul shouted back, 'What reason will I give them for you not being available, Deirdre?', to which Deirdre shouted back, 'Tell them I am with the gas man.'

Amidst promises to pay the bill immediately (indeed Paul was instructed to go straight down to the Gas Company to pay the bill) the gas man was gently encouraged towards the exit. When the door finally closed Deirdre returned and we all looked silently at each other and then spontaneously broke into howls of laughter at the incongruity of the situation. In Deirdre's case however, there was also a mixture of relief at having once again avoided another catastrophe happening to one of her productions.

I remember sitting there at the time still looking at the rain pouring down the back wall of the stage and understanding completely why I was there and relishing every minute of my involvement.

For Deirdre however, the sheer daily grind of maintaining a Theatre on a shoestring was just a part of her life which she accepted with great stoicism and humanity. At the same time, that struggle was something which an artist of her stature and immense talent should not have had to endure. Nevertheless she rarely spoke about it unless things got very tight, in which case the inevitable rabbit would be pulled from the hat at the eleventh hour and 'the show would indeed go on'.

That was Deirdre – all art and heart. She was a true artist in the real meaning of that word, and since her passing we all carry her in our hearts.

13 | Deirdre on Film: Reflections in A Golden Eye

Ronan O'Leary

My first movie connection with the Focus Theatre came in 1985. I had been working as a TV producer-director for PBS in Los Angeles, and was about to make a film of the Synge classic *Riders To The Sea*, to star the great American actress Geraldine Page from the Actors Studio and the young Broadway star Amanda Plummer. We decided to film on location in Ireland, with a cast that would also include Irish actors Barry McGovern and Joan O'Hara.

Arriving in Dublin, we needed some suitable space to rehearse in, and Deirdre kindly made the Focus available to us. For Deirdre and Geraldine, it was love and bonding at first sight; they had both studied with Lee Strasberg in the Actors Studio, and their mutual friendships included Stella Adler, Marlon Brando and Marilyn Monroe. Soon they were inseparable, happily sipping wine together in Hourican's Pub, deep in conversation about the art and the craft.

The theatre space itself proved to be a perfect arena in which the cast, coming from diverse acting traditions and principles, was able to explore the human and mythic elements of Synge's text and to experiment without fear. And, typical of Deirdre, when we tried to pay her the rental fee, she dug her hands deep inside her shawl, protesting that she couldn't possibly accept the money.

Some years later, I was approached by Tim McDonnell about the possibility of making a film of his award-winning one-man show *Diary Of A Madman*, an adaptation of the Gogol classic. This outstanding stage production, directed by Deirdre, had won Tim the Best Actor Harvey Award in Ireland, and a Best Actor Obie Award for its off-Broadway run, and Tim was keen to have his stage performance remembered on film.

For the film version, we needed to add further supporting roles to the cast, and Deirdre was very understanding that this film version of her stage production was inevitably, due to the demands of a different medium, going to have both additions and subtractions. The additional cast included the best of Irish acting talent available; Siobhan Miley, Conor Mullen, Mal Whyte, Daragh O'Malley, Derek Chapman and the veteran American actor O.Z. Whitehead who had been a great supporter of the Focus Theatre since arriving in Dublin in the Sixties.

The coup-de-grâce was to persuade Deirdre herself to play the role of Mavra, the kindly spinster neighbour who tends to the mentally disorientated Poprishkin and, in a final act of charity and deep love, dresses him for his departure to the asylum. Everyone in Dublin told me that there was no way that Deirdre would agree to appear in a film; but, miracle of miracles, she somehow said yes to the role. The film, she said, could not possibly interfere with her Studio work with her students; so, only in the afternoon, she would be whisked off by car to Ardmore Studios to shoot her scenes.

Deirdre was a huge hit with the crew, who were amused by her protestations before each take that she knew nothing about film acting whatsoever and then, as if reassured of imminent failure, got it absolutely right each time.

After the success in America of *Diary of A Madman*, I was asked to film another Focus Theatre stage production that had also been directed by Deirdre, *Hello Stranger*, an adaptation of a short story by Truman Capote. For this TV film, the cast featured Tim McDonnell and American actor Daniel J. Travanti, with O.Z. Whitehead and an eclectic supporting cast that included Tomás Mac Anna and Bill Golding. Again, Deirdre was supportive of the minor adjustments and additions that the TV film required and, again, the spirit and integrity of the original Focus production was dutifully retained.

Just when I thought my Focus filming days were over, I received an offer from an Irish documentary producer, Ann McRory, who wanted to make a definitive documentary history of the Focus Theatre and of its founder Deirdre O'Connell. Quite a brief. And one that I joyfully accepted. Already, Ann had a terrific title for the piece – *Hold The Passion*. Together, we plotted out the structure and shape of the documentary. We would film Deirdre teaching her students in the Studio, a vital part of the Focus Theatre's work. We would film a typical Focus Theatre production in rehearsal, charting the contours of its progress, and we would film extracts from the stage show itself, once it had opened. We would also capture the magic and excitement of the

Opening Night, and of the inevitable party afterwards in Hourican's Pub. And we would interview as many people as possible who were associated with the Focus down through the decades: from graduates such as Gabriel Byrne, Tom Hickey, Johnny Murphy and Sabina Coyne, to costume designer Joan Bergin and journalist Con Houlihan.

As fate would have it, the stage production that we chose to film, Lorca's *The House of Bernarda Alba*, turned out to be Deirdre's final stage performance. The play, a turbulent tale of family strife and stifled passion, had an all-female cast of twelve, and featured Deirdre as the formidable matriarch Bernarda. It also gave great acting opportunities to Focus actresses such as Margaret Twomey, Sile Nugent and Stephanie Dunne, under the watchful eye of director Jayne Snow. Filming these performances, and Deirdre's, was a special treat for me, such was the honesty, truth and Bergmanesque intensity that they brought to their roles.

The completed film, *Hold The Passion*, survives as a unique and valuable documentation of Deirdre's own work and teachings, and of her place in the Irish cultural landscape of the twentieth century. For this, we are forever in debt to the film's producer, Ann McRory, who had the courage and the foresight to undertake it.

14 | The 'Last Night' Speech at the Focus Theatre

Joe Devlin

[This is an edited transcript.]

I've worked at the Focus for ten years...I'm just going to speak from my heart. It's a very emotional night. I inherited the Focus Theatre from Deirdre who had died eleven years ago, and she was an extraordinary woman. And she brought a level of complexity and training into this country that this country never saw before. We were virtually a third-world country in 1963, and this amazing visionary who was 23 years old arrived, and basically frightened the living day lights out of all of them. And she found this place with her husband, Luke Kelly, and they turned Irish theatre upside down. Our President Michael D. Higgins said that post-war she's the most important theatre figure and that she revolutionized Irish theatre, and she did. And it was all done from this stage. All the teaching and all the productions.

And we're not going to stop because we're moving off this site. Our funding was axed last year, but we're committed to our art form, we're not committed to buildings. We come to theatre to engage on a profound human level, and when you get performances like you have seen tonight, it's the reason why we're here. Certainly the reason why I keep doing what I do. And I hope you'll come and see our work in other venues. We are looking for a new space, but will be doing our next, new, 50th anniversary season, and our next shows for this year, in other spaces. I think it's a huge loss to the Irish theatre community and to Dublin that we were allowed to close. But none of us should ever lose sight of what's important. It's not money, it's the art, and it's that that keeps us going. And it's about communicating at a profound level and not about filling seats. It's about the human soul and the human condition and sending joy and love and all those wonderful emotions, and sadness, too, which is what I'm feeling tonight.

But I'm also optimistic about the future, because we have a future and we have a full season. And next year we have the 50th anniversary coming up. So please keep a look out for us in the press. And thank you all very much, and if we could all give a big round of applause to the late Deirdre O'Connell for giving the gift of her life. Perhaps you'll join us for a glass of wine and sign the book on the way out. Just leave some comments and some happy thoughts, and thank you all very much. Goodnight.

15 | Afterword

Brian McAvera and Steven Dedalus Burch

After two years of (hard?) labour, one begins to see the wood for the trees. Perhaps the most significant aspects to have emerged from the research for, and collation of, this book, are that Deirdre O'Connell, and then Joe Devlin, were well in advance of their times.

In the 1960s the major new development in theatre in terms of the UK or Ireland was the Royal Court Theatre, firstly under George Devine and then under William Gaskill. As Philip Roberts in his *The Royal Court Theatre* makes clear, Devine and company wanted theatre 'to relate to what was happening outside its doors'. They wanted to appeal to a new public and they wanted to (and did) train actors, directors and dramatists, designers and musicians. There were weekly classes for authors (such as Bond, Arden, Jellicoe, Wesker, and Soyinka), education was regarded as a priority, and in the phrase coined by the director, Tony Richardson, what was important to a theatre like the Court, was 'the right to fail'.

There was a Specialized Actors' Group (which included classes in Method acting), Devine's interest – sparked by the Berliner Ensemble's visit in 1956 – was very much in the establishing of an ensemble actors' group; and such was the interest in education that the Studio actors at the Court worked with five different London training colleges, as well as various regional ones. When Devine resigned (officially in 1965) he noted that during his tenure there had been 145 productions at the Court as well as 87 of the famous 'Sunday Nights' which were effectively productions without décor – tryouts to test the worth of a play. Astonishingly 126 of these plays were new plays by contemporary writers.

Devine wanted to disturb his public, to challenge them. In a statement reminiscent of what was to come for Deirdre in Ireland, he once remarked that '...in our minds we know that to be accepted completely by the middle, to be smiled upon by the top, is the first sweet kiss of death. So we carry on, flirting with death in order to live'. Devine never 'made it big' but he has gone down in history as the man who changed the face of British Theatre from the late fifties onwards. He ushered in a generation of playwrights, actors, directors and designers who utterly re-aligned the face of the then contemporary theatre. And it is a salutary experience to realize that, although he always had supporters, there was no shortage of critical brickbats. Arden's *Sergeant Musgrave's Dance*, now regarded as a classic, was described by the critic Harold Hobson, at the time, as 'another frightful ordeal' and played to pitifully small audiences. Indeed many of the early Court productions played to as little as thirteen per cent, but that did not stop Devine supporting the writers, the idea of the ensemble, and the need to educate in all areas.

When we look at Irish theatre from the 1960's onwards, what is striking is how close Deirdre O'Connell came – albeit on a much smaller scale – to the ideals of a George Devine. She did not have the resources, the backers or (relative to the times) the broader platform that a city like London offered. Dublin, although it did not like to think of itself as such, was, like Belfast, provincial, narrow, and hidebound. What Deirdre did was to open it up to the sophistication of the New York world. Education was her mantra. Teaching was the necessity. And the seeds that she sowed have continued to flourish, often, admittedly, on somewhat stony ground, but they did take root. Irish theatre was never to be the same after her. No one would claim that she was perfect but, like any teacher working in hostile circumstances, the Miss Jean Brodie effect was definitely there. She won the hearts of her pupils and she shaped them for life.

It is typical of Irish theatre that her successor, Joe Devlin, has to confront the same uphill battles. Money is in short supply and the more you can demonstrate that you can provide quality productions at a fraction of the price needed by the major companies, the less you are given. Under Joe's tenure there has been a broadening out of the teaching strategy; a cross-fertilization with other theatre disciplines; and a greater emphasis upon the development of new work.

But the really notable aspect of Focus Theatre is that it has always drawn into its fold new generations of committed theatre people. New energies arrive. New developments take place. As the Royal Court actor

Bernard Gallagher remarked, reviewing his time at the theatre in the sixties, '...it *wasn't* all wonderful. How could it be with so many ambitious people of energy and talent together in a small space...we had our fair share of late night recriminations, weeping at parties and strong silence in rehearsals. There were times when treachery and ingratitude lurked in the wings. No common enterprise...has ever held together in its original form...overall my memory is of good times, of a small, manageable friendly stage within spitting distance of the audience, a warm, close house you could take in at a glance, shabby but hospitable dressing rooms...I am sure I was not the only one to find it a watershed in my working life'.

Appendix One:

Plays Produced at the Focus Theatre, 1967-2013
*A single asterisk in the tables below signifies a performance by a visiting company

1967

September	*Play with a Tiger*	Doris Lessing

1968

February	*Kelly's Eye*	Henry Livings
April	'Evening Without Angels':	
	Hello Out There	William Saroyan
	In the Zone	Eugene O'Neill
	Portrait of a Madonna	Tennessee Williams
July	*Miss Julie*	August Strindberg
	The Wedding	Anton Chekhov
October	*Toys in the Attic*	Lillian Hellman

1969

February	*Antigone*	Jean Anouilh
June	*Exiles*	James Joyce
		(cancelled)
July	*In Camera (No Exit)*	Jean Paul Sartre
October	'You're a Lovely Girl, Gertrude Dietrich':	Charles Mee
	Constantinople Smith	
	The Creation	Lee Gallagher
	Lunch Hour	John Mortimer

1970

January	*Uncle Vanya*	Anton Chekhov
May	*Hedda Gabler*	Henrik Ibsen
	Happy Days	Samuel Beckett

| November | *Mooney and His Caravans* | Peter Terson |

1971

February	*Happy Days*	Samuel Beckett (extended run)
April	*Le Malentendu(Cross Purpose)*	Albert Camus
November	*A Doll's House*	Henrik Ibsen

1972

| August | *The Father* | August Strindberg |

1973

February	*The Nuns*	Eduardo Manet
April	*The Lady of Larkspur Lotion*	Tennessee Williams
June	*Krapp's Last Tape*	Samuel Beckett
	Play	Samuel Beckett
October	*To Clothe the Naked*	Luigi Pirandello
	The Trespasser	Declan Burke-Kennedy

1974

January	*Night of the Iguana*	Tennessee Williams
March	*Before Breakfast*	Eugene O'Neill
	Uncle Wiggly in Connecticut	J.D. Salinger
April	*La Musica*	Marguerite Duras
May	*The Typists*	Murray Schisgal
August	*John Gabriel Borkmann*	Henrik Ibsen
October	*Hardly Any Brecht*	Bertolt Brecht
December	*When the Wind is Cold*	John Kendrick (cancelled)
	Shelter	Alun Owen
	Good Day	Emmanuel Peluso

1975

| April | *A Delicate Balance* | Edward Albee |

	Birdbath	Leonard Melfi
	Lunchtime	Leonard Melfi
June	*Hello and Goodbye*	Athol Fugard
August	*Occupations*	Trevor Griffiths
November	*Alpha Beta*	E.A. Whitehead
December	*Circus Animals' Desertion*	W.B. Yeats

1976

March	*Rosmersholm*	Henrik Ibsen
May	*Fire and Ice*	Robert Frost
June	*The Advertisement*	Natalia Ginzburg
	Little Fears	Emmanuel Peluso
July	*'Selections from Dylan Thomas'*	St. David's Day Society
	'Brief Encounters'	
	Thoughts on the Instant of Greeting a Friend on the Street	Jean Claude Van Italie & Sharon Thie
	Camera Obscura	Robert Patrick
	The Unexpurgated Memoirs of Bernard J. Mergendeiler	Jules Feiffer
August	*It's Called the Sugarplum*	Israel Horowitz
	Days in the Trees	Marguerite Duras
September	*Daughters*	John Morgan Evans
November	*A Month in the Country*	Ivan Turgenev

1977

April	*Curtains*	Tom Mallin
June	*Playboy of the Western World*	J.M. Synge
	Will	Peter O'Shaughnessy
November	*Tchin-Tchin*	François Billetdoux

1978

January	*Treats*	Christopher Hampton
February	*Émigrés*	Slawomir Mrozek
March	*Waiting for Beckett*	Jim Sheridan

June	*A Collier's Friday Night*	D.H. Lawrence
September	*The Little Foxes*	Lillian Hellman
October	*Dance of Death*	August Strindberg

1979

January	*Alice in Wonderland*	Lewis Carroll
March	*McGonagall*	Pat Abernathy & Dave Marsden
	I'm Pat, He's Just the Pianist	Pat Abernathy & Dave Marsden
	'Opening':	
	Endgame	Samuel Beckett
	Not I	Samuel Beckett
June	*He Who Gets Slapped*	Leonid Andreyev
August	*Old Times*	Harold Pinter
September	'Annex':	
	Contrivance	Tony Browne
	Mirror, Mirror	Lee Gallagher
October	*Blind Salad*	Jimmy Brennan

1980

January	*The Golden Goose*	Jacob and William Grimm
March	*The Lovers of Viorne*	Marguerite Duras
April	*Enter the Photographer*	Mary Elizabeth Burke-Kennedy
	Day of the Mayfly	Declan Burke-Kennedy
May	*Jumble Sale*	Robert Emmet Meagher
	Potatoes	Tony Cafferky
June	*Legends*	Mary Elizabeth Burke-Kennedy
	Marriages	William Trevor
July	*The Lady from the Sea*	Henrik Ibsen
October	*Currigh the Shapeshifter*	Mary Elizabeth Burke-Kennedy

December	*Evening Light*	Alexei Arbuzov

1981

March	'Two Plays by Federico Garcia Lorca':	
	The Shoemaker's Prodigious Wife	Federico Garcia Lorca
	The Love of Don Perlimpli.	Federico Garcia Lorca
June	*The Price*	Arthur Miller
July	*This Property is Condemned*	Tennessee Williams
	Winners	Brian Friel
August	*Shelter*	Alun Owen
September	*Legends*	Mary Elizabeth Burke-Kennedy
	Forever Yours, Marie-Lou	Michel Tremblay
October	*The Wind that Shook the Barley*	Declan Burke-Kennedy

1982

January	*La Ronde*	Arthur Schnitzler
March	*Cement*	Tony Cafferky
	Corporation Flat	Tony Cafferky
July	*Creditors*	August Strindberg
September	*Louvain-1915*	Barbara Field

1983

January	*Skirmishes*	Catherine Hayes
May	'Tennessee Williams':	
	The Strangest Kind of Romance	Tennessee Williams
	Talk to Me like the Rain...	Tennessee Williams
	The Lady of Larkspur Lotion	Tennessee Williams
June	'Plays from the USSR':	
	The Promise	Alexei Arbuzov
	Journey into the Whirlwind	Eugenia Ginzburg
	The Nose	Nikolai Gogol
July	*Mooney and His Caravan*	Peter Terson

	The Lady of Larkspur Lotion	Tennessee Williams
	Birdbath	Leonard Melfi
August	*The Tiger*	Murray Schisgal
	'Two Alone':	
	Mooney and His Caravan	Peter Terson
	Birdbath	Leonard Melfi
	Fancy Footwork	Miriam Gallagher
	A Pocket Romeo and Juliet	William Shakespeare
October	*I Must be Mad*	Pat Ingoldsby
	Success Woman	Alexei Arbuzov

1984

February	*A Lesson From Aloes*	Athol Fugard
May	*Silicon Sweethearts*	Donal O'Kelly
July	*'Night Mother*	Marsha Norman
October	*Poor Ol' Joe*	Tom Laidlaw
	'Two Views':	
	Out of the Beehive	Ena May
	Flotsam	Joe Taylor
	'A Brace':	
	Monologue	Samuel Beckett
	The Zoo Story	Edward Albee
December	*A Christmas Carol*	Charles Dickens

1985

April	*Ghosts*	Henrik Ibsen
June	*Waiting for Godot*	Samuel Beckett
September	*Hello and Goodbye*	Athol Fugard
December	*Two Way Mirror*	Arthur Miller

1986

January	*Doctor Faustus*	Christopher Marlowe
June	*The Nuns*	Eduardo Manet
September	*The Sea Horse*	Edward J. Moore
October	*Third Class Carriage*	Jack Kendrick
	Have a Nice Day	Tommy O'Neill

1987

February	*The Widowing of Mrs. Holroyd*	D.H. Lawrence
March	*Shades of the Jelly Woman*	Peter Sheridan
April	*Huis Clos*	Jean Paul Sartre
May	*Taken in Marriage*	Thomas Babe
July	*Beware of the Dog*	Anton Chekhov
August	*The Dumb Waiter*	Harold Pinter
October	*Each His Own Wilderness*	Doris Lessing
	Another Day	Tommy O'Neill
	Diary of a Madman	Nikolai Gogol
November	*PVT Wars*	James McLure

1988

January	*Stags and Hens*	Willie Russell
April	*A Question of Geography*	John Berger & Nella Bielski
May	*The Caretaker*	Harold Pinter
July	'Lunchtime Season of James McLure':	
	Lonestar	James McLure
	Laundry and Bourbon	James McLure
September	*She's Your Mother Too You Know*	Ena May
October	*Radio City*	Martin Murphy

1989

February	'Focus on Pirandello':	
	The Vice	Luigi Pirandello
	The Man with the Flower in His Mouth	Luigi Pirandello
April	*When the Wind Blows*	Raymond Briggs
July	*Orphans*	Lyle Kessler
November	*Crystal Clear*	Phil Young

1990

January	*Who's Afraid of Virginia Woolf?*	Edward Albee
March	*Crystal Clear*	Phil Young
April	*Rise and Shine*	Sean McCarthy
May	*Lunchtime*	Leonard Melfi
	Love Letters	A.R. Gurney
July	*Rocket to the Moon*	Clifford Odets
October	*Little Eyolf*	Henrik Ibsen

1991

February	*Small Craft Warnings*	Tennessee Williams
March	'Go on Red':	
	Foggy Hair and Green Eyes	Tom Mac Intyre
	Jack Be Nimble	Tom Mac Intyre
	Fine Day for a Hunt	Tom Mac Intyre
May	*The Secret Rapture*	David Hare
	'Programme of Scene Studies':	
	John Gabriel Borkman	Henrik Ibsen
	The Children's Hour	Lillian Hellman
	The Madwoman of Chaillot	Jean Giraudoux
	Blood Knot	Athol Fugard
July	*San Antonio Sunset*	Willy Holtzman
	Self Accusation	Peter Handke
August	*Dolores*	Edward Alan Baker
	Hello Stranger	Truman Capote
September	'Blue America':	
	San Antonio Sunset	Willy Holtzman
	Dolores	Edward Allan Baker
	Hello Stranger	Truman Capote
October	*A View from the Bridge*	Arthur Miller
November	*Waiting for Godot*	Samuel Beckett

1992

February	*Bourke and Blake*	Kevin O'Connor
April	*The Balcony*	Jean Genet
June	*The Master Builder*	Henrik Ibsen
July	*Brendan*	Ulick O'Connor
	The Misogynist	Michael Harding
August	'Encounters 3':	
	Time's Up	Carmel Winters & Patrick McCabe
	Small Box Psychosis	Barry McKinley
September	*Personal Ad*	Paul Ryan
October	*Summer*	Edward Bond
	All Livia's Daughters	Peter O'Shaughnessy
November	'Three Great One Act Plays from the Irish Revival':	
	The Cat and the Moon	W.B. Yeats
	The Rising of the Moon	Lady Gregory
	The Shadow of the Glen	J.M. Synge
December	*Alice Through the Looking Glass*	Lewis Carroll

1993

April	*A Place with the Pigs*	Athol Fugard
August	*All My Sons*	Arthur Miller
November	'Bloomin' Women':	
	Molly Bloom	Mary Linehan
	Maisie	Mary Linehan
December	*An Actor's Nightmare*	Christopher Durang

1994

February	*The Rape of Lucrece*	William Shakespeare
April	*Strawberry Fields*	Stephen Poliakoff
May	*A Lie of the Mind*	Sam Shepard
August	*Buried Child*	Sam Shepard
November	*Seachange*	John Banville
	The Kiss	Michael Harding

1995

February	*Men without Shadows*	Jean Paul Sartre
April	*Le Malentendu*	Albert Camus
	(Cross Purposes)	
June	'Mixed Doubles':	
	Lovers	Brian Friel
	The Glass Menagerie	Tennessee Williams
	Summertime	Ugo Betti
	The Zoo Story	Edward Albee
	Plenty	David Hare
September	'Three for Tennessee	
	Williams':	
	Auto-da-Fé	Tennessee Williams
	Talk to Me like the Rain...	Tennessee Williams
	The Lady of Larkspur Lotion	Tennessee Williams
October	*Thérèse Raquin*	Emile Zola

1996

April	*Precious Sons*	George Furth
September	'Garden District':	
	Something Unspoken	Tennessee Williams
	Suddenly Last Summer	Tennessee Williams
November	*Private/PVT Wars*	James McLure

1997

May	*'Night Mother*	Marsha Norman
July	'Naked Truth: An Evening of	
	Scene Studies': *The*	
	Widowing of Mrs. Holroyd	D.H. Lawrence
	Betrayal	Harold Pinter
	Richard's Cork Leg	Brendan Behan
	Someone Who'll Watch Over	Frank McGuinness
	Me	
August	'Ceasefire':	
	Absent Comrades	Bill Murphy
	Trade Me a Dream	Lindsay Sedgwick
September	*Jack's Too Open*	Paula Clamp
October	*Picnic*	William Inge

1998

February	*Playing Sinatra*	Bernard Kops
March	*Jordan*	Anna Reynolds
May	*Anna Christie*	Eugene O'Neill
July	'Lunchtime at the Focus: A Season of New Irish Writing':	
	Healing the Dead	Johnny Hanrahan
August	*Him and Her*	Lorcan Roche
	Death of a Dog	Gerry O'Malley
September	*The Watchman*	Sean Lawlor
November	*The Saga of Gudridur*	Brynja Benediktsdóttir

1999

February	*The House of Bernarda Alba*	Federico Garcia Lorca
June	'Naked Truth: An Evening of Scene Study':	
	Little Malcolm and His Struggle Against the Eunuchs	David Halliwell
	Kiss of the Spider Woman	Manuel Puig
	Skylight	David Hare
	Hedda Gabler	Henrik Ibsen
	The Lonesome West	Martin McDonagh
	Dolores	Edward Allan Baker
July	*Last Man Down*	Tommy O'Neill
August	*Stump*	Liam Brennan
	Pizza Boy	Pat Garret
November	*Journeyman*	Frank Shouldice

2000

May	*Awake and Sing!*	Clifford Odets
July	'Naked Truth: An Evening of Scene Study':	
	Low in the Dark	Marina Carr
	The Lonesome West	Martin McDonagh

	Skylight	David Hare
August	'Lovett for Lunch' or	
	'Absolution':	
	Watchdog	Tara Maria Lovett
	The Shape	Tara Maria Lovett
October	*Tillsonburg*	Malachy McKenna

2001

April	*Lips Together, Teeth Apart*	Terrence McNally
June	*The Gallant John-Joe*	Tom Mac Intyre
October	*A Close Shave with the Devil*	Ena May

2002

March	*A Delicate Balance*	Edward Albee
June	*Dead Boys*	Pius Meagher
July	*Miss Canary Islands 1936*	Conall Quinn
August	*The Gallant John-Joe*	Tom Mac Intyre
(Touring:		
Edinburgh		
Fringe Fest)		
September	*Talking Through His Hat*	Michael Harding
October	*John Gabriel Borkman*	Henrik Ibsen

2003

March	*Tillsonburg* (National Tour)	Malachy McKenna
April	*The Gallant John-Joe* (NY	Tom Mac Intyre
	Tour)	
	Stuck	David Rubinoff
May	*Talking Through His Hat*	Michael Harding
June	*The Gallant John-Joe*	Tom Mac Intyre
September	*Proof*	David Auburn

2004

January	*Proof* (Andrews Lane)	David Auburn
	Fallen Angels Cabaret	Devised
May	*Very Heaven*	Ann Lambert

August	*Jesus Hopped the 'A' Train*	Stephen Adly Guirgis
September	*The Robb'd That Smiled**	Gemma Doorly
	*The Marowitz Hamlet**	Charles Marowitz
	*Passport**	Gustavo Ott
October	'You Don't Feel It Here'	
	Bones for Otto*	Lia Bugner
	*Lucky Helps Those Who Dare**	Franz Xaver Kroetz

2005

February	*Playing Burton**	Mark Jenkins
May	*Decadence**	Stephen Berkoff
	*Harlequin's Lesson in Love**	Pierre Marivaux
June	*Hedwig and the Angry Inch**	John Cameron Mitchell & Stephen Trask
August	*Ladybird*	Vassily Sigarev
September	*Talk To Me Like the Rain...*	Tennessee Williams
	Stop the Tempo	Gianina Carbunariu
	*See No Evil**	Devised
	*Tramps and Vamps**	Sam Slater & Robert Murtagh
	*Lunch**	Stephen Berkoff
	The Friends of Jack Kairo	Simon Toal
October	*Shooters**	Jack Gilhooley

2006

March	*Lonestar/Laundry & Bourbon**	James McClure
**Venue Closed		
July	*Two Rooms* (Andrews Lane Studio)	Lee Blessing
August	*Mother Teresa is Dead* (Project Cube)	Helen Edmundsun
November	*The Friends of Jack Kairo* (Bucharest Tour)	Simon Toal

2007

June	*The Friends of Jack Kairo* (Prague Tour)	Simon Toal
October	'Picasso's Women' (New Theatre & Mill Theatre):	
	Fernande	Brian McAvera
	Olga	Brian McAvera
	Gaby	Brian McAvera

2008

June	*Picasso's Women*: Gaby (Mill/Tour)	Brain McAvera
	The Friends of Jack Kairo (Mill/Tour)	Simon Toal

2009

May	*Walnuts Remind Me of My Mother** (Cobalt Café)	Elizabeth Moynihan
	Picasso's Women: Gaby (RHA/Tour)	Brian McAvera
June	*The Friends of Jack Kairo* (Mermaid/Tour)	Simon Toal
	The Kiss (Mill/Tour)	Michael Harding
August	*The Wilder Wisdom of Auld Ones**(James Joyce Centre)	Nuala Hayes
	I Am of Ireland (James Joyce Centre/Tour)	Edward Callan
September	*Love, Death & Balloon Modelling* (Bewley's)	Simon Toal

2010

January	*I Am of Ireland* (Bewley's)	Edward Callan
March	*The Tinker's Curse* (Bewley's/Tour)	Michael Harding
May	*Slaughterhouse Swan* (New Theatre)	Elizabeth Moynihan

Theatre)
The Kiss (Bewley's)   Michael Harding

**Focus
Re-Opens

June	*The Tower*	Joe Joyce
August	*Baglady**	Frank McGuinness
	Tic	Elizabeth Moynihan
September	*7 Deadly Sins* (Ranelagh Arts Fest)	Devised
	*Scent of Chocolate**	Radoslaw Paczocha
October	*Orphans*	Denis Kelly
November	*Men of Tortuga**	Jason Wells
December	*Jo Bangles**	David Lordan

2011

February	'Love In Dublin':	
	Love Me in the Rain	Paul Kennedy
	Down By the River	Paul Kennedy
April	'Beckett X 4':	
	Catastrophe	Samuel Beckett
	Rockaby	Samuel Beckett
	Play	Samuel Beckett
	A Piece of Monologue	Samuel Beckett
June	*Francis & Frances*	Brian McAvera
	*Pinching for my Soul**	Elizabeth Moynihan
July	*Breathing Water**	Raymond Scannell
September	The New York Monologues (New Version)	Mike Poblete
	The Hen Night Epiphany Focus/Tour	Jimmy Murphy

2012

January	Hollywood Valhalla	Aidan Harney
	The Hen Night Epiphany (Tour)	Jimmy Murphy
April	'Before Vanishing...: Four Plays by Beckett:	

	Ohio Impromptu	Samuel Beckett
	Footfalls	Samuel Beckett
	That Time	Samuel Beckett
	Come and Go Teacht Is Imeacht (Irish Language Version	Samuel Beckett
	Hollywood Valhalla Focus/Tour	Aidan Harney

**Venue
Closed

June	Griswold (Play of New York) (Civic/Tour)	Arnold Thomas Fanning
September	Down by the River (Ranelagh Arts Festival and Tour)	Paul Kennedy
December	'Fathers and Children' (New Theatre):	
	First of the Day	Andrew Hinds
	Anaemia	Andrew Hinds
	Morning	Andrew Hinds

2013

| **May** | Bankers | Brian McAvera |

Appendix Two: A Short History of the Focus

This is a short history, as printed in their first programmes, probably written by Deirdre, though it is unsigned.

Dublin Focus Theatre – The Past

In May 1963 the Stanislavski Studio of Dublin was founded by Deirdre O'Connell, actress and director from Erwin Piscator's Dramatic Workshop and life-member of Lee Strasberg's Actors Studio. In New York she had taken part on and off Broadway in plays by Strindberg, Chekov [sic], Synge, O'Neill, Wilder, Saroyan and others.

The first home of the Stanislavski Studio was the Pocket Theatre, Ely Place. The Studio's two-fold purpose was to serve initially as an actors' training centre, and ultimately as the artistic foundation of a permanent repertory theatre. It was intended that the Studio would present plays at regular intervals, but the sale of the Ely premises put an end to the Pocket and to the possibility of continuing productions for quite some time. The Studio's only production at the Pocket was *For Madmen Only*, an adaptation by Saul Colin of the Nobel Prize-winner Hermann Hesse's *Steppenwolf*.

With the loss of the Pocket began a lean period for the Studio, which consisted of moving from place to place in search of suitable premises. After stays at Westland Row, Kildare Street, the Pike Theatre and Fitzwilliam Square, it was painfully clear that the aims of the Studio would not be realized until it had found a permanent theatre of its own. Deirdre O'Connell then left Dublin for a year to attempt fund-raising in London. She kept the Studio alive by coming back to Dublin at weekends as often as she could.

During the 1965 Theatre Festival many of the Studio's actors were involved in Meryl Gourley's highly praised production of Yeats' *Calvary* and *Resurrection* in the Players Theatre, Trinity. The following summer, Allen Miller of the Actors' Studio spent two months in Dublin, as guest teacher at the Studio. Since September 1966 much of the Studio's energies have been absorbed in the founding of Dublin Focus. After an intensive search, number 6 Pembroke Place was finally found. A fund-raising campaign was launched towards the costs of converting this disused factory into a theatre. Many people responded to this request and it is hoped more people will do so in the future.

For the first six months of 1967 the Studio gave improvisational performances approximately every second week-end. These had to be limited to invited audiences in the Studio's Fitzwilliam Square premises, but can now be performed publicly between productions.

Dublin Focus Theatre was formed in July 1967 and its first production, the Irish Premiere of Doris Lessing's *Play With a Tiger* was rehearsed in Fitzwilliam Sq. and Stephen's Green, while the Pembroke Place premises was being converted. In January 1968 we presented *Kelly's Eye*, by Henry Livings, another Irish Premiere. *Evening without Angels*, three short American plays by O'Neill, Williams and Saroyan, followed in April, and Strindberg's *Miss Julie*, and *The Wedding* by Chekov [sic] were offered for the summer season.

For 1968's Theatre Festival, we had the Pulitzer Prize play *Toys in the Attic* by the American dramatist, Lillian Hellman, and this was followed by *Antigone* by the leading French dramatist, Jean Anouilh. Though we fully prepared a production of James Joyce's *Exiles* for the summer of 1969, we were refused the rights at the last moment, as a London management was 'considering' a Dublin production of the play, and having the money we hadn't, was able to tie up the rights indefinitely. However, we set to, and had our production of *In Camera* by Jean-Paul Sartre, ready by July.

For the last Theatre Festival we presented our first original play, The *Creation* by Lee Gallaher. Next came Anton Chekhov's *Uncle Vanya*, our longest run to date, from January 1970 for 10 weeks.

Despite the pressure of running a theatre, with a membership of between twenty-five and thirty actors, working together for at least two three-hour periods a week, the Studio has continued to function as a distinct training centre and will continue to do so, alongside the Theatre, making Dublin Focus the only unsubsidized Irish Theatre with its own premises and its own school.

Appendix Three: Two Excerpts on the Focus

These are excerpts from an Irish Times article in 1970, and in 1987 an article by Peter Thompson discussing the Focus Theatre and its Stanislavski training, and Irish theatre in general.

From *The Irish Times*, 'The Actors Schooling, Part Three' by Kay Kent, September 18, 1970:

'Walk into the Focus Theatre on a Saturday afternoon and you might think a group from Grangegorman had taken over. Grunts, shrieks and moans, gurgles and wild laughter will assault your ears. Turn to the tiny stage and you will hardly be reassured by the sight of six or more actors, totally self-absorbed, vacant eyed, making sudden movements and mysterious gestures, uncommunicative, but obviously of great importance to themselves. Perhaps they are rehearsing for an unscheduled performance of the *Marat/Sade*? No, says their teacher, Deirdre O'Connell, this is the 'warm up.'

'They must be totally unconcerned with projecting to anyone in this exercise. The purpose is to actualize their own conception of an idea through concentration and deliberately abstracted sound and movement.

'Relaxation, concentration and observation are the main points of this exercise,' explains Deirdre O'Connell, an intense ginger-haired young woman dressed all in black.

'All three are basic needs for the actor. Muscular tension interferes with both physical and emotional response, and lack of concentration ruins many performances which could otherwise be first rate.'

'Fifty percent of her actors' work,' she goes on, 'is on themselves – developing their own inner resources, their powers of involvement in an idea, becoming more sensitive and fully alive. Anyone who trains himself in this way automatically increases his ability to communicate.

'Even so, with an actor of small talent, the Stanislavski Method can do more harm than good. And it is these less gifted people, particularly in America, who have caused many of the misunderstandings about the Method itself. They have become over-dependent on the system, and are unable to leave the exercise stage behind, even on performance.'

Because of this danger, Miss O'Connell selects her pupils with great care, accepting them only after they have attended classes as spectators for some weeks. She gives her pupils graded exercises and homework according to their individual progress, along with improvisations.

But Focus is aware, too, of the need for standard voice and movement training. Pupils are advised to go for these to the RIAM and Evelyn Burchill.

Brendan Smith, Dublin's 'standard' teacher par excellence since 1943, aims to give his students everything but the Method, not that he is opposed to it, but that he considers that the Western world theatres, poorly subsidized, have not the time for it. In Dublin stage training is done on a part-time basis, based on the Coquelin-Diderot theory of 'dual control.' 'This is not as fancy as it sounds. In fact, it is the method used by any actor naturally whether he knows it or not. On stage he has two personalities functioning simultaneously, his own and his character's. The important thing is that the first must be in control of the second throughout the performance.'

Smith helps his students towards physical expressiveness in his mime and movement classes. Both the strength and weakness of the class is that it admits many students who have neither hope nor intention to be professional stage actors.

Phyllis Ryan, Dublin product and ex-actress, asks whether acting can be taught. 'Basically there either is talent or there is not. There is only a limited amount that can be taught – voice and movement training and one's general approach to the job.'

As Deirdre O'Connell says in her intense, decisive way:

> The Irish do tend to nourish the rather complacent notion that they are so temperamentally suited to the acting profession that they can get away without any hard work or training. There's an enormous amount of talent here, I agree, but I'd like to see the whole thought process reversed. Every actor and actress must be willing to work so hard that eventually they transcend work and achieve real art. There are not many actors in Dublin, in my opinion, who have done that.

From *Theatre on Ireland Retrospective*, 1987, by Peter Thompson, pp. 30-35:

> Indeed, the introduction of the Stanislavski methods of training into Dublin by Deirdre O'Connell was not exactly greeted by the theatrical establishment of the time with open arms. 'Stanislavski wasn't the done thing,' recalls Tom Hickey. 'The tradition in the (Irish) theatre had been 'Talent' was enough.' Deirdre O'Connell remembers with amusement references to her as 'the snot-nosed kid from America who had come over to Ireland to teach the Irish how to act.' It was a prejudice which survived long after the Focus itself had been established. Speaking of the public improvisations at the Theatre during

1971, Mary Elizabeth Burke-Kennedy recollects that 'there was quite a degree of hostility from some other members of the profession. There was this idea around that you didn't have to learn your craft. Young people today are much more aware of the need for training.' (31)

Deirdre O'Connell:

They found it difficult to consider that actors must train like any artist or crafts person. That thought was anathema to them. It was: either the actor has it or hasn't. The young Abbey for example, was not so much a training process as a preparation-for-performance process, whereas the Stanislavski system is a very precise, systematic and gruelling if rewarding, study of principles into practice. And THAT was a process they didn't understand.

Her studying with Erwin Piscator, who had been expelled from the USA for being a communist, and her marriage to Luke Kelly, himself a member of the Irish Communist Party, ruffled many feathers. 'Obviously the fact that Luke is my husband meant that people knew where my feelings lay.'

While politics doubtless played a part, the psychological and sexual implications of Stanislavski's method were, in Deirdre's view, far more central to the unwillingness of Irish people to accept it. Perhaps theatre people were afraid of the beast lurking in the Irish psyche which Stanislavski might have unleashed...

Nobody can deny that the Irish have a temperament which is prone to self-analysis, and an inner life that is conducive to spirit, imagination and a certain wildness,' Deirdre argues. 'There is an innocence, a rawness – but we are nervous of that, of our emotionality. There is also a darkness we mask with laughter. But we must not forget the sexual dimension to it. In that respect, we are very conservative, or at least we were 25 years ago. And Stanislavski deals with all those things that make life dangerous. We don't want to live dangerously. We see ourselves as religious and conservative though I don't believe we are, internally.'

Tapping psycho-sexual forces, a la Freud, and, worse still, accepting rather than repressing what you find, can also be seen as heresy by the peddlers of religion who've exerted such a stranglehold on Irish society this century.

'They may have seen it as placing the self above everything and everyone else,' Deirdre comments.

Or rather self-indulgent in the sense that you are ploughing around in muddy waters where even angels fear to tread. And we had the gall, this young company, to march in there and stoke up those murky waters in the individual and maybe collective consciousness, both through the way we approached the work and in the plays themselves.'

Deirdre admits that the lines are not drawn as severely now as they once were. 'We have infiltrated well,' she laughs. 'It's all over the place now. But we go gently, not bursting through doors. It's still resented in many places, but we've proved the legitimacy of the approach.'

Appendix Four: Press responses in the early Focus years

Not all of it negative or hostile. In fact, the press was largely attuned to what Deirdre O'Connell and company were doing.

Nusight May 1968 p.18: 'Flann O'Connor writes on Theatre'

[Re: currently performing *Evening Without Angels* (Tennessee Williams's 'Portrait of a Madonna', William Saroyan's 'Hello out There,' Eugene O'Neill's 'In the Zone').]

'It looks as if the Dublin Focus Theatre is here to stay and a good thing too.' [Two previous productions] '...drew excellent 'write-ups' from the critics but did not attract the audiences which they deserved...' 'Opening night saw at the Focus an amazing position – half an hour before the curtains were due to rise, one hundred and thirty people were crammed into the seventy-five seat theatre, sitting and standing in the aisles and doorways and a growing crowd accumulating outside. ...

'Audience research has shown that ninety-five per cent (sic) of the audience have come on the recommendation of friends and acquaintances who have already had the pleasure of seeing these three short plays.' The article's author [Flann O'Connor] felt the company needed to be recognized by the leaders of Irish theatre; included lengthy paragraph on their being disciples of Stanislavski and the Method, referenced current Method-trained American stars then appearing in films (Brando, Poitier etc.) named the Focus' noted patrons – John Huston, Lady Longford, Clancy Brothers – and ended his article with 'The time has come for the leaders of Irish theatre to throw their support and assistance behind this group and help to give Dublin the additional theatre and school it so badly needs.' (19)

Letter to the Editor, The Irish Times March 31, 1969 titled 'METHOD':

Sir, – Before my arrival in Ireland, I was under the belief that gross misunderstanding and 'misinterpretation' of Stanislavski and 'The Method' had generally died in the late forties and early fifties in the decaying remnants of the Pasadena Playhouse and Actors Studio. Through my years of theatre training, every method for the beginning actor had been touched on, as one would touch on schools of philosophical thought, and only then, as a glossary or cursory outline for the development of individual method. One basic premise hammered into our heads since we first carried a prop on to a stage was, 'The playwright is first.' In Edwin Duerr's excellent and 'dialectically complete history, *The Length and Depth of Acting*, this major conclusion stands out: the great moments of world theatre have been the great moments of the world's playwrights.

If one is not capable of reviewing a play if one 'walks out' half way through, then I am not capable of giving a honest review of The Focus production *Antigone*. I am under the belief, however, if I had remained, I would have seen little more of *Antigone*. [Jean] Anouilh [author of the play] was unrecognizable.

The 'play' opened with the two guards flipping flags to the accompaniment of their appropriate anthems. Why? To show universality? Perhaps it was a kind of apology for the 'poor' poetry of the playwright and he intended it to be universal after all. Perhaps we're all in kindergarten and require picture stories?

As the play commenced, Anouilh's line scattered into the realms of improvisation. Entire speeches were turned up-side-down. Phrases were backward. Soliloquies were lengthened. Random additives were frequent and irrelevant. The most striking example of 'spontaneity' (I use the term loosely) was the up-turned face in the down-stage right corner extending a speech to nearly three times its original length. The more appropriate title to this fiasco should have been, 'Based on Anouilh's *Antigone*'.

Lack of direction or inadequate acting are all forgivable in the realms of theatre criticism; but, to alter lines at random, at one's own 'emotional' discretion, based on no pre-conceived formulae or dialectic is sinful, not only to Anouilh, but to Stanislavski, who in no way ever implied his 'beginning method' to be the key to the final performance of a play.

The Irish people surely would not tolerate this kind of alteration for Synge; let us give the same respect to another of the world's great playwrights Anouilh. – Yours, etc, Leo Charles Greene c/o Conor Cruise O'Brien, Whitewater, Summit, Howth'

'Improvisational theatre at Focus' by Kane Archer, *The Irish Times*, Monday, June 18, 1973

Improvisation, as a part of the actor's preparation, is an important part of the work both of the Stanislavski Studio which it incorporates. Given as a part of that theatre's fund-raising week, Thursday night's programme of improvisations by five actors without director or set dialogue – but prepared among themselves beforehand through discussion of the characters and their positions, their background, their situation – sets a series of problems for the critic that are not to be solved this side of an extended consideration of the place and purpose of such exercises.

What part, for example, is the audience to play? Mute witness to the actor's self-preparation; provider of a challenge of nerve; or a body to be moved by the myriad means at the actors' command directed by them to that end? To name, that is, but a small number of possibilities out of many.

It became increasingly clear on this occasion that so far had all the options been left open that in the event itself it had proved impossible for the players to choose between them – with the result that for the want of clear thinking none were taken up. Improvisation, with or without an audience, whether that audience is the paying public or a group of fellow actors, can indeed be valuable. The circumstances, however, must be reckoned with. Beyond such observations, criticism of this particular evening would be invidious.

'Five Years of Focus', *The Irish Press*, Thursday, November 9, 1972

It [the Method] has been misunderstood and mispresented (sic), even by other actors, and yet it is, essentially, a way of taking apart and then putting together the things that many a good actor discovers for himself through long, painful process of trial and error. It consists of two disciplines; the actor's work on himself, and the actor's work on his part.

In the first, an actor carries out certain 'exercises' which are designed to heighten his sensitivity to the experiences of his senses; to what he sees, hears, smells, tastes and touches, and then to attempt to recreate those experiences by using his imagination and his memory, his body and his voice.

At Studio classes Deirdre sits at the back of the theatre while students work on the stage. The exercises seem far removed from 'acting.' One actor is being a camel, another an earth mover; one is handling an invisible object in space, another is imagining himself scalded in the bath.

The gyrations and the sounds seem more suited to Bedlam than to the innocent inside of a theatre. But it is all directed to the time when an actor begins to work on his part, so that he can then call on an image, a sensation or a movement that will 'work' for him.

In his second stage the actor at first works alone in a series of 'character studies' which he composes himself, putting his character into a variety of situations in order to discover and create his way of thinking, feeling, moving and speaking. Then together, the actors improvise.

Two characters in an imaginary situation that precedes the time of the play, confront each other for the purpose of revealing the nature of their relationship. There may be several such background improvisations before the actors begin to improvise on the scene itself.

Finally they will work on the text of the scene, using the lines of the play, but still experimenting with movement, activities, responses. It is from these 'on text' improvisations that the Director shapes his play. If the method works as it is designed to, the result is a kind of ensemble playing that bears the stamp of real human relationships.

According to Deirdre O'Connell, Focus 'had been invited by the Peacock two times to bring a successful production into their larger houses but both times was blocked by the Irish Actors' Equity because Focus's company members work full time and do house/technical assistance for productions as well as cleaning. It is a situation that could easily defeat a lesser woman, or at least cause regret. 'I'm too single minded, possibly even thoughtless, to have regrets. I have none whatsoever. If I were going to go about doing what I'm doing, and have a damn rough time of it, I'd much prefer to do it here. I'm not nationalistic in the banner waving sense, but I have a sense of where I'm more me – and I'm just more me here, as far as I can measure that...' It's important for me to communicate with people, and yet it's hard. All that we do in life that gets in the way – well, I'm not doing it while I'm acting, and I think it's just a marvellous, beautiful thing not to be doing it."

'Inside Holy Russia' by John Jordan, Hibernia 6 February 1970:

...that Mr. [Jim] Fitzgerald was responsible for the idea of keeping almost all the characters on the stage almost all of the time: those technically off stage retire to open niches where they sit frozen, pathetic ikons who in Paul Staple's setting are an insistent reminder that this play [*Uncle Vanya*] is a tragic-comedy from Holy Russia.

'A devoted 'Hedda Gabler' – but' by David Nowlan January 1970:

That the production is ponderous must be because the director conceived it in that way and encouraged his actors so to execute it. Likewise it is slow because it was meant to be slow; and where lines were played against the grain of the writing it was intentionally done. There need, of course, be no quibble with all of this: it is the director's prerogative to conceive of his interpretation of the play and so design his production of it that will best meet his own ideas. Had Declan Burke-Kennedy been directing this 'Hedda Gabler' as an exercise in which his players could best develop their interpretive techniques or extend their understanding of Ibsen's charactors (sic) for their own benefit, all would have been well. Had it even been a purely workshop production all might have been well. But the audience is an integral part of any theatrical event and the fatal flaw in this production is that little thought has been given to the audience. Actors may well be able to sustain their characterizations through 30-second pauses of no great dramatic import, but they cannot expect always to carry their audience with them. It may be perfectly all right – so far as the players are concerned - - to play a scene in such soft voices that only they can hear, but someone must then supply the audience with a script.

'Box Office': Paul Condon's Saturday column, *Evening Press*, Saturday, 20 June 1970:

Recently I was engaged in conversation with a young actress from the Focus Theatre where the play is being put on. On the subject of acting, I fear I rather dirtied my bib, for I expressed myself thus on the profession (and I didn't say it was Mrs. Warren's even).

Acting is a trade. Almost exactly like boot-making. Now I have no disrespect whatsoever for trade. It's a very valuable, highly worthwhile activity. We need it – and without the tradesmen's entrance. I'm for them coming in the front door in silks if possible. But acting and bootmaking are trades nonetheless, not arts which involve creation, as it were, from nothing, from the personality...

Anyway that's shortly what I think about acting. There is a difficulty though, in that acting is a public gesture which imitates reality and since imitations of reality are often dangerous to it, acting is more prone than other trades to the disfigurement of life.

If I understand the Stanislavski method correctly, however, that disfigurement of life [next line cut off] correct me if I'm wrong but I take the method of the 'method' to mean that the actor works his performance out from the character of the part by becoming as much as possible possessed of the same springs of action as the character.

This would mean that in performance the actor's behaviour is not a collection of words learned by rote conjoined with a series of actions and movements which suit the words, but that the words he uses, because of his preparation, become the only words he could possibly speak and the actions that he makes would be the actions which the character would make.

To a large extent acting by necessity instead of acting by technical device. (Which is not to say, of course, that the Stanlavski (sic) method is not a technique)'

[Goes on to talk about how it is unfortunate that this is not a professional company in that the actors have to have side jobs and rehearse part-time]

That's not to say that the actors don't know their lines or that this is any less good than any professional production at present available in Dublin but that the interdependence of the players is weak in places. One or to (sic) of the actors haven't developed (or haven't been able to develop perhaps) their character sufficiently to draw the best reactions from those who have.

'Liberate Women' Theatre by Mary Manning, *Hibernia*, 3 December 1971)

Considering their handicaps – the smallness of the stage and the auditorium and above all the lack of funds with which to dress their actors and the stage, the Focus production is remarkable for its taste and efficiency.

Every famous actress in every European country has essayed Nora and with varying success...Mary Elizabeth Burke-Kennedy in this Focus production made a brave shot at it. She is a graduate of Miss O'Connell's Stanislavski studio and therefore a product of the method. She has already shown great promise in previous roles as a sensitive, intelligent performer. She does not as yet have the technique for Nora, which is an extremely taxing characterization, but within her limited range she gave us an interesting and touching performance...Frank McDonald was very good as the doomed Dr Rank, except when he had moments of theatricality, and the Stanislavski method has not yet purged him of doing odd things with his voice.

'Women Liberated Kids Enthralled' Anthony Lennon At The Cinema (no dateline) [re: Doll's House]

When the sixth Earl of Longford died in 1961, Dublin was cut off from periodic helpings of two of the world's greatest dramatists, Ibsen and Chekhov. With the establishment of the minute Focus Theatre in 1967, the lacuna has been filled in. Now we can be certain of a whiff of greatness in dramatic literature at least twice a year...As usual, where settings are concerned Focus has made the best possible silk purse out of a sow's ear.'

'Focus Theatre in New Ross with Some Remarks by 'Random' (South Leinster Advertiser, Enniscorthy, Friday, May 26, 1972)

...and provided an experience in audience involvement that nowadays is alas! All too rare in the down-the-country theatre. More power to Focus' daring! By deciding on an Ibsen play (and *Doll's House* is no exception) they accepted its challenge of a series of word-drawn situations racing each other so that they could be lost with anything but the very best of interpretation. Never lost are they. Focus is giving us Ibsen! Ibsen here is giving us Focus! The result – unforgettable involvement in a great Theatre experience.'

[*Doll's House* toured Limerick, Galway, Athlone, Cork and Kilkenny (where it was sponsored by a Beer Festival) In Limerick there was an Improvisational performance.]

'Limerick-bound: FOCUS – Helen Buckley's Leisure Page', *Limerick Leader*, Saturday 8April 1972

...A number of them are full-time professional actors who survive by splitting their time between Focus and the more commercially viable enterprises that employ them as actors. Others are employed in teaching, secretarial work design, house-keeping, copper worker, and other activities during the day, but devote every second of their free time to Focus. All are committed in a way which their theatre work reflects, and are resolved, with the help of public and private subsidy, to make the Focus a full-time repertory theatre.

...also presents each week an evening of Improvisational Theatre that is to say, of spontaneous performances on an agreed theme, where the company work together to explore in dramatic terms a situation (sometimes suggested by the audience) without any script or agreed dialogue. A play is therefore created communally before one's eyes. This highly stimulating experiment, like the high degree of 'integrity' and 'discipline' that Focus productions are acclaimed for, is without parallel in Irish theatrical life.'

Theatre: Work at the Focus' by John Jordan *The Catholic Standard* **16March 1973**):

Indeed, so uniformly have the critics been on the side of Focus that so far as I can make out, only Miss Mary Manning and myself have ever written a harsh word.'

Appendix Five: Stanislavski Studio Exercises at the Focus. Questions to ask yourself as an actor

Below is a selection of exercises that would be in Part One of the Stanislavski process. (It informs and enlightens actors about their strengths and weaknesses). They are by no means the complete exercises. This is an example of what the students would be involved with while nurturing and nourishing their talent. Part Two would be the actors' work on character and the actors' work on the play including a first reading.

Transposition of the Object

This exercise requires the actor to explore an object or series of objects sensorially and imaginatively, with the objective of using the object/objects in a manner suggested by the sensory/imaginative exploration.

Sense Memory

The sense memory exercise is used to enable the actor on a basic level to discover how their innate sensorial talent can be nurtured and eventually used within an imaginative context of their choosing.

Personalization of the word.

Requires the actor to make manifest in sound only what a specific word suggests and to endeavour also to capture and bring dramatic shape to the personalized sound that is expressed. With two actors this exercise can eventually be brought into improvisation, the objective of which is to establish a specific imaginative relationship between the two actors.

Personalization of Abstract Painting into Sound and Eventual Impositional Improvisation.

This exercise requires the actor to select an abstract painting that affects him/her on a deep personal level. Ergo the selection of the painting should in no way be of a casual nature otherwise the exercise proper would be undermined in terms of its specific rigour and dramatic possibilities. Assuming all of the above are in place the actor then proceeds to explore and express the response to the painting only in sound. (As in the personalization of the word exercise) seeking out once again the dramatic shape that is evoked and developed by the specific response. With two actors this exercise can be richly developed into what is called an impositional improvisation where the objective is to establish a specific relationship imaginatively and economically within the imaginative choice imposed by one actor on the other. The impositional choice must be a logical process resulting from the dramatic experience the actor has explored with the abstract painting.

Jump Improvisation.

The jump improvisation usually (but not always) involves just two actors placed in an imaginative situation in which each has to try and realize a specific objective through a series of dramatic actions (put simply: a dramatic action or sequence of dramatic actions is the way in which each actor endeavours to accomplish their individual objectives). The objective and dramatic actions are always chosen by the actors involved in the exercise. The objective must always be imperative, not forgetting of course that the underlying purpose of the exercise is to create relationship. The development of dramatic shape is of primary importance in this particular exercise.

Justification of an Action

(Getting dressed to go out to a party. Packing a suit-case. Burning old letters)
In the justification of an action exercise the actor is again required to choose an imaginative set of circumstances/situation that bring the actor to whatever action they have chosen. As in the 'Jump Improvisation' situation the circumstances are imperative and never casual choices.

Personalization of the Object

The above exercise will once again require the actor to decide on an imaginative set of circumstances in which the relationship with a specific object (not an object belonging to the actor!) palpably suggests and resonates with the specifics of a relationship that is above and beyond the mere physical reality of that object.

The Portrait Exercise.

This is the first exercise in which the actor has to inhabit an objective reality. An objective reality that in this exercise is predefined by the portrait itself. (Perhaps a moment where a cup of tea is about to be drunk, a cigarette about to be sucked in or not. A cigarette to be stubbed out. Etc., etc.) For this exercise it is imperative that the actor be imaginatively moved by what the portrait suggests to him/her personally. The choice as to what is the specific life and reality of the person portrayed remains completely with the actor (the specifics of that particular day remain within the actor's imaginative domain.) What must be observed is the absolute responsibility of the actor to the details of the portrait. Attention must be paid to particular dress modes especially in portraits of the 19th Century. This aspect of the exercise whether 19th Century or in the present day must be appropriated rigorously. The fascinating aspect of this exercise is not only the actors ability to turn the character in the portrait into understandable insightful and imaginative behaviour equally. Once the position of the portrait has been appropriated the exercise then can take a turn into an unexpected shape or form. The actor must be open at all times to this possibility. (This exercise begins to prepare the actor for the demands and responsibility of an actual play).

Questions to ask yourself as an Actor

What are the given circumstances (What are the actual facts of the play?)
What are the relationships – immediate and surrounding?
Where am I coming from?
Where am I going?
What is the same about today? What is different about today?
What do I want? (What is my Object?)
How do I proceed to accomplish what I want? (Which simply means my dramatic actions to get my objective?)
What is the dominant situation reality?
What is my inner life reality?
What kind of clothes do I wear?

Comb script for as much information about your character as you can find. Look at what you say about your own character and what other characters say about your character.
When you do make imaginative choices for your character, make sure that they can be supported by the script.

Appendix Six: Preparing the body to work with the Elements

While standing have your feet shoulders width apart. Keep knees relaxed – do not lock them. Find your centre of gravity and keep the spine aligned.

Imagine a laser beam of light energy travelling from the sky through the top of your head, down your spine, into your legs, feet, and then on into the ground, right through the crust of the earth into the core of the planet. Then imagine the energy of the planet rising up to support you. Feel completely grounded to the earth. See and feel the laser travelling through your body back up into the sky and on into the universe.

- First breathe out all the air in your body
- In a moment feel the need to breathe
- Breathe in the life force/chi
- See the energy of the life force or chi moving through your own spine
- Breathe wide and deep with the colour of the chi
- Then breathe out all the energy 'held' within

The 4 Elements

1. Fire
2. Air
3. Water
4. Earth

The Body Chambers and the Elements

Visualize the body broken up into four chambers.

1. The **Fire Chamber** in the Head
2. The **Air Chamber** in the throat and chest
3. The **Water Chamber** in the stomach
4. The **Earth Chamber** below the waist line to the soles of the feet

Then work with sound vibration in each chamber.

Fire   **HEE:** Feel the resonance in the head
Air   **HOW:** Feel the resonance in the throat
Water **HOO:** Feel the resonance in the heart
Earth **HAW:** Feel the resonance in the solar plexus
ZZZ: Feel the vibration through the spine
HUM: Feel the sonic shower through the body

Then speak:

Fire   **'I inform'**   Head
Air   **'I soothe'**   Throat
Water **'I empower'** Heart
Earth **'I mourn'**   Solar Plexus

Listen into distance for sound.
Feel the stillness.
Connect with each sense to feel truly present.

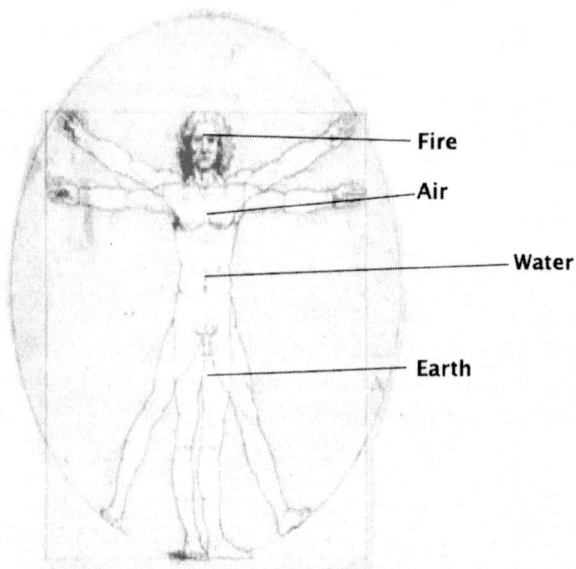

Appendix Seven:

'What the arts mean to me: The President, Mrs Mary Robinson, talks to Paddy Woodworth About the place of the arts in her life and in Irish Society'

The Irish Times, Monday 24 June 1991

I didn't act at college, but I joined the Focus for a short time, and took part in Stanislavski Method classes with Deirdre O'Connell. I can remember in the early stages being encouraged to think of becoming something very familiar. As I was studying law, the most familiar object was my briefcase...so there I was, busy becoming my briefcase, and then Deirdre's voice came up saying: 'Mary, you have to keep your eyes open', and I opened my eyes and the whole thing was gone. I continued to go to plays at the Focus, and was interested in that approach, but then I grew away from it. I thought it was too 'achieved' in a mechanical way.

Short Biographies: the Editors

Steven Dedalus Burch is currently an Associate Professor of theatre history and playwriting for the Department of Theatre and Dance at the University of Alabama in Tuscaloosa. In addition to the essays and interviews in this collection, he has published *Andrew P. Wilson and the Early Irish and Scottish National Theatres, 1911-1950.* He has also written articles for *Journal of Dramatic Theory and Criticism, Theatre Journal, Theatre History Studies,* and *Theatre Symposium.* He is also an award-winning playwright (New York Foundation for the Arts Playwriting Fellowship for *Love Nor Money*) and actor, and currently is the artistic director of the Rude Mechanicals, a free Shakespeare in the park company in Tuscaloosa, Alabama where he lives with his wife, Deborah Parker.

Brian McAvera is a playwright, director, art critic and historian whose best-known work, the cycle of eight plays called *Picasso's Women,* is currently translated into seventeen languages. He has written over thirty plays for the theatre, including *Yo! Picasso!, Kings of the Road,* and *Francis & Frances,* some eighteen radio plays, and two television films, one of which he directed. He has also directed for the theatre since the late 1960's, was co-founder of various theatre companies including New Writers' Theatre, and is an Artistic Adviser to the Focus. He is a member of the Theatre Committee of the Writers' Guild of Great Britain and is currently the Royal Literary Fund Fellow at Queens University Belfast. As an art critic and historian he has written thirteen books including *Art, Politics and Ireland,* and biographical and critical studies of Irish artists *Patrick Pye, Victor Sloan, Jim Manley, Michael Cullen and Eamon Colman,* the Indian artist *Avtarjeet Dhanjal,* and over fifty catalogues.

Short Biographies of Contributors, Interviewees, and Witnesses

Mary Elizabeth Burke-Kennedy is a director, actress, and playwright. She was a founder member of the Focus Theatre and formed the Second Studio there. More recently she established Storytellers Theatre. Among the plays she directed at Focus are *Alice in Wonderland*, *Women in Arms*, *Daughters,* and *Currigh the Shape Shifter*.

Geraldine O'Connell Cusack is the sister of Deirdre O'Connell. She had written about Deirdre and the Focus Theatre in her family biography, *Children of the Far Flung*.

Sabina Coyne Higgins was an actress and is currently the First Lady of Ireland. She was a founder member of the Stanislavski Studio and the Focus Theatre. Among her productions are *A Doll's House*, *Uncle Vanya*, and *Antigone*.

Ena May is an actress and author and a mainstay of the Focus Theatre during Deirdre's years. Among her performances are *A Delicate Balance*, *Night of the Iguana*, and her own one-woman show, *Close Shave with the Devil*. Plays produced at Focus include *Out of the Beehive* and *She's Your Mother Too You Know*.

Tim McDonnell is an actor, director, and teacher who was the Head of the Acting Studio at Focus (2002-2008), a founder member of the Stanislavski Studio and the Focus Theatre. Among his acclaimed performances are *A Delicate Balance*, *The Zoo Story*, and the award-winning *Diary of a Madman* (including a Harvey's Best Actor and an Obie in NYC).

Elizabeth Moynihan is an actress and playwright, whose years at Focus include both of its artistic directors, Deirdre O'Connell and Joe Devlin. Among her performances at Focus are *'Night Mother*, *The House of Bernada Alba*, and *Mother Teresa is Dead*. Focus has also produced her scripts, *Pinching for My Soul* and *Tic*.

Mary Moynihan is a creative artist working in professional theatre and film as a theatre director, writer, actor and facilitator. Mary is a founder member and current Artistic Director of Smashing Times

Theatre Company Limited and she lectures in drama and theatre studies for the Honours Bachelor of Arts in Drama (performance) at the Conservatory of Music and Drama, Dublin Institute of Technology. Mary has an honours M.A. in Film Production from the Dublin Institute of Technology and an honours B.A. in Drama and Theatre Studies from Trinity College Dublin. Mary trained as an actor and director at Focus Theatre under the direction of Deirdre O'Connell, her friend and mentor, and today continues her involvement as an associate director/artist.

Jimmy Murphy is one of Ireland's best-known younger playwrights. His plays for the Abbey Theatre include *Brothers of the Brush* (Winner of the Dublin Theatre Festival Best New Play Award 1993), *A Picture of Paradise* and *The Muesli Belt*. He is a former Writer-in-Residence at NUI, Maynooth, a member of the Abbey Theatre's Advisory Council, and in 2004 he was elected a member of Aosdána.

Ronan O'Leary began his career as a producer-director for PBS in Los Angeles in 1984, making drama-documentaries on the philosophers Thoreau and Emerson, and profile-interviews with the filmmakers Oliver Stone and Sir David Puttnam. He returned to his native Ireland in 1986 to film the Abbey Theatre classic play *Riders to the Sea* for PBS, starring Oscar-winner Geraldine Page and Amanda Plummer. He subsequently filmed the Pulitzer-nominated book *Fragments of Isabella*, starring Gabrielle Reidy, based on the memoirs of Auschwitz survivor Isabella Leitner. He then filmed *Diary of a Madman* based on the classic Russian novella by Nicolai Gogol, starring Tim McDonnell, and filmed *Hello, Stranger* for PBS, based on a screenplay by the legendary Truman Capote. More recently, Ronan directed and co-scripted the psychological film drama *Driftwood* starring James Spader, for Goldcrest Films.

Cathal Quinn is Head of Voice at The Lir, Trinity College. He trained as an actor at the Royal Scottish Academy, acted throughout Scotland and Europe, took his own play about Keats to Toronto, Edinburgh, London and Florida, then started directing and teaching Voice at Langside College, Glasgow. He trained as a Voice Teacher at Central School of Speech and Drama 1997-98 and taught at Oxford School in Woodstock before becoming Head of Voice at the Gaiety School of Acting, 1998-2012. He did a Masters top-up at Central with a dissertation on Beckett, and is now Artistic Director of Mouth on Fire

Theatre Company who have taken Beckett's work all over Ireland, to Southampton, Tokyo, and will shortly be travelling to Belgium, Russia and Canada.

Joe Devlin was Artistic Director of Focus Theatre 2002 to 2011. Directing credits include *Griswold, Hollywood Valhalla, The Hen Night Epiphany, Tic, Gaby* from *Picasso's Women, Mother Teresa is Dead, Stop The Tempo!, Jesus Hopped The 'A' Train,* and *Proof.* Executive Director 2011 to 2013. Highlights include *Francis & Frances, Blood Ties* and *Bankers.* Artistic Director of Rattle Bag Theatre Company:. highlights include *A Brusque Affair* (Edinburgh Fringe Festival 1990); *Julius Caesar* (Nominated for Irish Times Award 2001). For the Lyric Theatre, Belfast – *Potestad, Put Out That Light,* and *Cirque du Cinema* (Belfast Circus School). Associate Director for the Playhouse, Derry 1995 to 1999: *Energy* and *The Fire King* opera. Artistic Director of Pointfields Theatre Company, Belfast 1993 to 1996. Highlights include *Picture of Tomorrow* and *Angels with Split Voices.* Other Productions include: *Poor Superman* (Muted Cupid/Project); *Bonjour Mucker* (O.M.A.C); and *Talbot's Box* (Belfast Festival). He won the Beck's Award for new work in N.Ireland and The Writers Guild of Great Britain Award for the Encouragement of New Work at the Focus Theatre. Joe holds a degree in Theatre and Art & Design from John Moore's University, Liverpool. He has taught performance at the University of Ulster, Coleraine and Trinity College, Dublin. He currently teaches Stanislavski and Shakespeare performance at the Focus Acting Studio in Dublin. Joe now also works as a theatre producer.

Index

Nugent, Sile, 187

O

O'Brien, Colm, 147, 151
O'Brien, Eoin, 12
O'Brien, Kevin, 171, 181
O'Casey, Sean
Juno and the Paycock, 59
O'Connell, Kevin
Fire King, The, 39, 236
O'Connor, Flann, 217
O'Donoghue, Maurice, 182
O'Driscoll, Ann Maloney, 17, 20
O'Kelly, Donal, 22, 146, 200
O'Leary, Ronan, 17, 19, 126, 185
O'Malley, Daragh, 186
O'Malley, Mary, 102
O'Neill, Eugene
Anna Christie, 18, 205
In the Zone, 12, 195, 217
O'Neill, Tommy, 11, 200-201, 205
O'Toole, Peter, 158
Obie Award, 162, 185
Odets, Clifford
Rocket to the Moon, 18, 202
Olivier, Laurence, 61
Ouspenskaya, Maria, 62

P

Pacino, Al, 63
Paczocha, Radoslaw
Scent of Chocolate, 42, 209
Page, Geraldine, 63, 134
Pantakin Theatre, 53
Parr, Chris, 28
Pavlovsky, Eduardo
Potestad, 33, 236
Peacock Theatre, 17, 133, 220
Pearce, Stewart, 50

Pembroke Place, 6, 10, 20-23, 60, 152, 165, 177, 210, 211
Personalization of an Object, 70
Personalization of the word, 224
Pike Theatre, 9, 210
Pirandello, Luigi
Man with the Flower in his Mouth, The, 182
To Clothe the Naked, 129, 196
Piscator, Erwin, 5, 7, 135, 210, 215
Players Theatre, 9, 210
Plunkett, Geraldine, 151
Pocket Theatre, 8, 9, 127, 210
Point Fields, 33-34, 38
Poliakoff, Stephen
Strawberry Fields, 132, 203
Polus, 62
Priestly, J.B.
An Inspector Calls, 102
Project Art Gallery, 9
Project Arts Centre, 17, 21
Provincetown Playhouse, 66
Psychological Gesture, 135
Puig, Manuel
Kiss of the Spiderwoman, 19
Purple Heart Theatre, 21

Q

Questions to ask yourself as an actor, 224, 226
Quinn, Cathal, 3, 42, 52, 114, 126, 144, 147, 157, 235
Quinn, Michael, 101

R

Radio Three, 101
Ranelagh Arts Centre, 43, 47
Rattlebag Theatre Company, 37, 39
Raynor, Paul, 22
Rea, Stephen, 102